Faster than a speeding bullet

More powerful than a locomoti

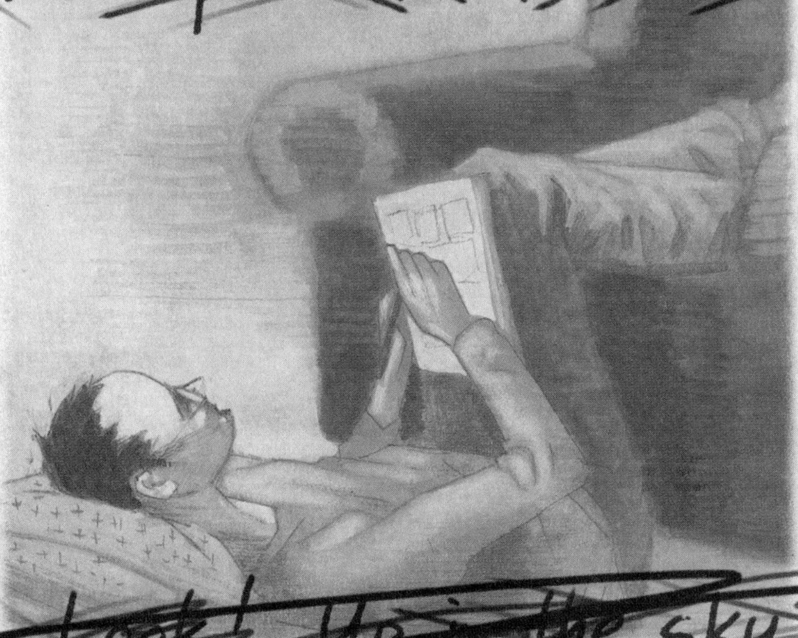

Look! Up in the sky!

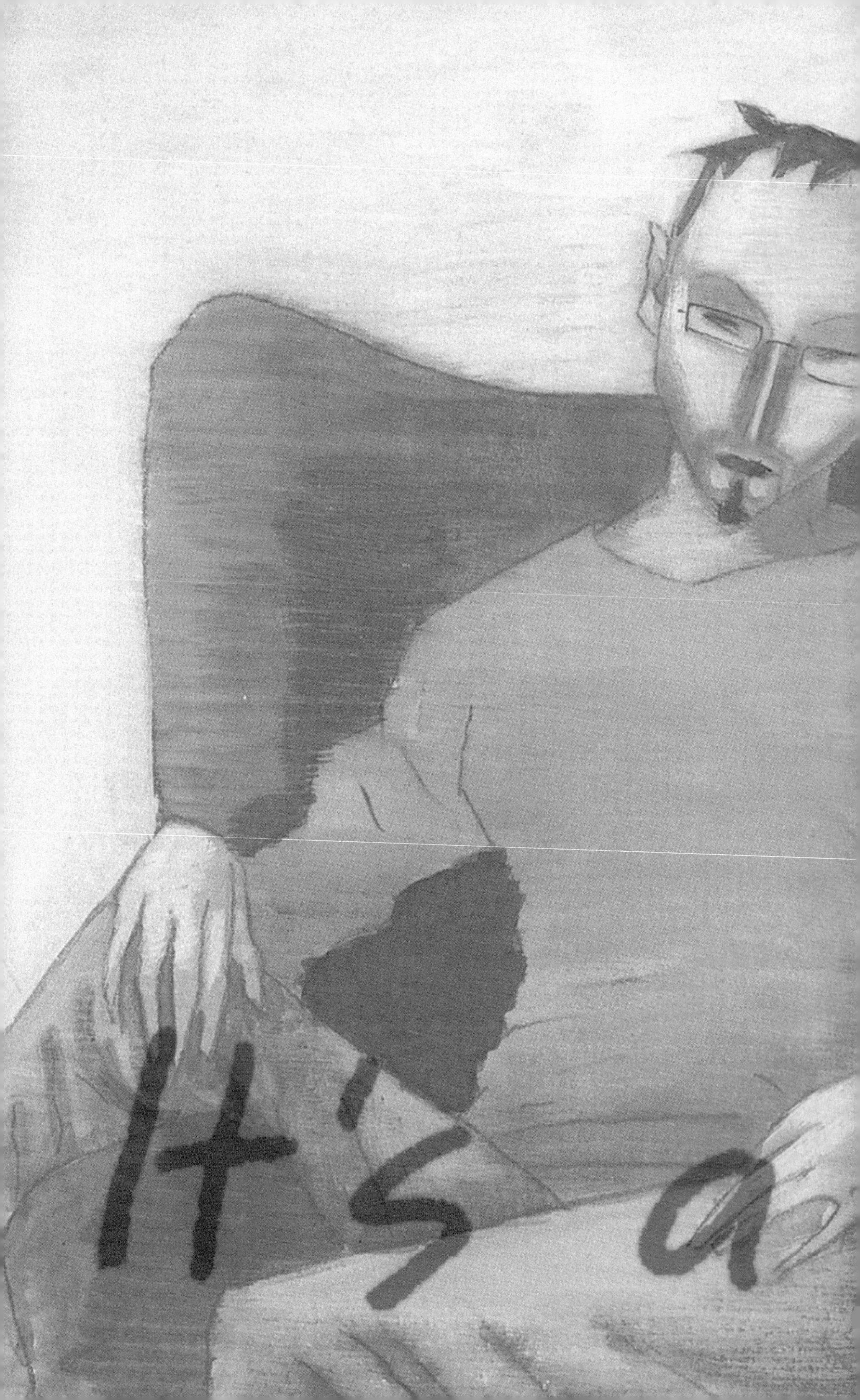
It's a

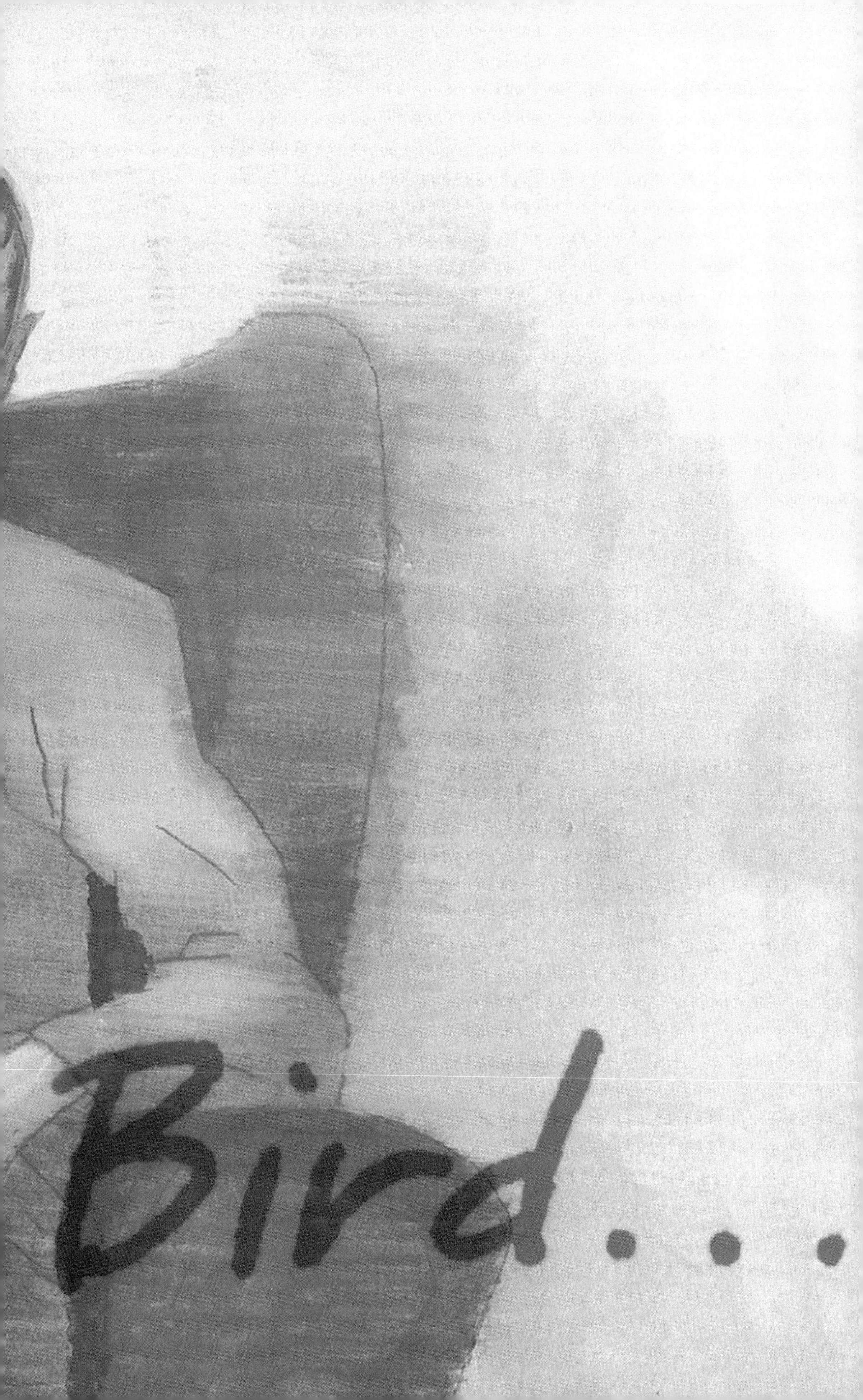
Bird....

DC Comics

Karen Berger *VP – Executive Editor*

Pornsak Pichetshote *Assistant Editor*

Amie Brockway-Metcalf *Art Director*

Paul Levitz *President & Publisher*

Georg Brewer *VP - Design & Retail Product Development*

Richard Bruning *Sr. VP - Creative Director*

Patrick Caldon *Sr. VP - Finance & Operations*

Chris Caramalis *VP-Finance*

Terri Cunningham *VP-Managing Editor*

Dan DiDio *VP-Editorial*

Alison Gill *VP – Manufacturing*

Lillian Laserson *Sr. VP & General Counsel*

Jim Lee *Editorial Director - WildStorm*

David McKillips *VP – Advertising & Custom Publishing*

John Nee *VP – Business Development*

Gregory Noveck *Sr. VP – Creative Affairs*

Cheryl Rubin *VP- Brand Management*

Bob Wayne *VP – Sales & Marketing*

It's a Bird...

hc isbn 1-4012-0109-1

sc isbn 1-4012-0311-6

cover artist Teddy Kristiansen

logo design Pete Friedrich

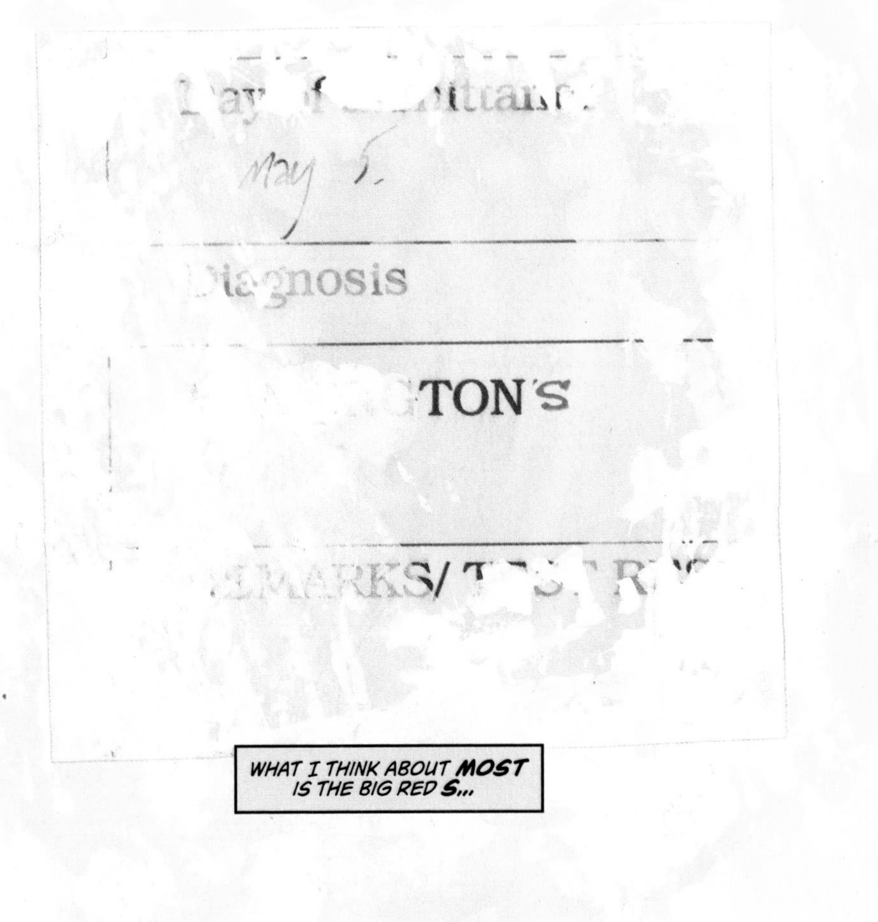

Day of admittance:

May 5.

Diagnosis

...GTON'S

...EMARKS/...

WHAT I THINK ABOUT **MOST**
IS THE BIG RED **S**...

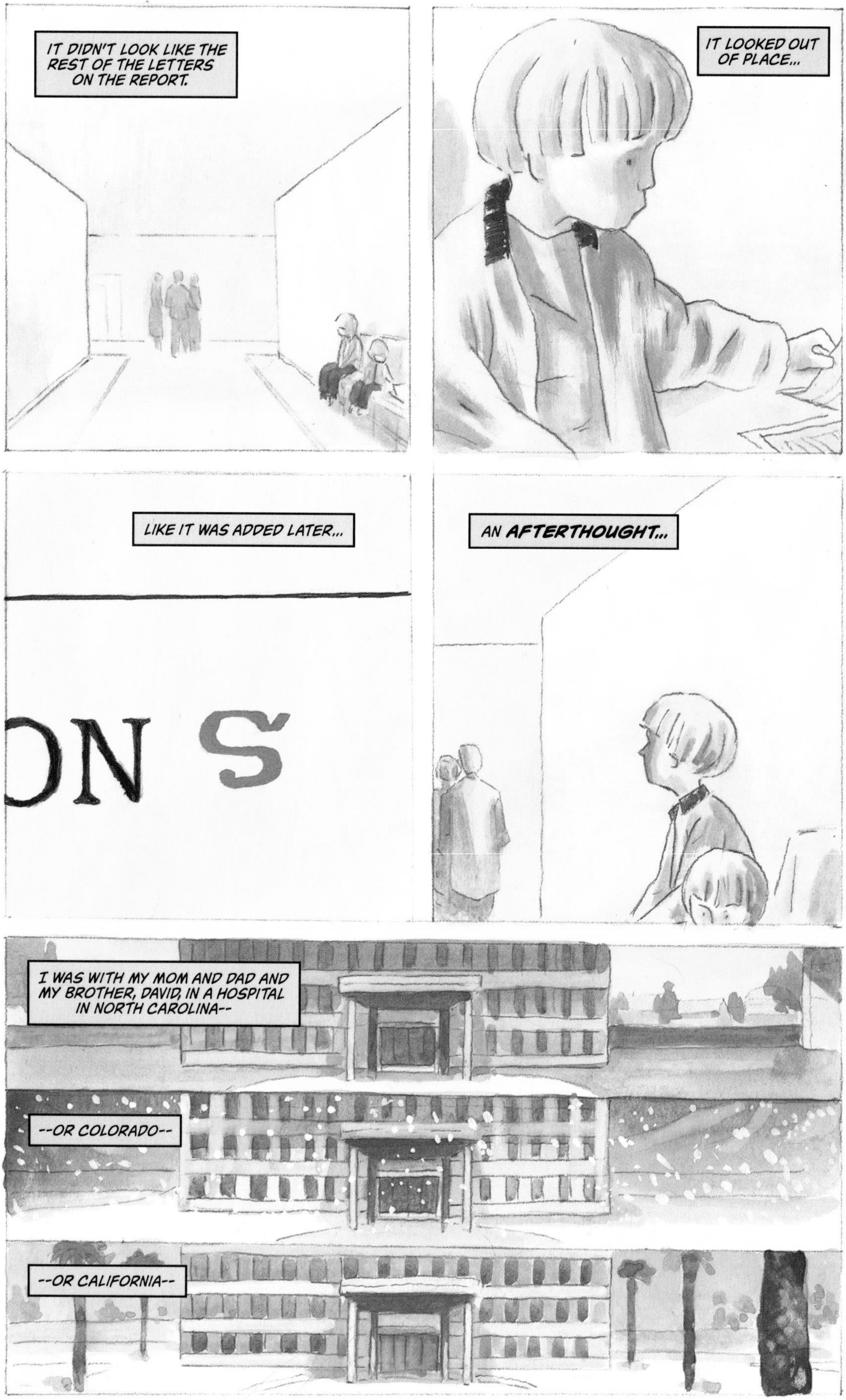
IT DIDN'T LOOK LIKE THE REST OF THE LETTERS ON THE REPORT.
IT LOOKED OUT OF PLACE...
LIKE IT WAS ADDED LATER...
ON S
AN AFTERTHOUGHT...
I WAS WITH MY MOM AND DAD AND MY BROTHER, DAVID, IN A HOSPITAL IN NORTH CAROLINA--
--OR COLORADO--
--OR CALIFORNIA--

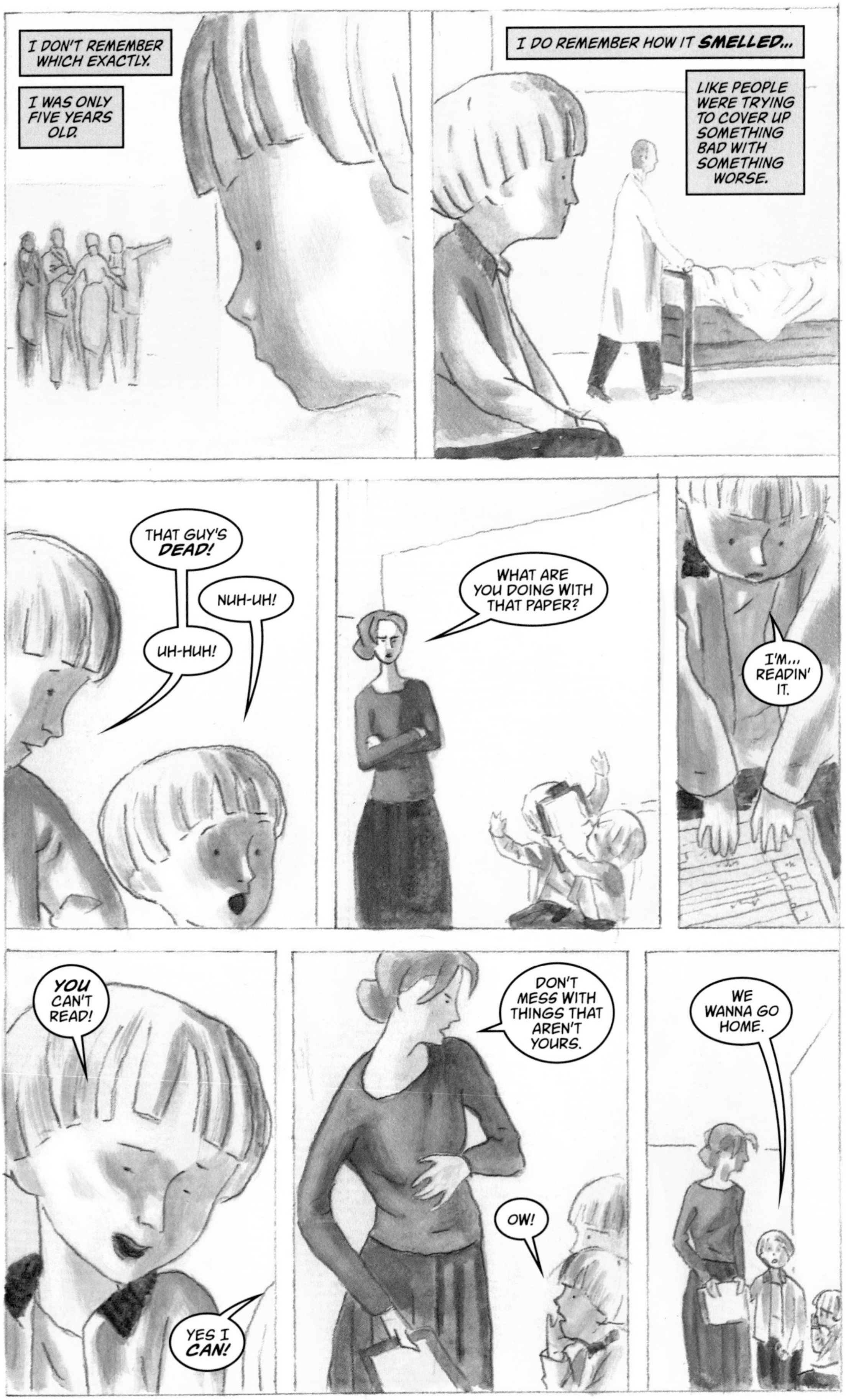
I DON'T REMEMBER WHICH EXACTLY.
I WAS ONLY FIVE YEARS OLD.
I DO REMEMBER HOW IT SMELLED...
LIKE PEOPLE WERE TRYING TO COVER UP SOMETHING BAD WITH SOMETHING WORSE.
THAT GUY'S DEAD!
UH-HUH!
NUH-UH!
WHAT ARE YOU DOING WITH THAT PAPER?
I'M... READIN' IT.
YOU CAN'T READ!
YES I CAN!
DON'T MESS WITH THINGS THAT AREN'T YOURS.
OW!
WE WANNA GO HOME.

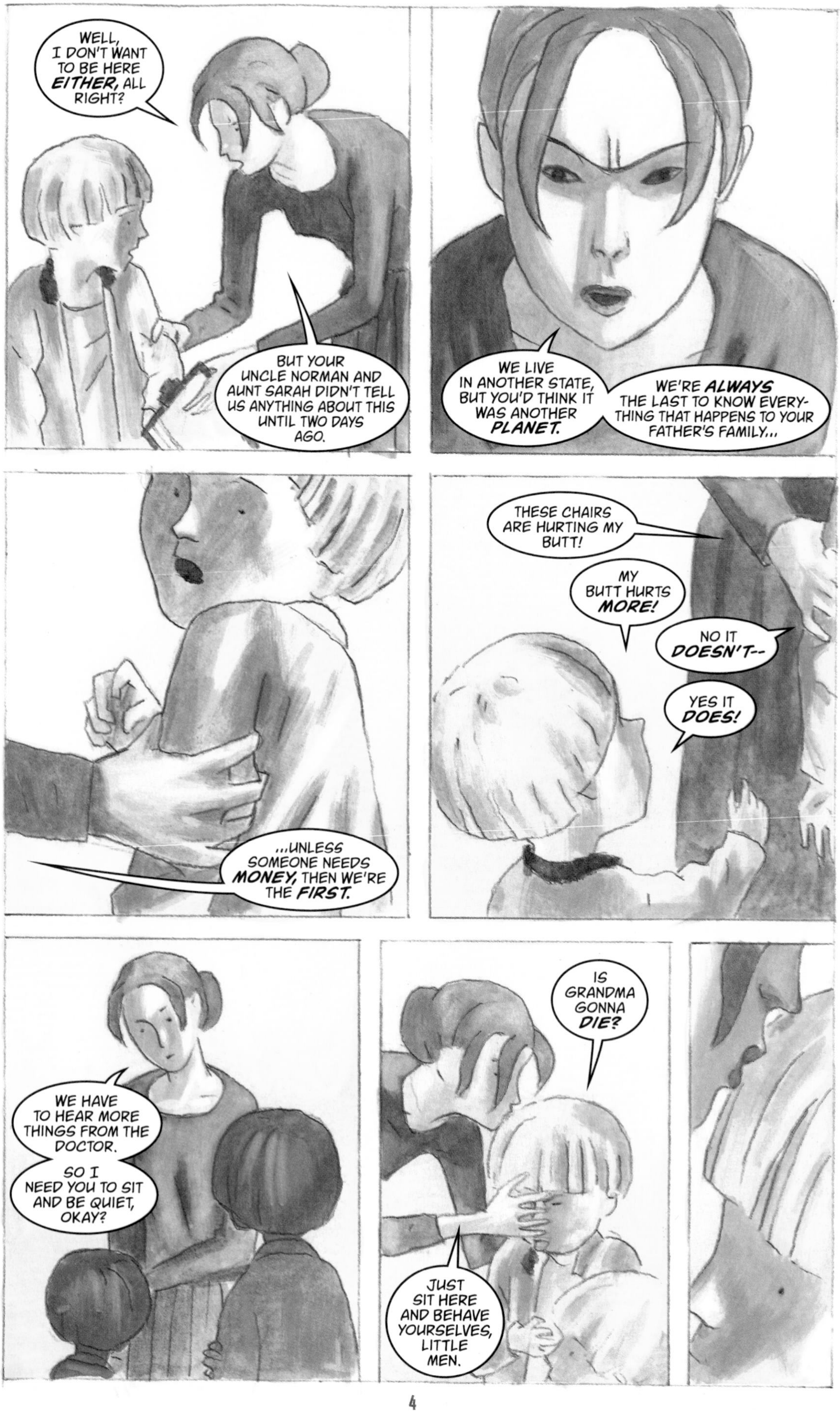
WELL, I DON'T WANT TO BE HERE EITHER, ALL RIGHT?
BUT YOUR UNCLE NORMAN AND AUNT SARAH DIDN'T TELL US ANYTHING ABOUT THIS UNTIL TWO DAYS AGO.
WE LIVE IN ANOTHER STATE, BUT YOU'D THINK IT WAS ANOTHER PLANET.
WE'RE ALWAYS THE LAST TO KNOW EVERY-THING THAT HAPPENS TO YOUR FATHER'S FAMILY...
...UNLESS SOMEONE NEEDS MONEY, THEN WE'RE THE FIRST.
THESE CHAIRS ARE HURTING MY BUTT!
MY BUTT HURTS MORE!
NO IT DOESN'T--
YES IT DOES!
WE HAVE TO HEAR MORE THINGS FROM THE DOCTOR.
SO I NEED YOU TO SIT AND BE QUIET, OKAY?
IS GRANDMA GONNA DIE?
JUST SIT HERE AND BEHAVE YOURSELVES, LITTLE MEN.

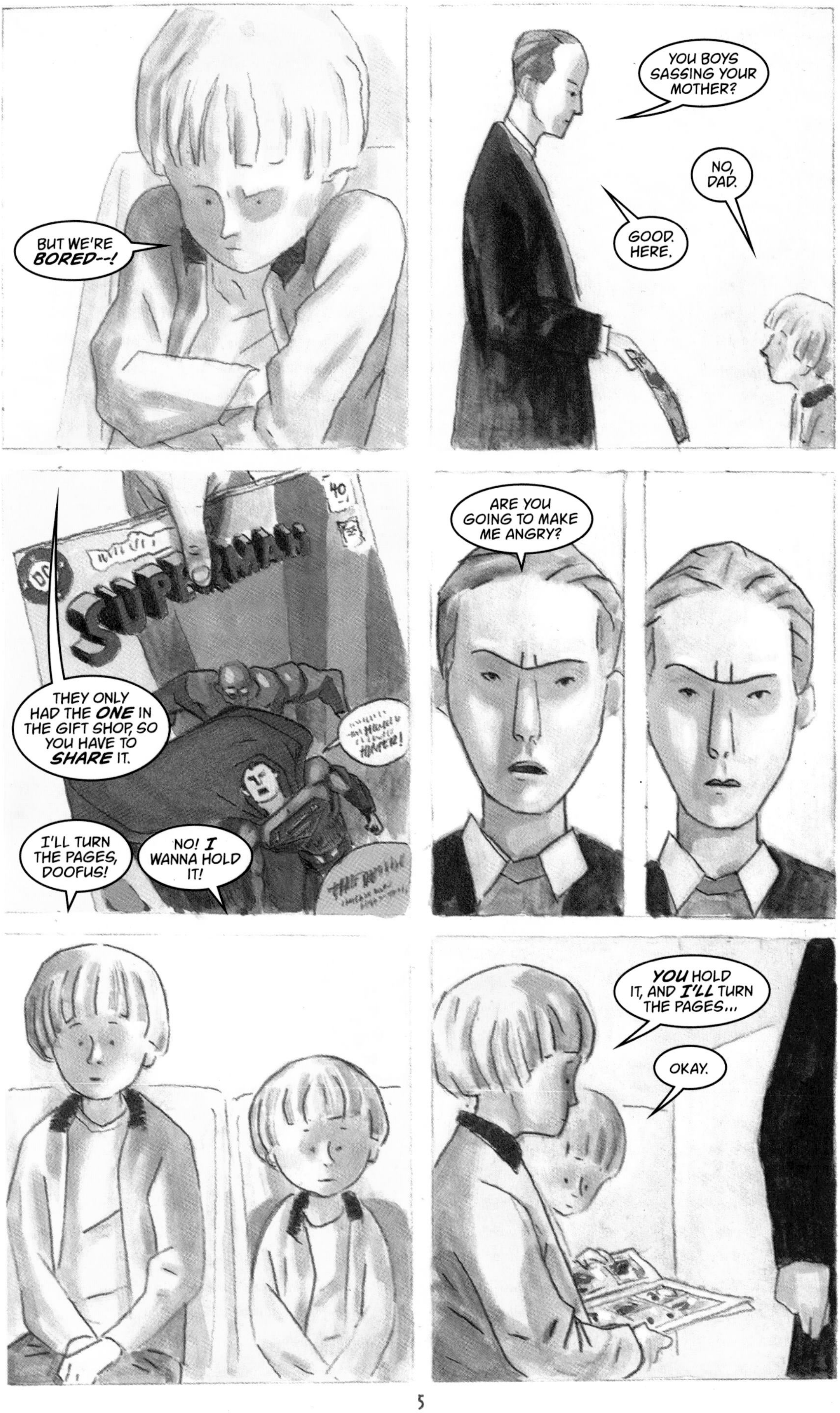
BUT WE'RE BORED--!
YOU BOYS SASSING YOUR MOTHER?
NO, DAD.
GOOD. HERE.
THEY ONLY HAD THE ONE IN THE GIFT SHOP, SO YOU HAVE TO SHARE IT.
I'LL TURN THE PAGES, DOOFUS!
NO! I WANNA HOLD IT!
ARE YOU GOING TO MAKE ME ANGRY?
YOU HOLD IT, AND I'LL TURN THE PAGES...
OKAY.

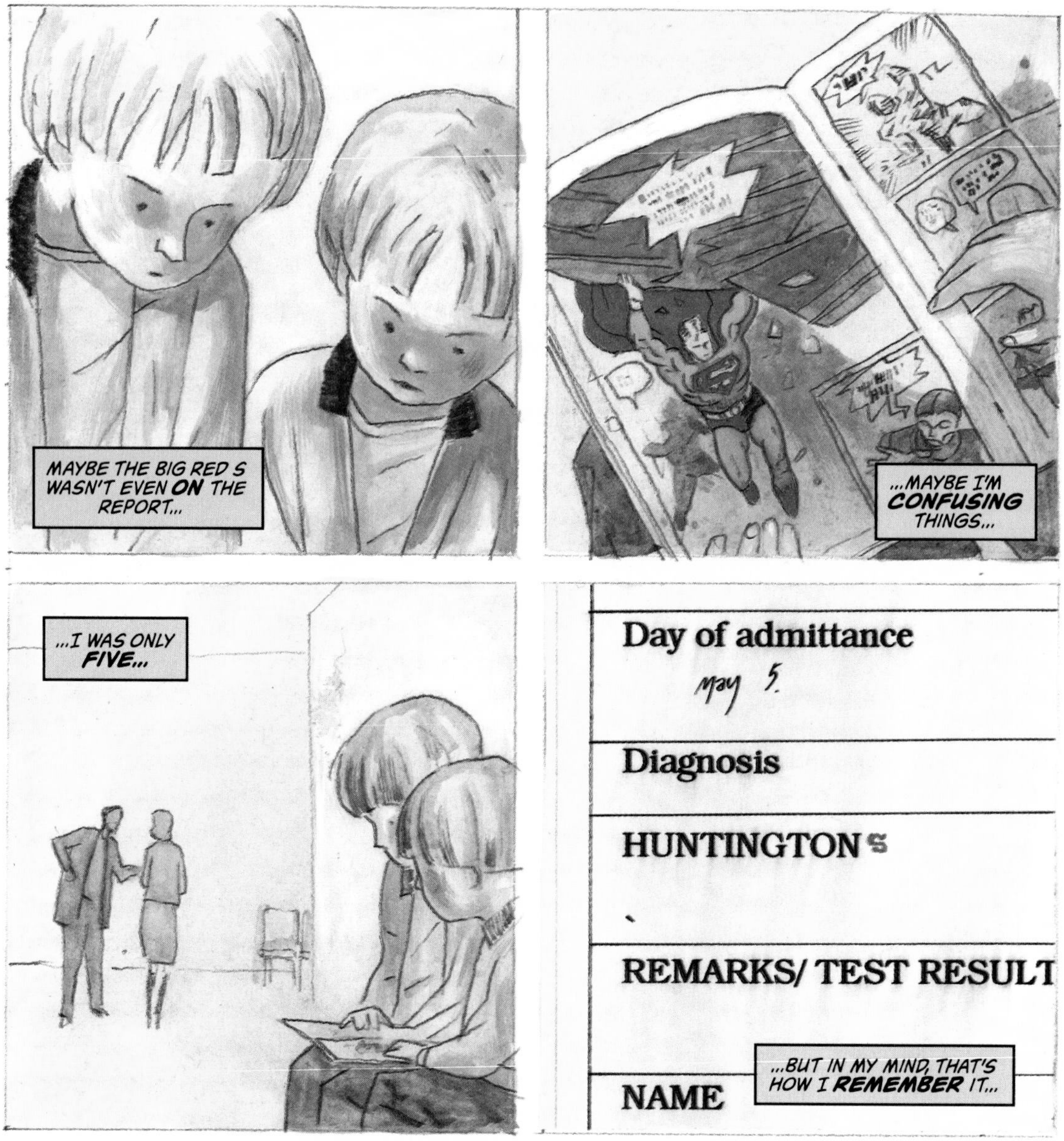
MAYBE THE BIG RED S WASN'T EVEN ON THE REPORT...
...MAYBE I'M CONFUSING THINGS...
...I WAS ONLY FIVE...
Day of admittance
may 5.
Diagnosis
HUNTINGTON'S
REMARKS/ TEST RESULT
NAME
...BUT IN MY MIND, THAT'S HOW I REMEMBER IT...

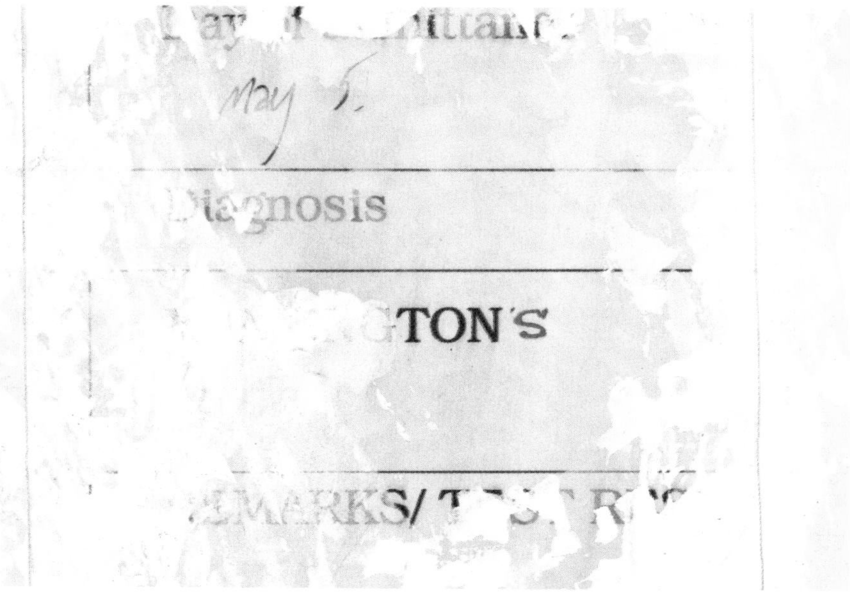
may 5.
Diagnosis

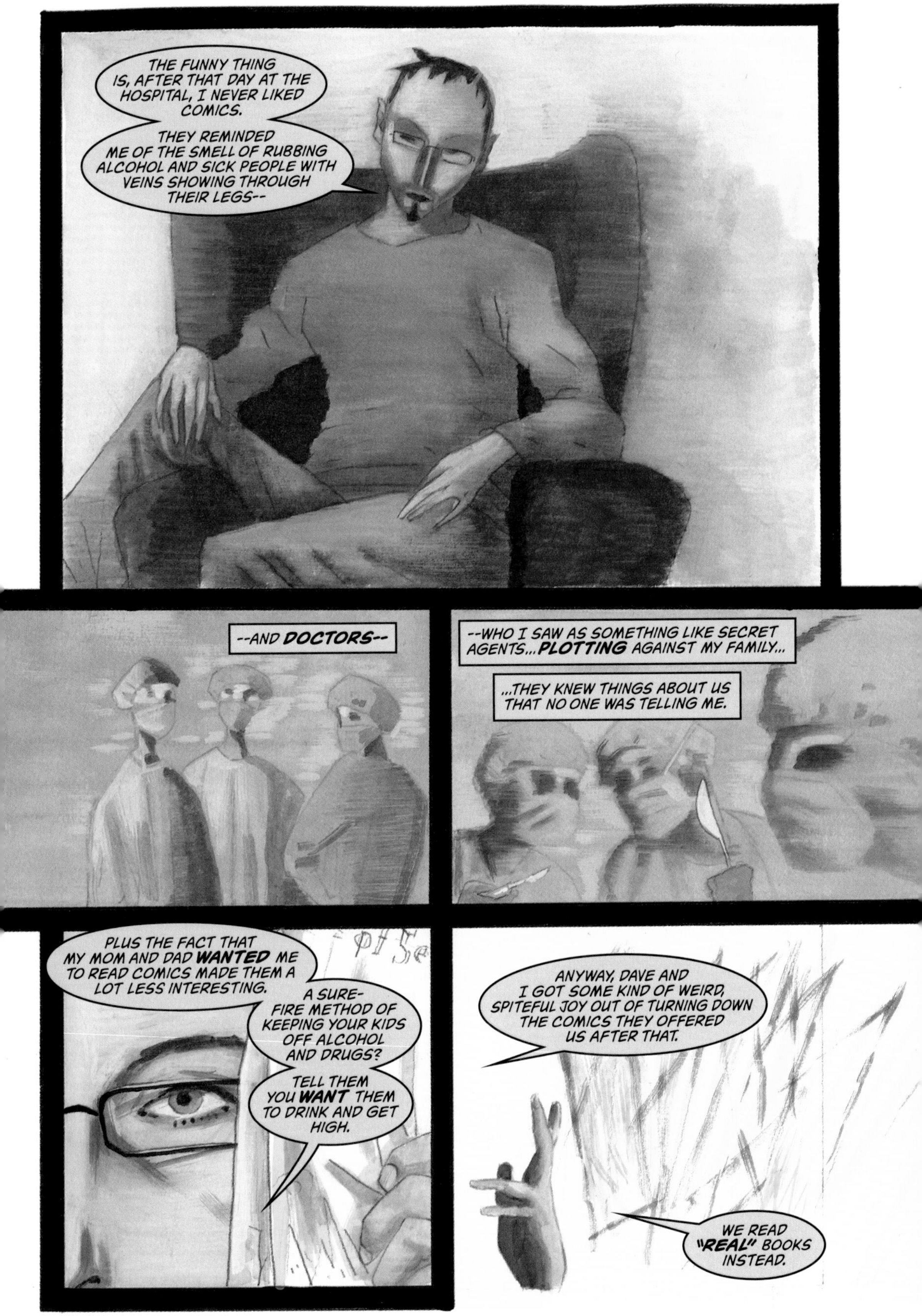
THE FUNNY THING IS, AFTER THAT DAY AT THE HOSPITAL, I NEVER LIKED COMICS.
THEY REMINDED ME OF THE SMELL OF RUBBING ALCOHOL AND SICK PEOPLE WITH VEINS SHOWING THROUGH THEIR LEGS--
--AND **DOCTORS**--
--WHO I SAW AS SOMETHING LIKE SECRET AGENTS... **PLOTTING** AGAINST MY FAMILY...
...THEY KNEW THINGS ABOUT US THAT NO ONE WAS TELLING ME.
PLUS THE FACT THAT MY MOM AND DAD **WANTED** ME TO READ COMICS MADE THEM A LOT LESS INTERESTING.
A SURE-FIRE METHOD OF KEEPING YOUR KIDS OFF ALCOHOL AND DRUGS?
TELL THEM YOU **WANT** THEM TO DRINK AND GET HIGH.
ANYWAY, DAVE AND I GOT SOME KIND OF WEIRD, SPITEFUL JOY OUT OF TURNING DOWN THE COMICS THEY OFFERED US AFTER THAT.
WE READ "**REAL**" BOOKS INSTEAD.

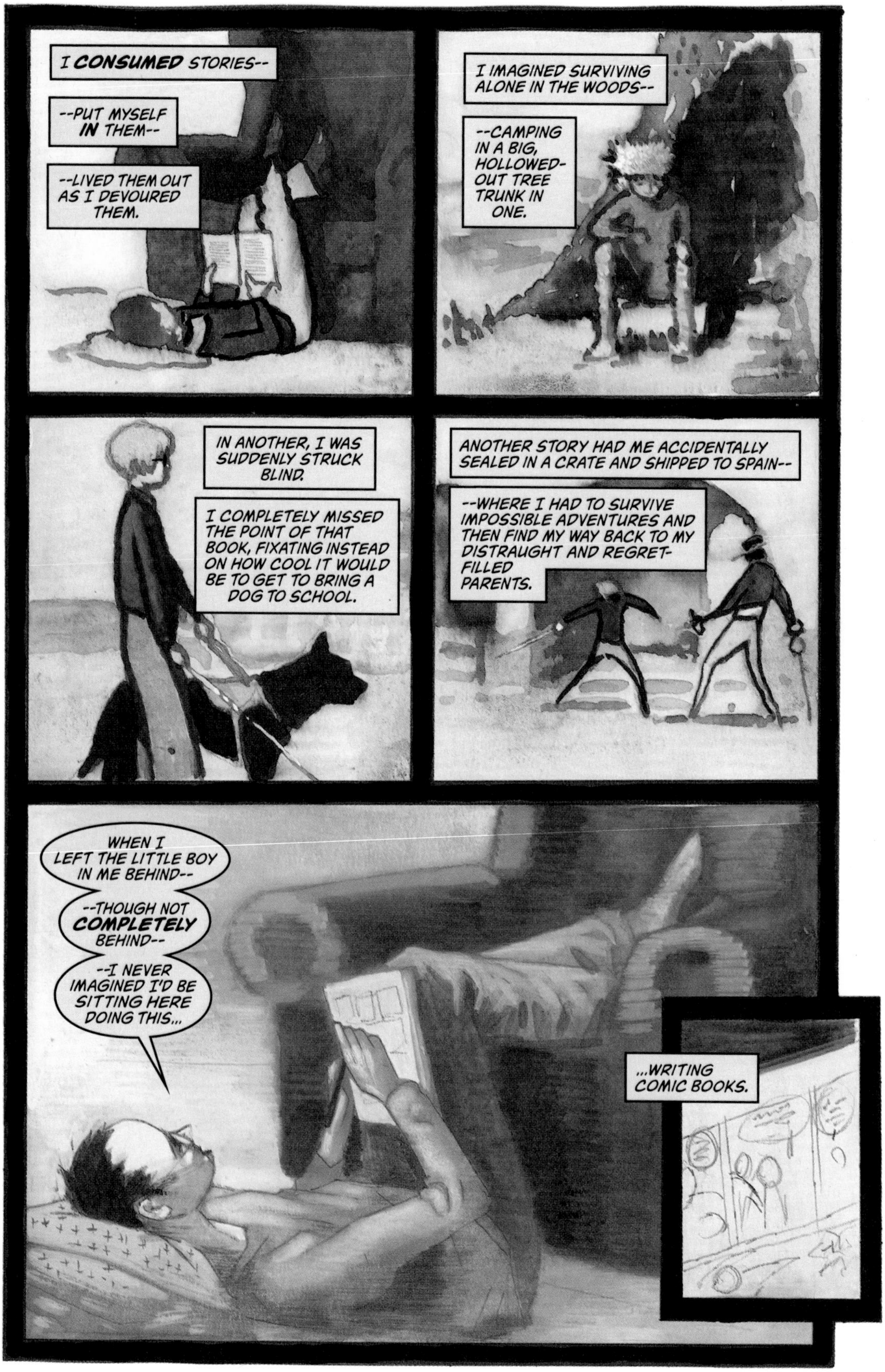
I CONSUMED STORIES--
--PUT MYSELF IN THEM--
--LIVED THEM OUT AS I DEVOURED THEM.
I IMAGINED SURVIVING ALONE IN THE WOODS--
--CAMPING IN A BIG, HOLLOWED-OUT TREE TRUNK IN ONE.
IN ANOTHER, I WAS SUDDENLY STRUCK BLIND.
I COMPLETELY MISSED THE POINT OF THAT BOOK, FIXATING INSTEAD ON HOW COOL IT WOULD BE TO GET TO BRING A DOG TO SCHOOL.
ANOTHER STORY HAD ME ACCIDENTALLY SEALED IN A CRATE AND SHIPPED TO SPAIN--
--WHERE I HAD TO SURVIVE IMPOSSIBLE ADVENTURES AND THEN FIND MY WAY BACK TO MY DISTRAUGHT AND REGRET-FILLED PARENTS.
WHEN I LEFT THE LITTLE BOY IN ME BEHIND--
--THOUGH NOT COMPLETELY BEHIND--
--I NEVER IMAGINED I'D BE SITTING HERE DOING THIS...
...WRITING COMIC BOOKS.

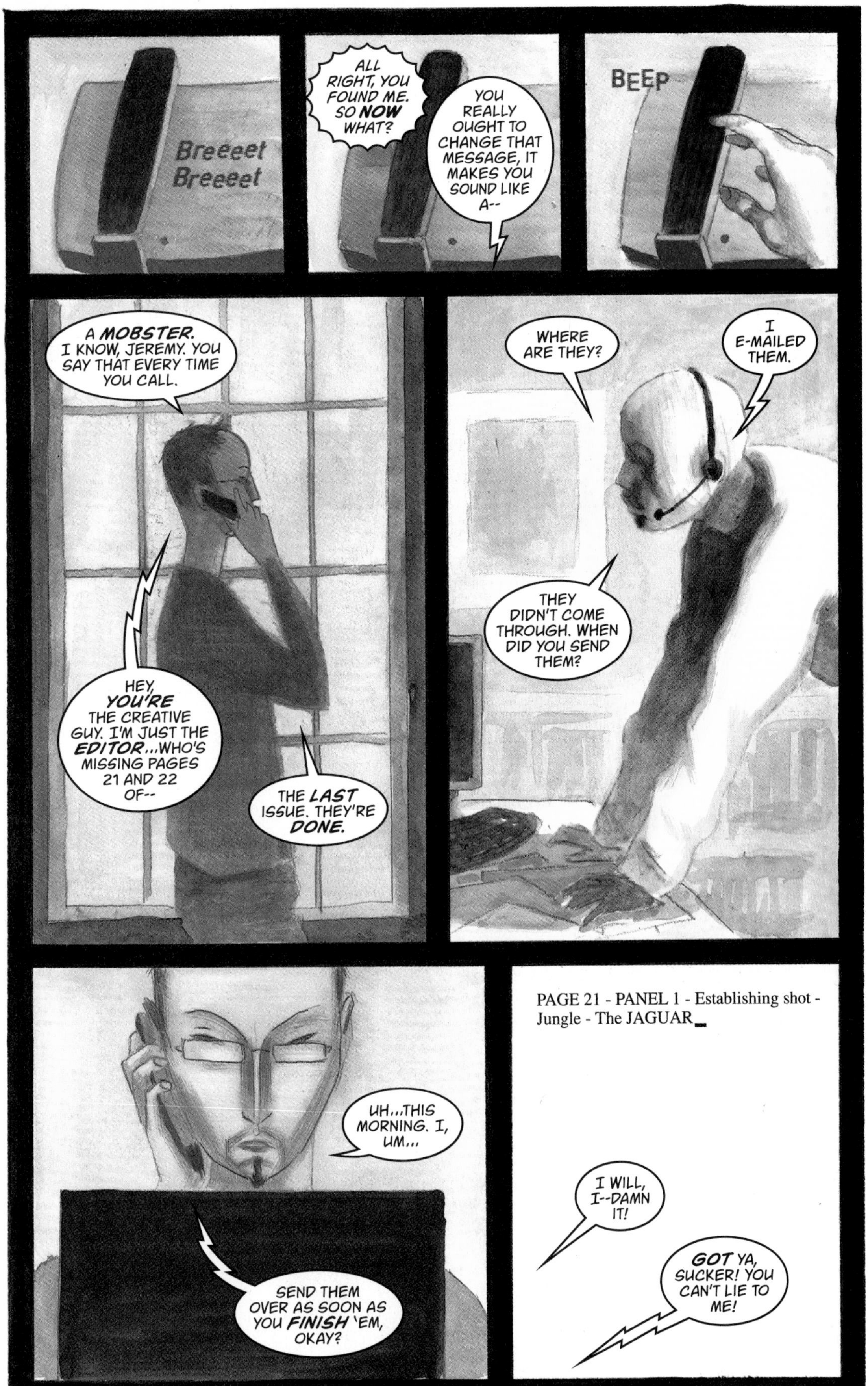
Breeeet
Breeeet
ALL RIGHT, YOU FOUND ME. SO NOW WHAT?
YOU REALLY OUGHT TO CHANGE THAT MESSAGE, IT MAKES YOU SOUND LIKE A--
BEEP
A MOBSTER. I KNOW, JEREMY. YOU SAY THAT EVERY TIME YOU CALL.
HEY, YOU'RE THE CREATIVE GUY. I'M JUST THE EDITOR...WHO'S MISSING PAGES 21 AND 22 OF--
THE LAST ISSUE. THEY'RE DONE.
WHERE ARE THEY?
I E-MAILED THEM.
THEY DIDN'T COME THROUGH. WHEN DID YOU SEND THEM?
UH...THIS MORNING. I, UM...
SEND THEM OVER AS SOON AS YOU FINISH 'EM, OKAY?
PAGE 21 - PANEL 1 - Establishing shot - Jungle - The JAGUAR
I WILL, I--DAMN IT!
GOT YA, SUCKER! YOU CAN'T LIE TO ME!

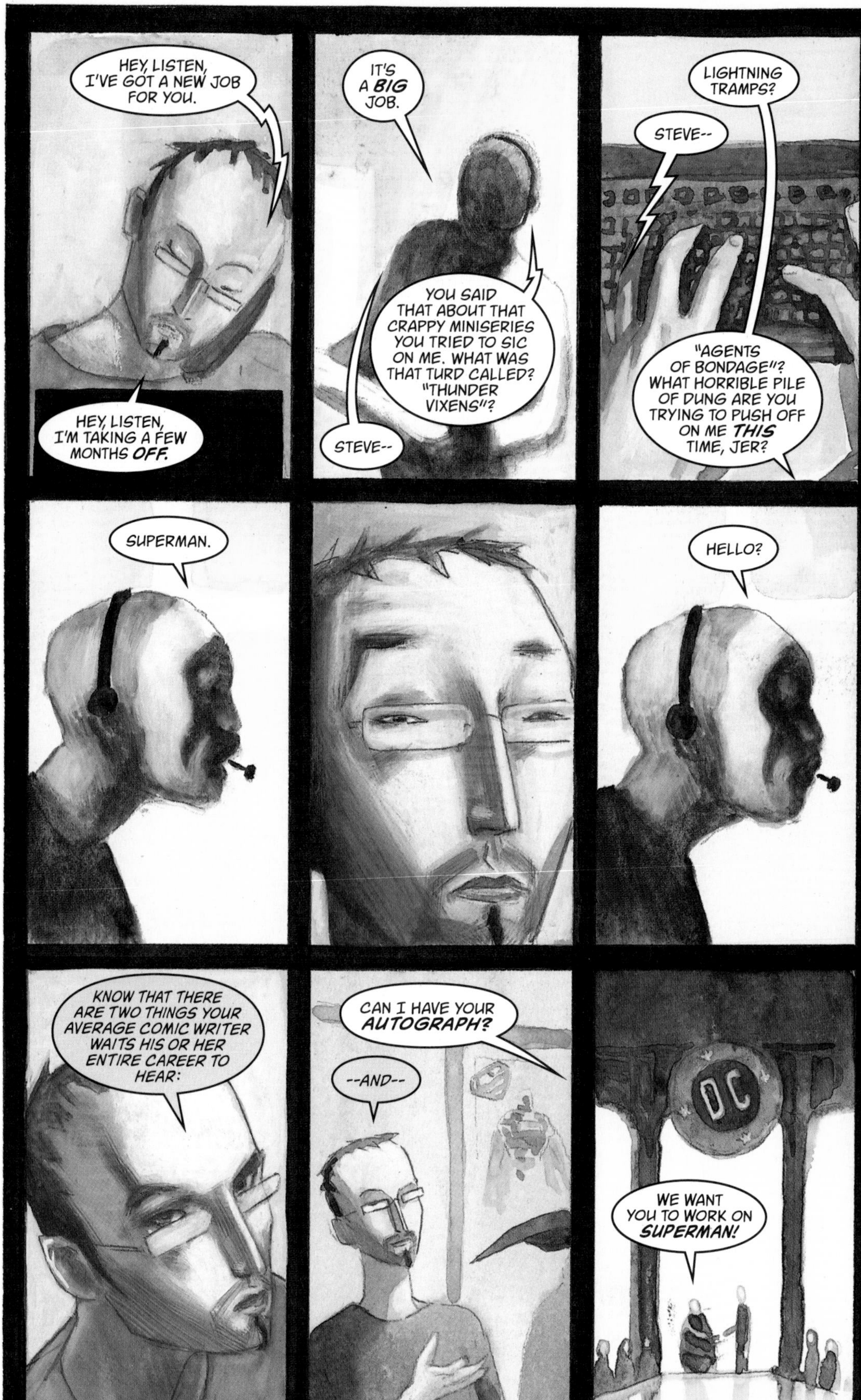
HEY, LISTEN, I'VE GOT A NEW JOB FOR YOU.
HEY, LISTEN, I'M TAKING A FEW MONTHS OFF.
IT'S A BIG JOB.
YOU SAID THAT ABOUT THAT CRAPPY MINISERIES YOU TRIED TO SIC ON ME. WHAT WAS THAT TURD CALLED? "THUNDER VIXENS"?
STEVE--
LIGHTNING TRAMPS?
STEVE--
"AGENTS OF BONDAGE"? WHAT HORRIBLE PILE OF DUNG ARE YOU TRYING TO PUSH OFF ON ME THIS TIME, JER?
SUPERMAN.
HELLO?
KNOW THAT THERE ARE TWO THINGS YOUR AVERAGE COMIC WRITER WAITS HIS OR HER ENTIRE CAREER TO HEAR:
CAN I HAVE YOUR AUTOGRAPH?
--AND--
DC
WE WANT YOU TO WORK ON SUPERMAN!

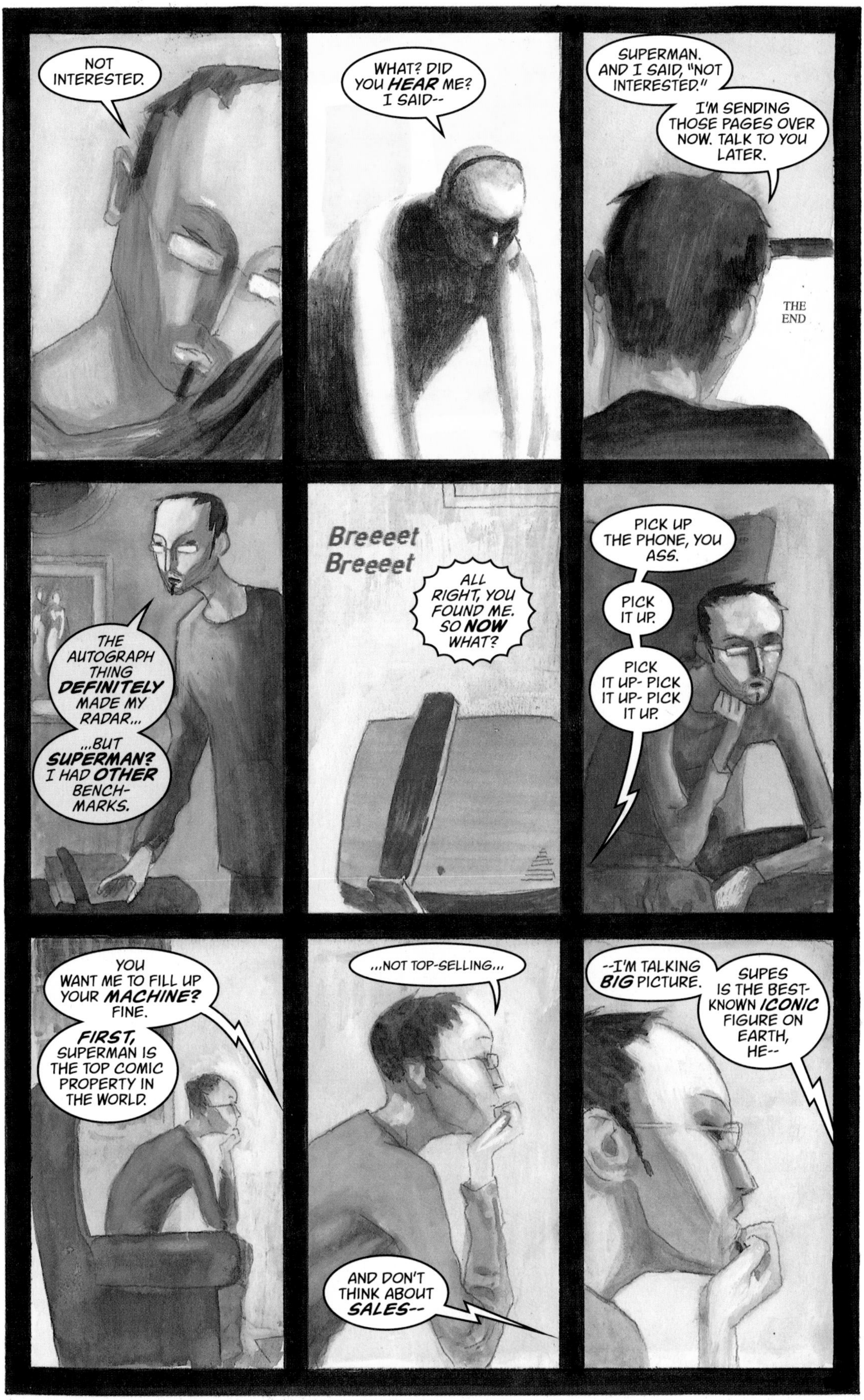

NOT INTERESTED.
WHAT? DID YOU HEAR ME? I SAID--
SUPERMAN. AND I SAID, "NOT INTERESTED."
I'M SENDING THOSE PAGES OVER NOW. TALK TO YOU LATER.
THE END
THE AUTOGRAPH THING DEFINITELY MADE MY RADAR...
...BUT SUPERMAN? I HAD OTHER BENCH-MARKS.
Breeeet Breeeet
ALL RIGHT, YOU FOUND ME. SO NOW WHAT?
PICK UP THE PHONE, YOU ASS.
PICK IT UP.
PICK IT UP- PICK IT UP- PICK IT UP.
YOU WANT ME TO FILL UP YOUR MACHINE? FINE.
FIRST, SUPERMAN IS THE TOP COMIC PROPERTY IN THE WORLD.
...NOT TOP-SELLING...
AND DON'T THINK ABOUT SALES--
--I'M TALKING BIG PICTURE.
SUPES IS THE BEST-KNOWN ICONIC FIGURE ON EARTH, HE--

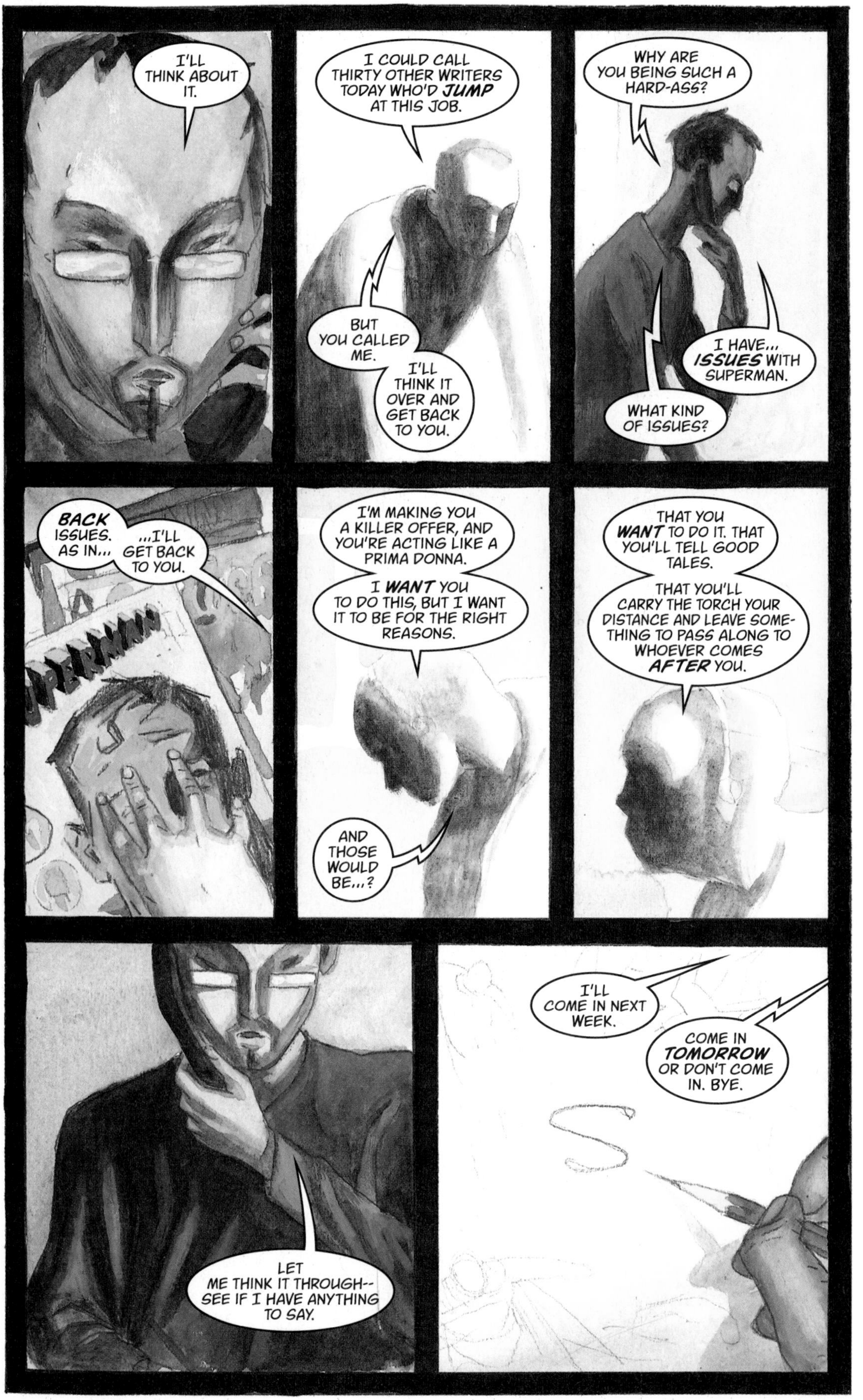
I'LL THINK ABOUT IT.
I COULD CALL THIRTY OTHER WRITERS TODAY WHO'D JUMP AT THIS JOB.
BUT YOU CALLED ME.
I'LL THINK IT OVER AND GET BACK TO YOU.
WHY ARE YOU BEING SUCH A HARD-ASS?
I HAVE... ISSUES WITH SUPERMAN.
WHAT KIND OF ISSUES?
BACK ISSUES. AS IN...
...I'LL GET BACK TO YOU.
I'M MAKING YOU A KILLER OFFER, AND YOU'RE ACTING LIKE A PRIMA DONNA.
I WANT YOU TO DO THIS, BUT I WANT IT TO BE FOR THE RIGHT REASONS.
AND THOSE WOULD BE...?
THAT YOU WANT TO DO IT. THAT YOU'LL TELL GOOD TALES.
THAT YOU'LL CARRY THE TORCH YOUR DISTANCE AND LEAVE SOMETHING TO PASS ALONG TO WHOEVER COMES AFTER YOU.
LET ME THINK IT THROUGH--SEE IF I HAVE ANYTHING TO SAY.
I'LL COME IN NEXT WEEK.
COME IN TOMORROW OR DON'T COME IN. BYE.

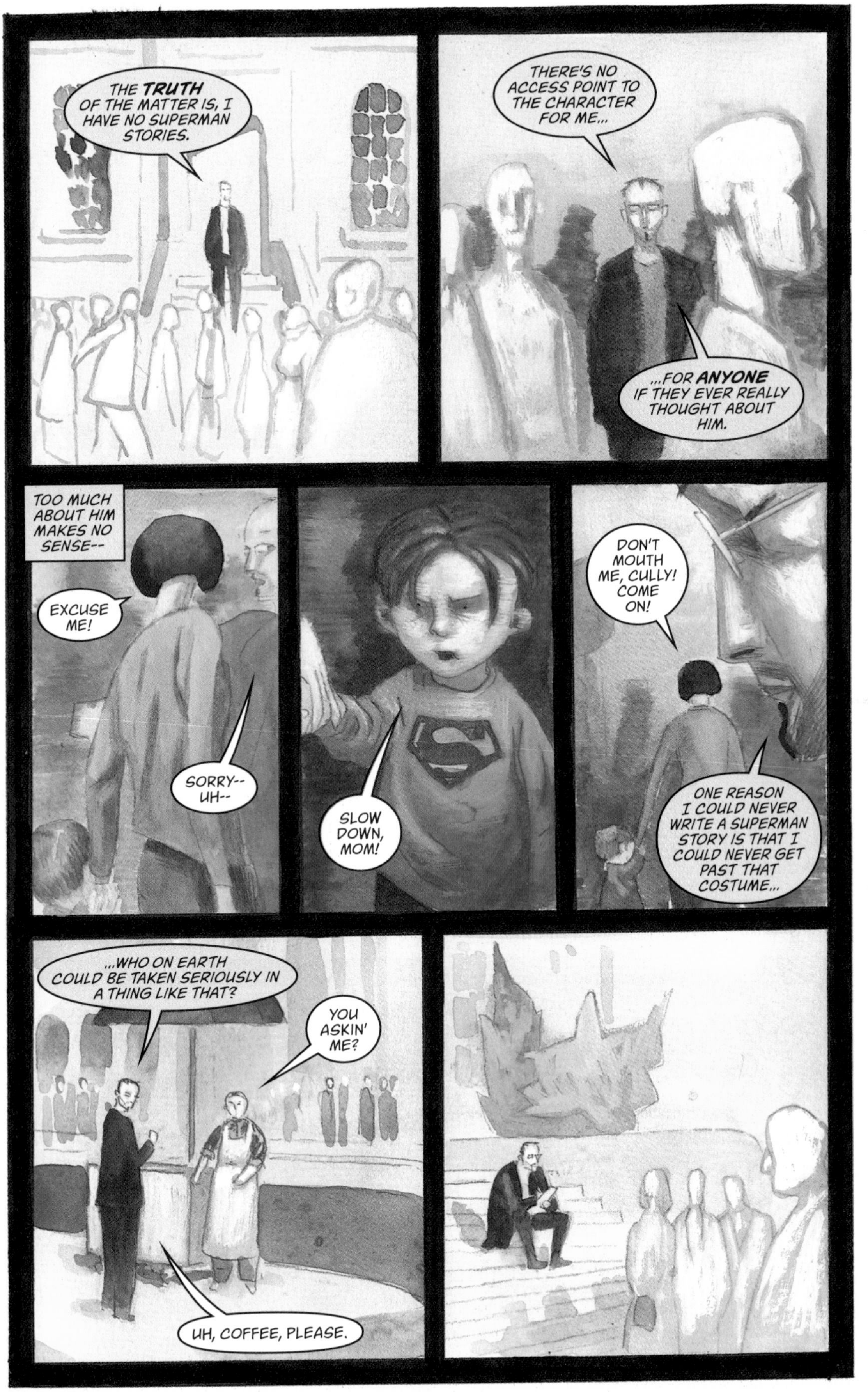

THE TRUTH OF THE MATTER IS, I HAVE NO SUPERMAN STORIES.
THERE'S NO ACCESS POINT TO THE CHARACTER FOR ME...
...FOR ANYONE IF THEY EVER REALLY THOUGHT ABOUT HIM.
TOO MUCH ABOUT HIM MAKES NO SENSE--
EXCUSE ME!
SORRY-- UH--
SLOW DOWN, MOM!
DON'T MOUTH ME, CULLY! COME ON!
ONE REASON I COULD NEVER WRITE A SUPERMAN STORY IS THAT I COULD NEVER GET PAST THAT COSTUME...
...WHO ON EARTH COULD BE TAKEN SERIOUSLY IN A THING LIKE THAT?
YOU ASKIN' ME?
UH, COFFEE, PLEASE.

THE COSTUME

SEVENTH GRADE WAS WHERE IT ALL STARTED TO GET WEIRD. SOME OF THE BOYS LOOKED LIKE KIDS, WHILE THEIR FRIENDS THE SAME AGE LOOKED LIKE MEN.

SOME OF THE GIRLS STILL PLAYED WITH DOLLS, BUT OTHERS BEGAN TO DRESS LIKE THEIR OLDER SISTERS.

AND THINGS THAT DIDN'T USED TO MATTER SUDDENLY DID.

THE KIDS CONGREGATED INTO GROUPS THAT WOULD ENDURE UNTIL GRADUATION DAY: THE JOCKS...THE BRAINS...THE GEEKS.

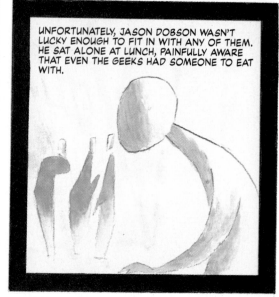

UNFORTUNATELY, JASON DOBSON WASN'T LUCKY ENOUGH TO FIT IN WITH ANY OF THEM. HE SAT ALONE AT LUNCH, PAINFULLY AWARE THAT EVEN THE GEEKS HAD SOMEONE TO EAT WITH.

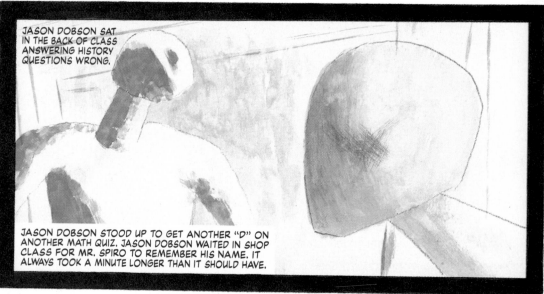

JASON DOBSON SAT IN THE BACK OF CLASS ANSWERING HISTORY QUESTIONS WRONG.

JASON DOBSON STOOD UP TO GET ANOTHER "D" ON ANOTHER MATH QUIZ. JASON DOBSON WAITED IN SHOP CLASS FOR MR. SPIRO TO REMEMBER HIS NAME. IT ALWAYS TOOK A MINUTE LONGER THAN IT SHOULD HAVE.

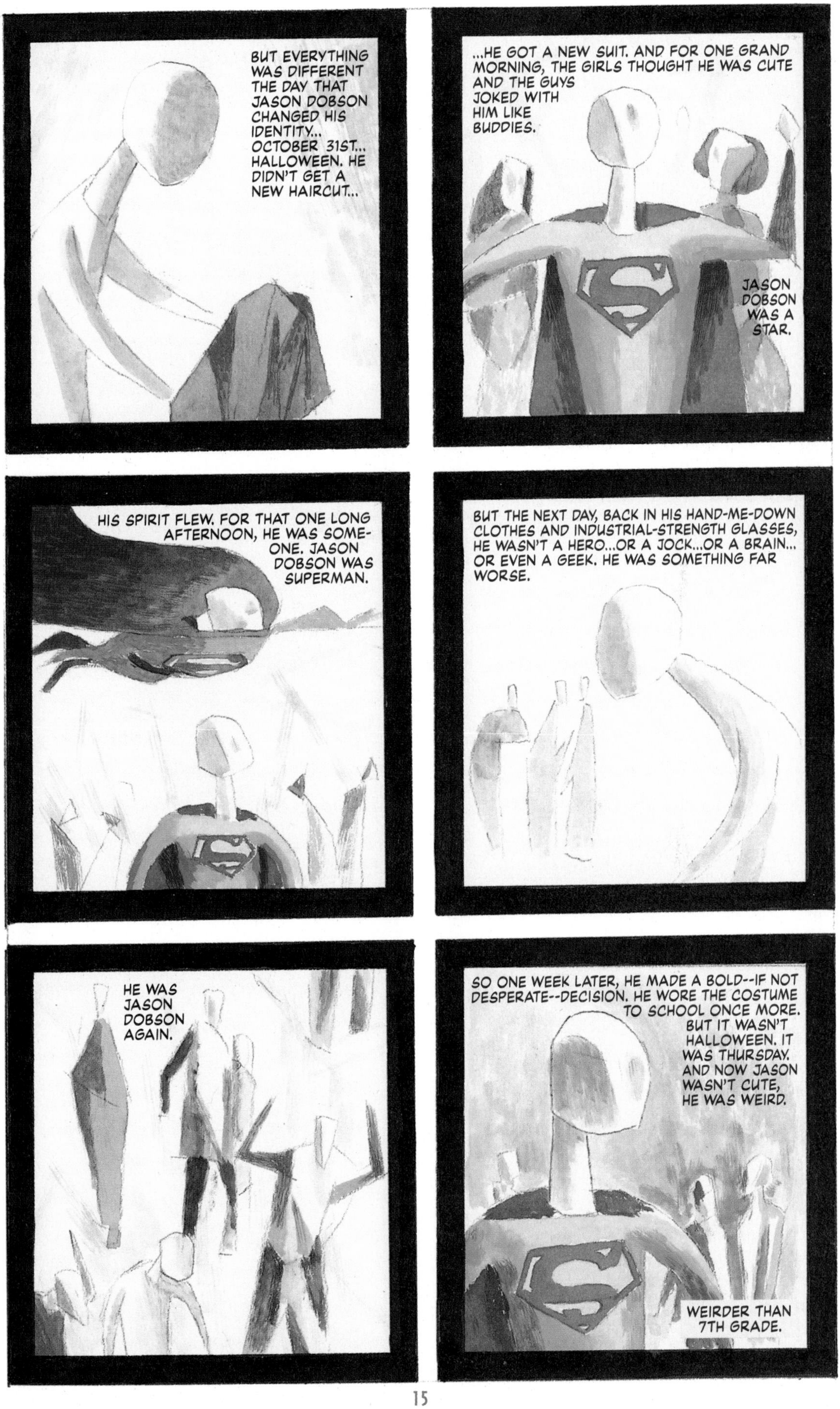
BUT EVERYTHING WAS DIFFERENT THE DAY THAT JASON DOBSON CHANGED HIS IDENTITY... OCTOBER 31ST... HALLOWEEN. HE DIDN'T GET A NEW HAIRCUT...
...HE GOT A NEW SUIT. AND FOR ONE GRAND MORNING, THE GIRLS THOUGHT HE WAS CUTE AND THE GUYS JOKED WITH HIM LIKE BUDDIES.
JASON DOBSON WAS A STAR.
HIS SPIRIT FLEW. FOR THAT ONE LONG AFTERNOON, HE WAS SOME-ONE. JASON DOBSON WAS SUPERMAN.
BUT THE NEXT DAY, BACK IN HIS HAND-ME-DOWN CLOTHES AND INDUSTRIAL-STRENGTH GLASSES, HE WASN'T A HERO...OR A JOCK...OR A BRAIN... OR EVEN A GEEK. HE WAS SOMETHING FAR WORSE.
HE WAS JASON DOBSON AGAIN.
SO ONE WEEK LATER, HE MADE A BOLD--IF NOT DESPERATE--DECISION. HE WORE THE COSTUME TO SCHOOL ONCE MORE. BUT IT WASN'T HALLOWEEN. IT WAS THURSDAY. AND NOW JASON WASN'T CUTE, HE WAS WEIRD.
WEIRDER THAN 7TH GRADE.

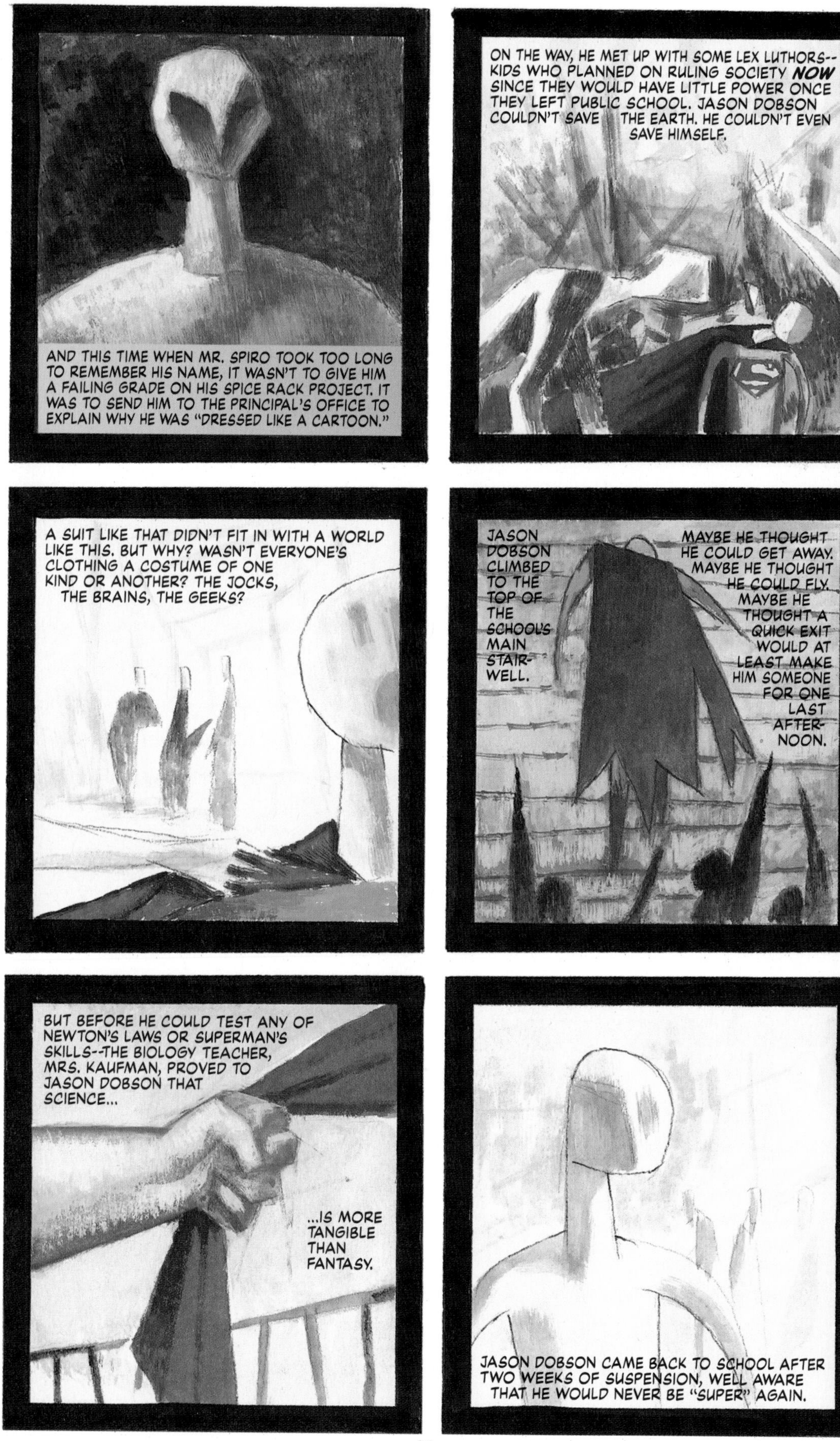
AND THIS TIME WHEN MR. SPIRO TOOK TOO LONG TO REMEMBER HIS NAME, IT WASN'T TO GIVE HIM A FAILING GRADE ON HIS SPICE RACK PROJECT. IT WAS TO SEND HIM TO THE PRINCIPAL'S OFFICE TO EXPLAIN WHY HE WAS "DRESSED LIKE A CARTOON."
ON THE WAY, HE MET UP WITH SOME LEX LUTHORS--KIDS WHO PLANNED ON RULING SOCIETY NOW SINCE THEY WOULD HAVE LITTLE POWER ONCE THEY LEFT PUBLIC SCHOOL. JASON DOBSON COULDN'T SAVE THE EARTH. HE COULDN'T EVEN SAVE HIMSELF.
A SUIT LIKE THAT DIDN'T FIT IN WITH A WORLD LIKE THIS. BUT WHY? WASN'T EVERYONE'S CLOTHING A COSTUME OF ONE KIND OR ANOTHER? THE JOCKS, THE BRAINS, THE GEEKS?
JASON DOBSON CLIMBED TO THE TOP OF THE SCHOOL'S MAIN STAIR-WELL.
MAYBE HE THOUGHT HE COULD GET AWAY. MAYBE HE THOUGHT HE COULD FLY. MAYBE HE THOUGHT A QUICK EXIT WOULD AT LEAST MAKE HIM SOMEONE FOR ONE LAST AFTER-NOON.
BUT BEFORE HE COULD TEST ANY OF NEWTON'S LAWS OR SUPERMAN'S SKILLS--THE BIOLOGY TEACHER, MRS. KAUFMAN, PROVED TO JASON DOBSON THAT SCIENCE...
...IS MORE TANGIBLE THAN FANTASY.
JASON DOBSON CAME BACK TO SCHOOL AFTER TWO WEEKS OF SUSPENSION, WELL AWARE THAT HE WOULD NEVER BE "SUPER" AGAIN.

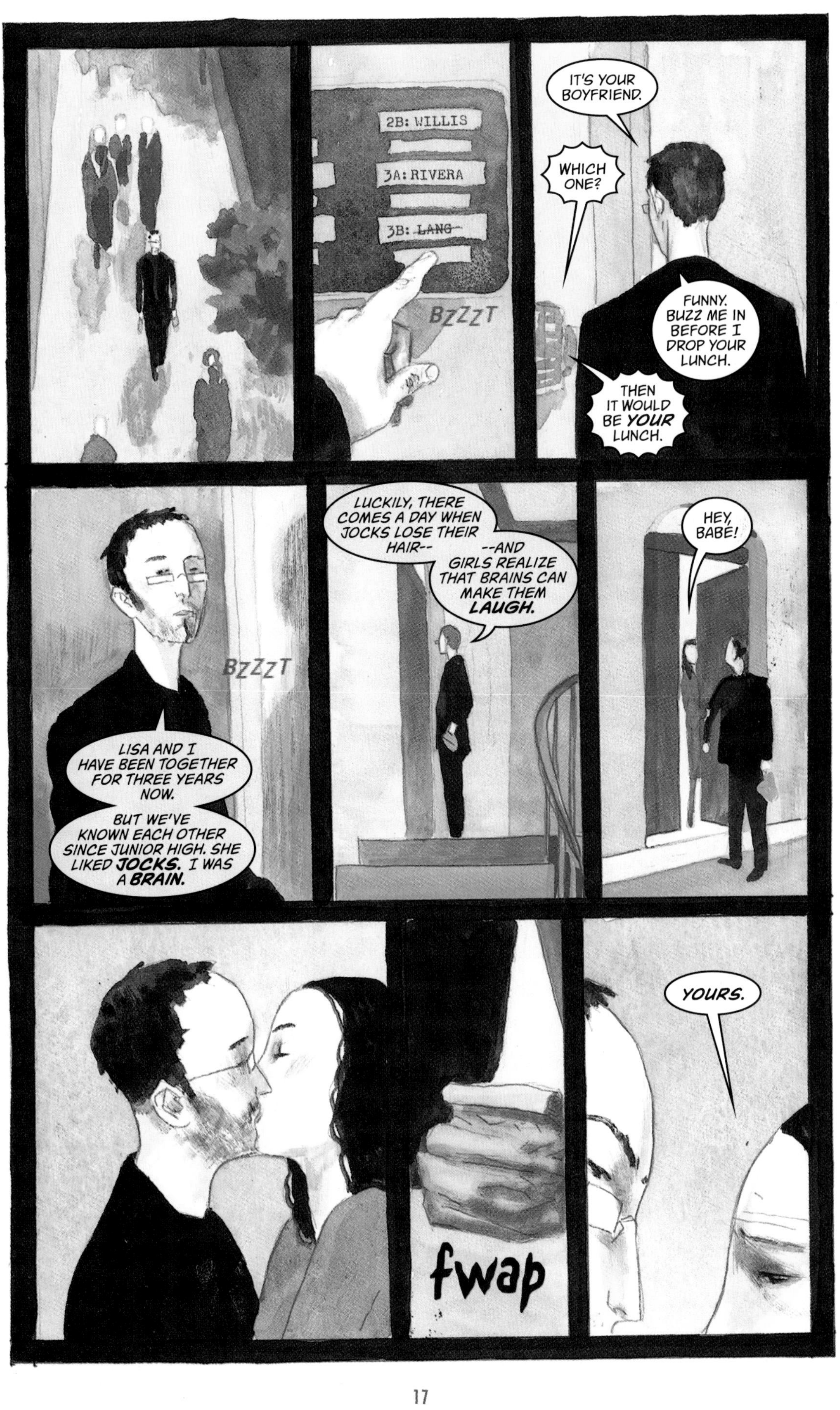
2B: WILLIS
3A: RIVERA
3B: LANG
BZZZT
IT'S YOUR BOYFRIEND.
WHICH ONE?
FUNNY. BUZZ ME IN BEFORE I DROP YOUR LUNCH.
THEN IT WOULD BE YOUR LUNCH.
BZZZT
LISA AND I HAVE BEEN TOGETHER FOR THREE YEARS NOW.
BUT WE'VE KNOWN EACH OTHER SINCE JUNIOR HIGH. SHE LIKED JOCKS. I WAS A BRAIN.
LUCKILY, THERE COMES A DAY WHEN JOCKS LOSE THEIR HAIR--
--AND GIRLS REALIZE THAT BRAINS CAN MAKE THEM LAUGH.
HEY, BABE!
fwap
YOURS.

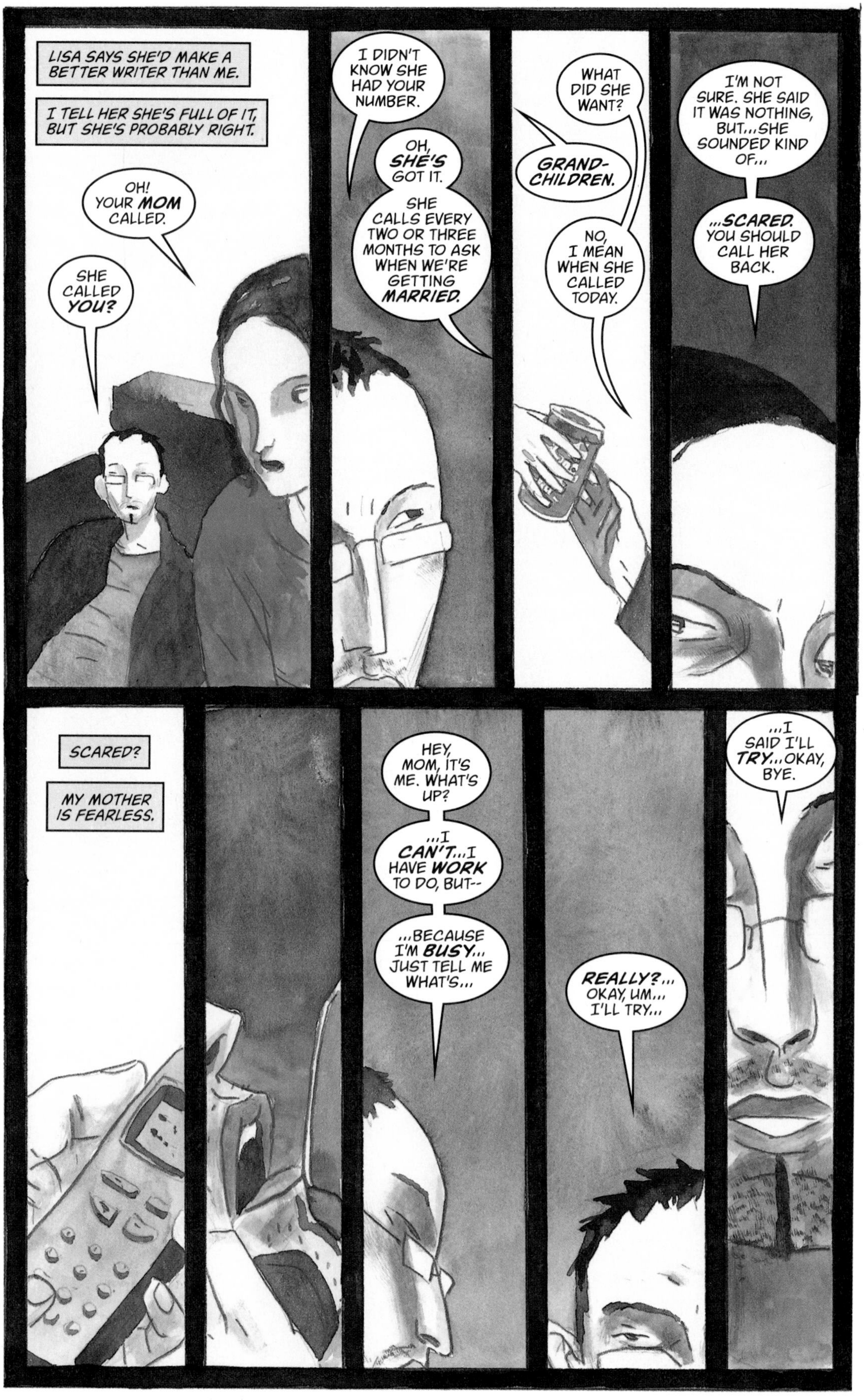
LISA SAYS SHE'D MAKE A BETTER WRITER THAN ME.
I TELL HER SHE'S FULL OF IT, BUT SHE'S PROBABLY RIGHT.
OH! YOUR MOM CALLED.
SHE CALLED YOU?
I DIDN'T KNOW SHE HAD YOUR NUMBER.
OH, SHE'S GOT IT.
SHE CALLS EVERY TWO OR THREE MONTHS TO ASK WHEN WE'RE GETTING MARRIED.
WHAT DID SHE WANT?
GRAND-CHILDREN.
NO, I MEAN WHEN SHE CALLED TODAY.
I'M NOT SURE. SHE SAID IT WAS NOTHING, BUT...SHE SOUNDED KIND OF...
...SCARED. YOU SHOULD CALL HER BACK.
SCARED?
MY MOTHER IS FEARLESS.
HEY, MOM, IT'S ME. WHAT'S UP?
...I CAN'T...I HAVE WORK TO DO, BUT--
...BECAUSE I'M BUSY... JUST TELL ME WHAT'S...
REALLY?... OKAY, UM... I'LL TRY...
...I SAID I'LL TRY...OKAY, BYE.

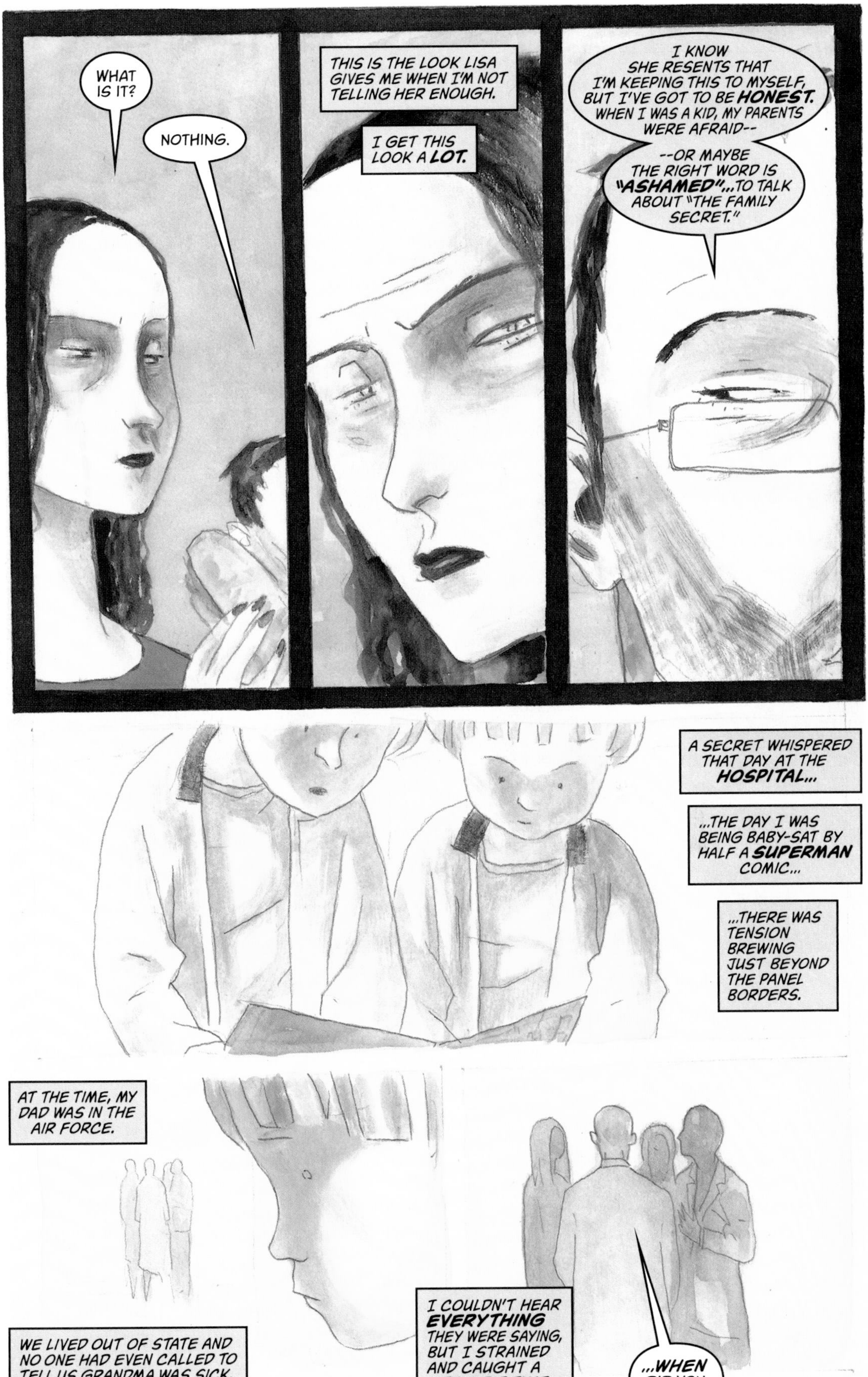

WHAT IS IT?
NOTHING.
THIS IS THE LOOK LISA GIVES ME WHEN I'M NOT TELLING HER ENOUGH.
I GET THIS LOOK A LOT.
I KNOW SHE RESENTS THAT I'M KEEPING THIS TO MYSELF, BUT I'VE GOT TO BE HONEST. WHEN I WAS A KID, MY PARENTS WERE AFRAID--
--OR MAYBE THE RIGHT WORD IS "ASHAMED"... TO TALK ABOUT "THE FAMILY SECRET."
A SECRET WHISPERED THAT DAY AT THE HOSPITAL...
...THE DAY I WAS BEING BABY-SAT BY HALF A SUPERMAN COMIC...
...THERE WAS TENSION BREWING JUST BEYOND THE PANEL BORDERS.
AT THE TIME, MY DAD WAS IN THE AIR FORCE.
WE LIVED OUT OF STATE AND NO ONE HAD EVEN CALLED TO TELL US GRANDMA WAS SICK.
I COULDN'T HEAR EVERYTHING THEY WERE SAYING, BUT I STRAINED AND CAUGHT A LITTLE BIT THAT STOOD OUT--
...WHEN DID YOU KNOW?

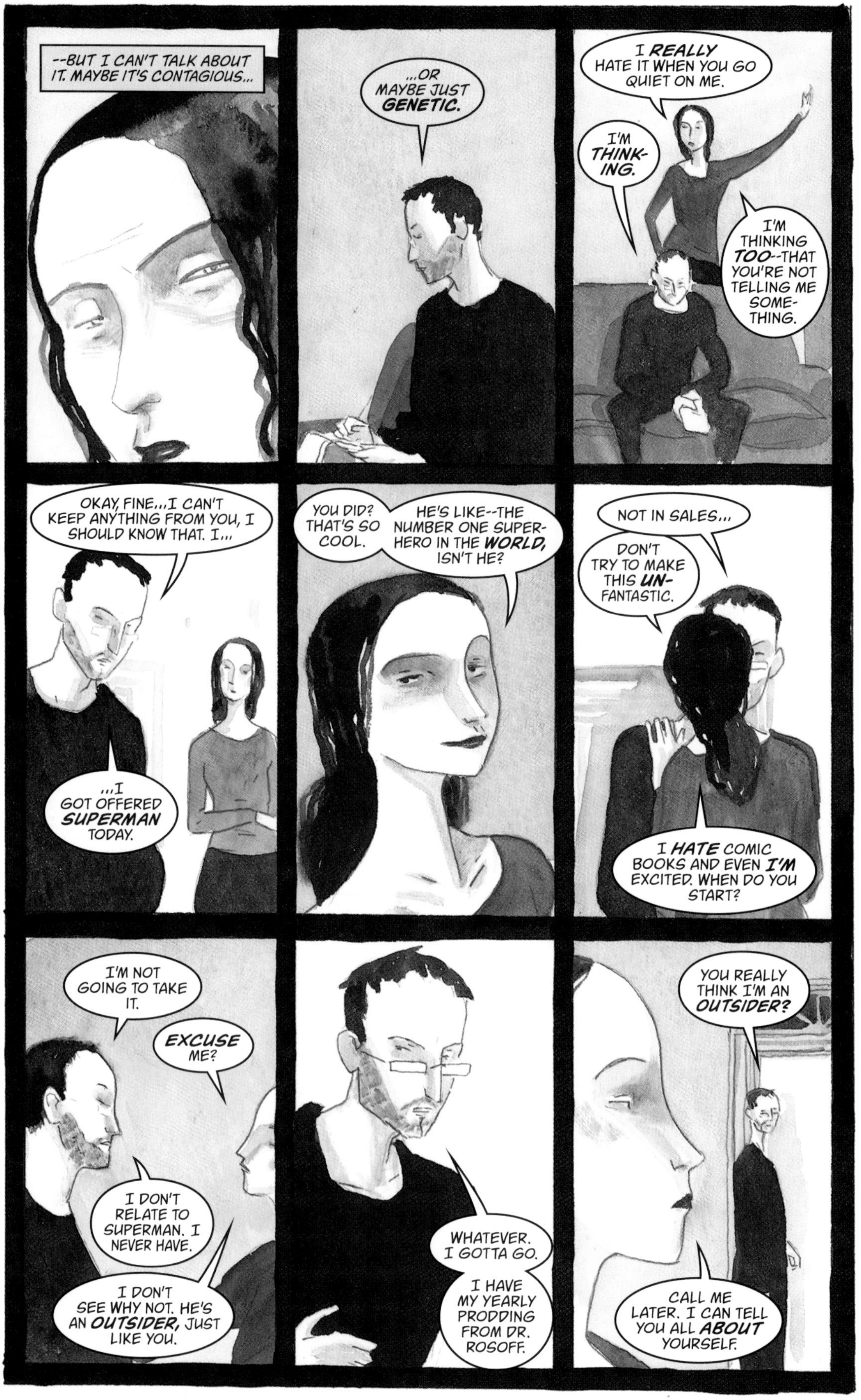
--BUT I CAN'T TALK ABOUT IT. MAYBE IT'S CONTAGIOUS...
...OR MAYBE JUST GENETIC.
I REALLY HATE IT WHEN YOU GO QUIET ON ME.
I'M THINKING.
I'M THINKING TOO--THAT YOU'RE NOT TELLING ME SOMETHING.
OKAY, FINE...I CAN'T KEEP ANYTHING FROM YOU, I SHOULD KNOW THAT. I...
...I GOT OFFERED SUPERMAN TODAY.
YOU DID? THAT'S SO COOL.
HE'S LIKE--THE NUMBER ONE SUPER-HERO IN THE WORLD, ISN'T HE?
NOT IN SALES...
DON'T TRY TO MAKE THIS UN-FANTASTIC.
I HATE COMIC BOOKS AND EVEN I'M EXCITED. WHEN DO YOU START?
I'M NOT GOING TO TAKE IT.
EXCUSE ME?
I DON'T RELATE TO SUPERMAN. I NEVER HAVE.
I DON'T SEE WHY NOT. HE'S AN OUTSIDER, JUST LIKE YOU.
WHATEVER. I GOTTA GO.
I HAVE MY YEARLY PRODDING FROM DR. ROSOFF.
YOU REALLY THINK I'M AN OUTSIDER?
CALL ME LATER. I CAN TELL YOU ALL ABOUT YOURSELF.

THE OUTSIDER

Suit and Tie
Hat and Glasses
Clark Kent fits
   right in
To the Walk-a-day
Work-a-day
Chit-chat
Clickity-clack
Paycheck and
   Collar-stay
Water-cooler
   world of
   Metropolis.

On that Oh-so-
   anticipated
   Lunch Break
There's always
   time for a
   Quick Change
A Quick Flight
Quick Work
For Would-be
   World-crushers
And then right
   back to
Suit and Tie
Hat and Glasses
Oh yes, Clark Kent
   fits right in.

But down in
   Accounting
Columns and Rows
And Linda Goldberg
   knows
The "Ha ha ha's" at
   the Water Cooler
Are Jokes about
   how "Her People"
Are always "the ones
   handling Money."
No Lunch Break
   long enough
To allow her a
   Quick Change
From her Heritage
   or its Critics.

Leather gloves
Denim fatigues
If DeRon Sanford
    didn't come to
    work
Everyone on The
    Planet would
    Notice
But when he Does
    come in
He doesn't Blend in
So much as
    Vanish in
Push and Sweep
    Plain Sight
The Invisible Man.

Until the Coffee
    Club Money
Goes Missing from
    Someone's Desk
No one looks at Clark,
    or even Linda
They don't say a Word
But don't really
    have to
And on his
    Lunch Break
There's no way
    DeRon can
Push and Sweep
    away the Skin
That makes him live
    Outside Himself.

And Greg Giddley
Whose legs are
    Aluminum Spokes
And Melissa
    Bandeau
Whose "Boyfriend"
    isn't a Boy at all
Join the Staff that
    Searches each
    day
For Suit and Tie
Hat and Glasses
That will bring
    them from the
    Outside
In.

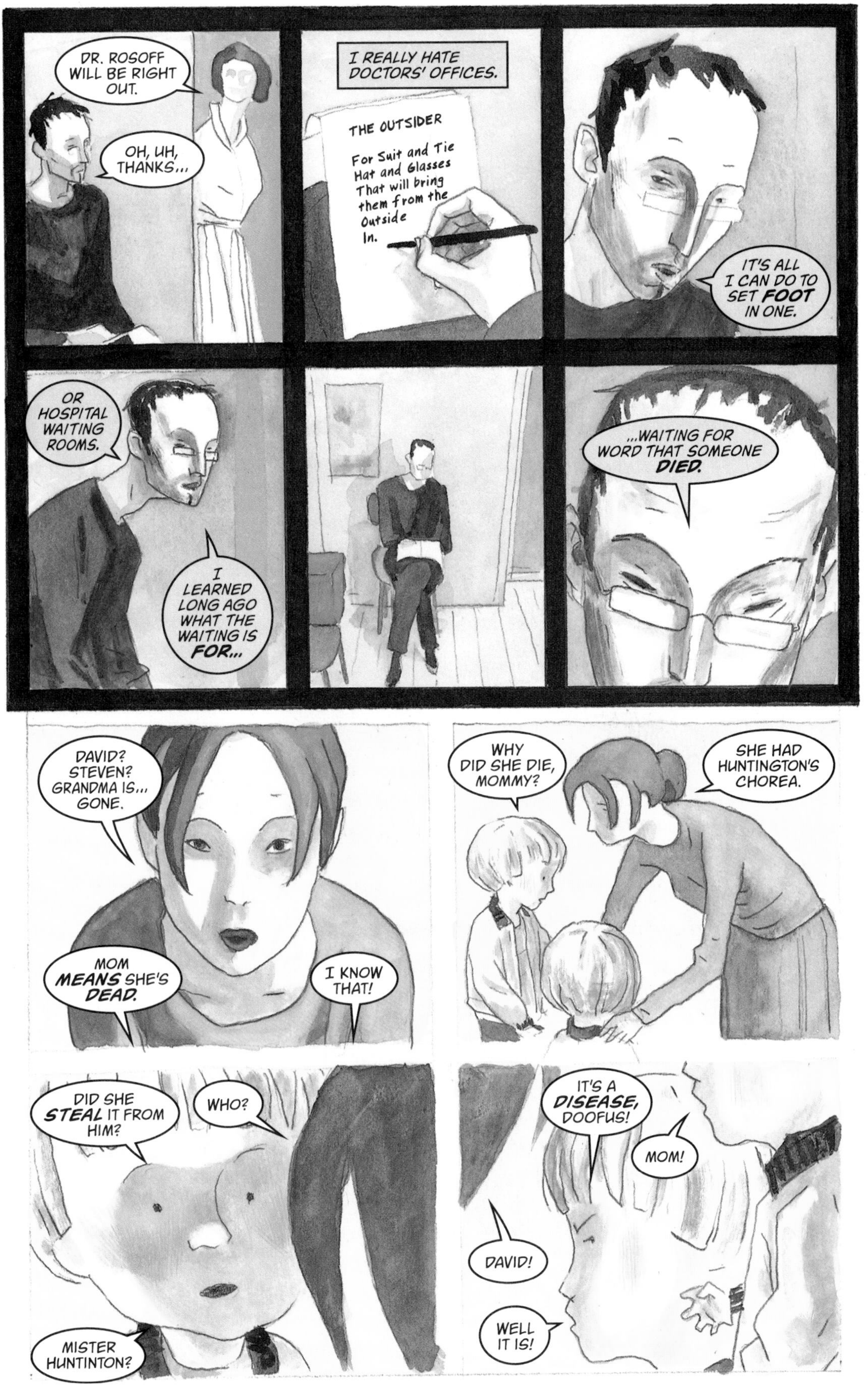
DR. ROSOFF WILL BE RIGHT OUT.
OH, UH, THANKS...
I REALLY HATE DOCTORS' OFFICES.
THE OUTSIDER
For Suit and Tie Hat and Glasses That will bring them from the Outside In.
IT'S ALL I CAN DO TO SET FOOT IN ONE.
OR HOSPITAL WAITING ROOMS.
I LEARNED LONG AGO WHAT THE WAITING IS FOR...
...WAITING FOR WORD THAT SOMEONE DIED.
DAVID? STEVEN? GRANDMA IS... GONE.
MOM MEANS SHE'S DEAD.
I KNOW THAT!
WHY DID SHE DIE, MOMMY?
SHE HAD HUNTINGTON'S CHOREA.
DID SHE STEAL IT FROM HIM?
WHO?
MISTER HUNTINTON?
IT'S A DISEASE, DOOFUS!
MOM!
DAVID!
WELL IT IS!

WELL IT *IS*...

FOR A FEW YEARS, I WROTE SOME "MUTANT" COMICS-- TRYING TO THINK OF EXCITING NEW *POWERS* THE HEROES' SECRET GENETIC STRUCTURES MIGHT GIVE THEM.

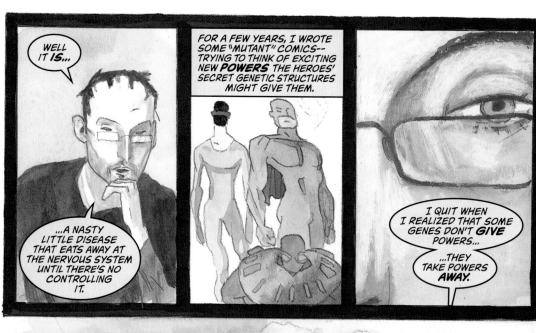

...A NASTY LITTLE DISEASE THAT EATS AWAY AT THE NERVOUS SYSTEM UNTIL THERE'S NO CONTROLLING IT.

I QUIT WHEN I REALIZED THAT SOME GENES DON'T *GIVE* POWERS...

...THEY TAKE POWERS *AWAY*.

THE POWER TO *WALK*.

THE POWER TO *SIT UP*.

THE POWER TO *EAT*.

THE POWER TO *SPEAK*.

MY PARENTS NEVER SPOKE MUCH ABOUT WHAT HAD KILLED MY GRAND- MOTHER.

THEY JUST SAID WHAT THEY KNEW:

THAT IT DAMAGES *NERVES* AND RUNS IN *FAMILIES*.

UNFORTUNATELY, WHAT THEY KNEW WASN'T MUCH BECAUSE HUNTINGTON'S CHOREA ISN'T A *GLAMOUR* DISEASE.

OKAY!

NOT ENOUGH *CASUALTIES*. NO *CELEBRITIES* HAVE DIED FROM IT...

...JUST PEOPLE LIKE MY *GRANDMOTHER*.

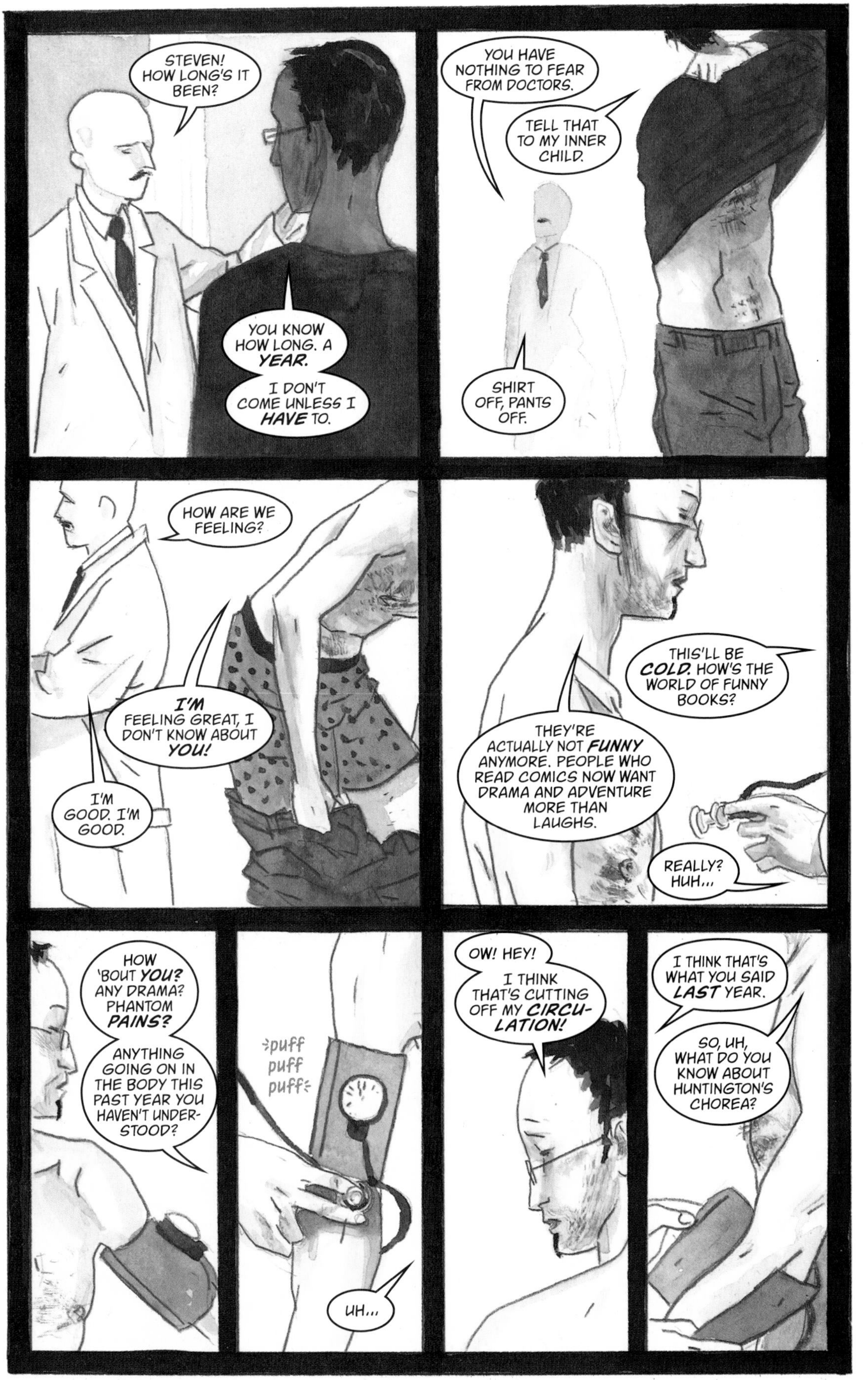
STEVEN! HOW LONG'S IT BEEN?
YOU KNOW HOW LONG. A YEAR.
I DON'T COME UNLESS I HAVE TO.
YOU HAVE NOTHING TO FEAR FROM DOCTORS.
TELL THAT TO MY INNER CHILD.
SHIRT OFF, PANTS OFF.
HOW ARE WE FEELING?
I'M FEELING GREAT, I DON'T KNOW ABOUT YOU!
I'M GOOD. I'M GOOD.
THIS'LL BE COLD. HOW'S THE WORLD OF FUNNY BOOKS?
THEY'RE ACTUALLY NOT FUNNY ANYMORE. PEOPLE WHO READ COMICS NOW WANT DRAMA AND ADVENTURE MORE THAN LAUGHS.
REALLY? HUH...
HOW 'BOUT YOU? ANY DRAMA? PHANTOM PAINS?
ANYTHING GOING ON IN THE BODY THIS PAST YEAR YOU HAVEN'T UNDERSTOOD?
puff puff puff
UH...
OW! HEY!
I THINK THAT'S CUTTING OFF MY CIRCULATION!
I THINK THAT'S WHAT YOU SAID LAST YEAR.
SO, UH, WHAT DO YOU KNOW ABOUT HUNTINGTON'S CHOREA?

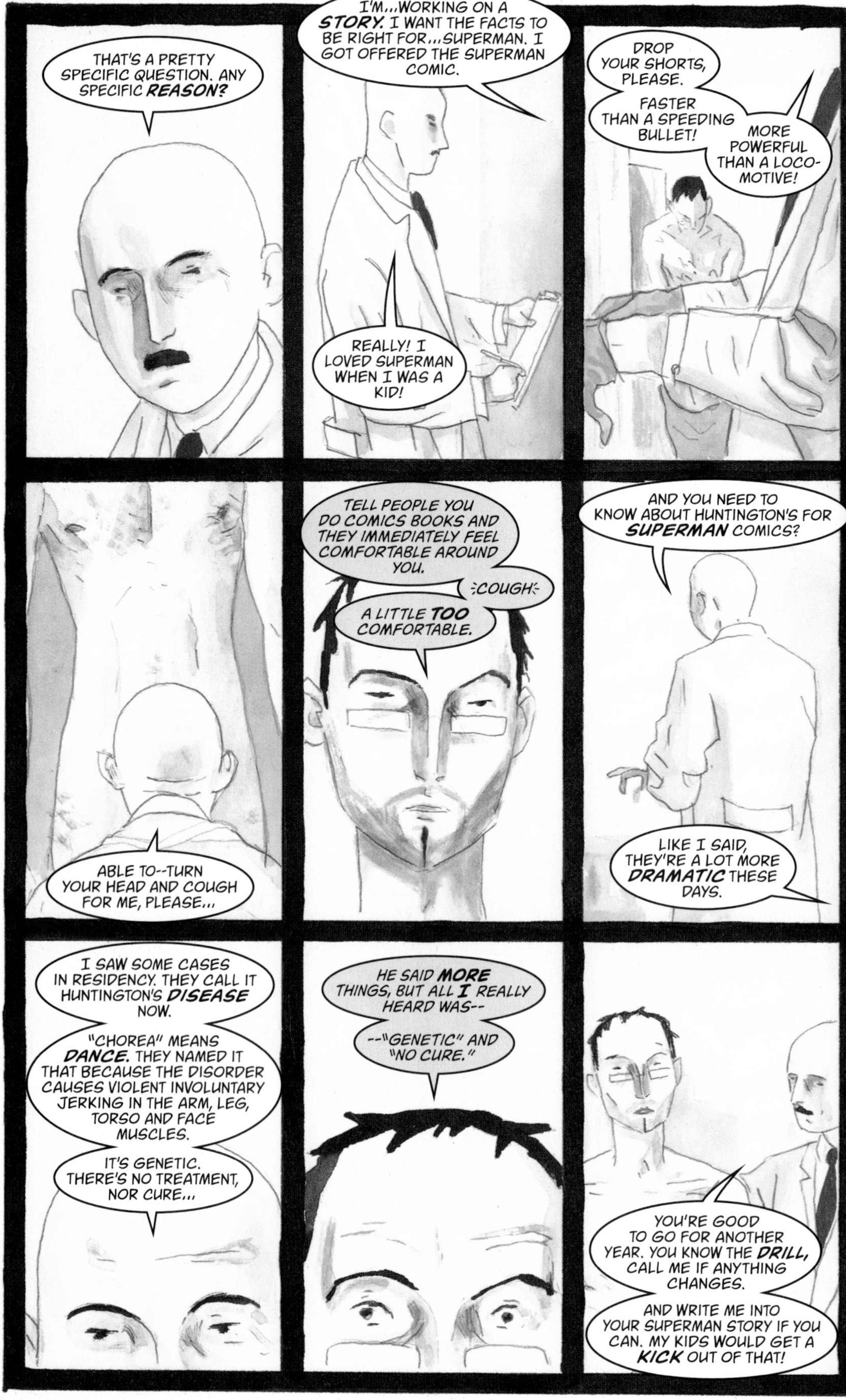
THAT'S A PRETTY SPECIFIC QUESTION. ANY SPECIFIC REASON?
I'M...WORKING ON A STORY. I WANT THE FACTS TO BE RIGHT FOR...SUPERMAN. I GOT OFFERED THE SUPERMAN COMIC.
REALLY! I LOVED SUPERMAN WHEN I WAS A KID!
DROP YOUR SHORTS, PLEASE.
FASTER THAN A SPEEDING BULLET!
MORE POWERFUL THAN A LOCO-MOTIVE!
ABLE TO--TURN YOUR HEAD AND COUGH FOR ME, PLEASE...
TELL PEOPLE YOU DO COMICS BOOKS AND THEY IMMEDIATELY FEEL COMFORTABLE AROUND YOU.
COUGH
A LITTLE TOO COMFORTABLE.
AND YOU NEED TO KNOW ABOUT HUNTINGTON'S FOR SUPERMAN COMICS?
LIKE I SAID, THEY'RE A LOT MORE DRAMATIC THESE DAYS.
I SAW SOME CASES IN RESIDENCY. THEY CALL IT HUNTINGTON'S DISEASE NOW.
"CHOREA" MEANS DANCE. THEY NAMED IT THAT BECAUSE THE DISORDER CAUSES VIOLENT INVOLUNTARY JERKING IN THE ARM, LEG, TORSO AND FACE MUSCLES.
IT'S GENETIC. THERE'S NO TREATMENT, NOR CURE...
HE SAID MORE THINGS, BUT ALL I REALLY HEARD WAS--
--"GENETIC" AND "NO CURE."
YOU'RE GOOD TO GO FOR ANOTHER YEAR. YOU KNOW THE DRILL, CALL ME IF ANYTHING CHANGES.
AND WRITE ME INTO YOUR SUPERMAN STORY IF YOU CAN. MY KIDS WOULD GET A KICK OUT OF THAT!

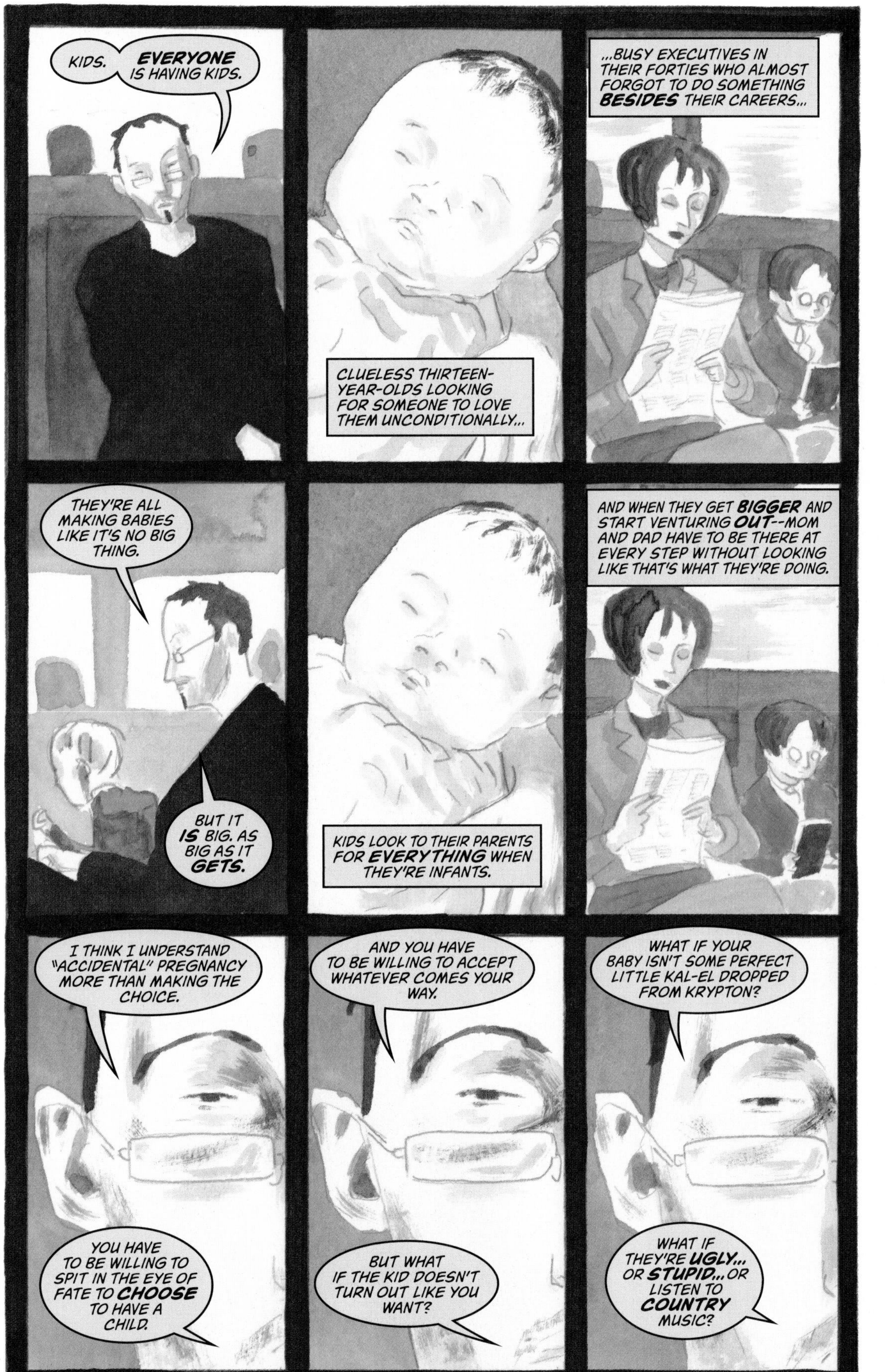
KIDS.
EVERYONE IS HAVING KIDS.
CLUELESS THIRTEEN-YEAR-OLDS LOOKING FOR SOMEONE TO LOVE THEM UNCONDITIONALLY...
...BUSY EXECUTIVES IN THEIR FORTIES WHO ALMOST FORGOT TO DO SOMETHING BESIDES THEIR CAREERS...
THEY'RE ALL MAKING BABIES LIKE IT'S NO BIG THING.
BUT IT IS BIG. AS BIG AS IT GETS.
KIDS LOOK TO THEIR PARENTS FOR EVERYTHING WHEN THEY'RE INFANTS.
AND WHEN THEY GET BIGGER AND START VENTURING OUT--MOM AND DAD HAVE TO BE THERE AT EVERY STEP WITHOUT LOOKING LIKE THAT'S WHAT THEY'RE DOING.
I THINK I UNDERSTAND "ACCIDENTAL" PREGNANCY MORE THAN MAKING THE CHOICE.
YOU HAVE TO BE WILLING TO SPIT IN THE EYE OF FATE TO CHOOSE TO HAVE A CHILD.
AND YOU HAVE TO BE WILLING TO ACCEPT WHATEVER COMES YOUR WAY.
BUT WHAT IF THE KID DOESN'T TURN OUT LIKE YOU WANT?
WHAT IF YOUR BABY ISN'T SOME PERFECT LITTLE KAL-EL DROPPED FROM KRYPTON?
WHAT IF THEY'RE UGLY... OR STUPID... OR LISTEN TO COUNTRY MUSIC?

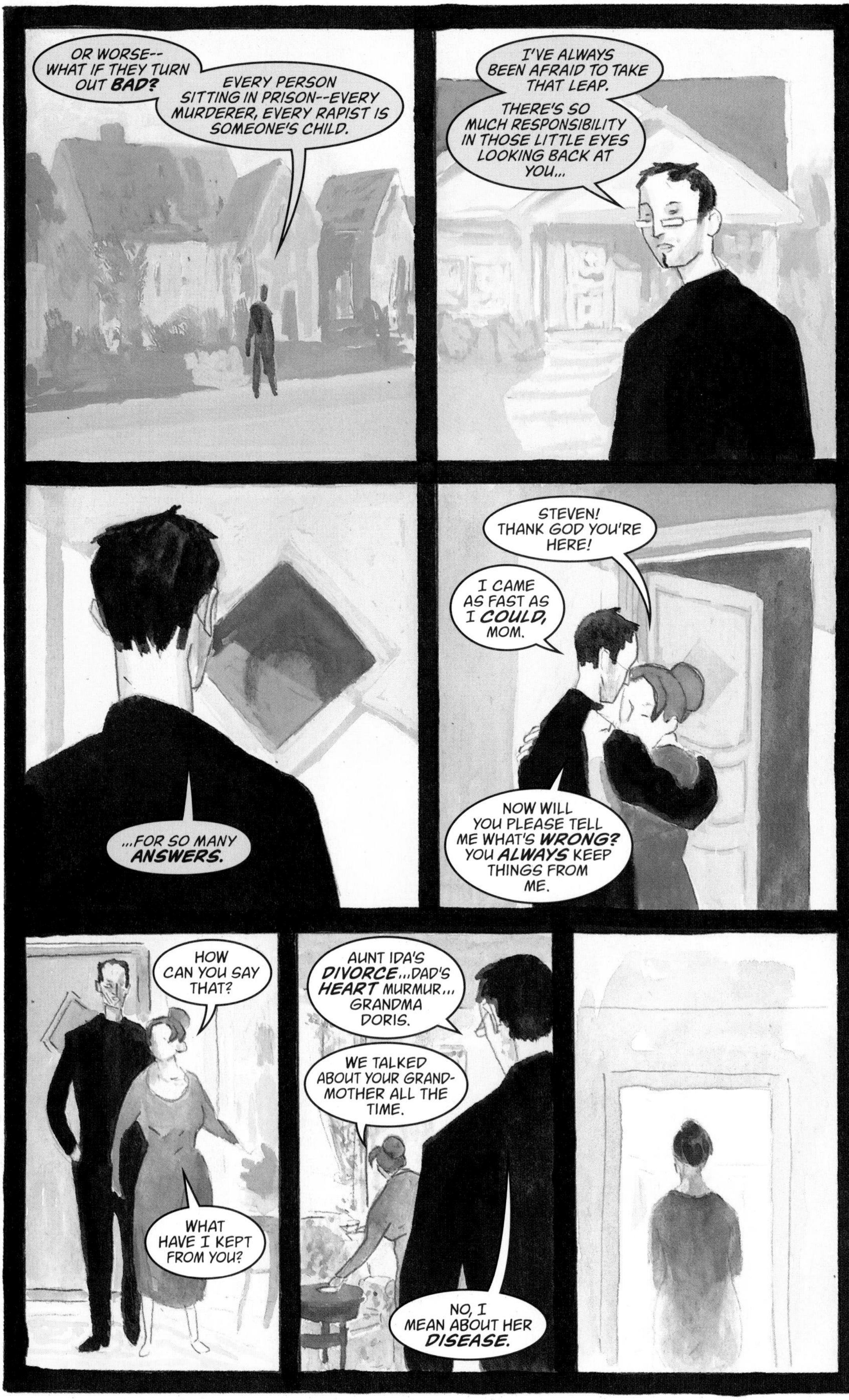
OR WORSE--
WHAT IF THEY TURN OUT BAD?
EVERY PERSON SITTING IN PRISON--EVERY MURDERER, EVERY RAPIST IS SOMEONE'S CHILD.
I'VE ALWAYS BEEN AFRAID TO TAKE THAT LEAP.
THERE'S SO MUCH RESPONSIBILITY IN THOSE LITTLE EYES LOOKING BACK AT YOU...
...FOR SO MANY ANSWERS.
STEVEN! THANK GOD YOU'RE HERE!
I CAME AS FAST AS I COULD, MOM.
NOW WILL YOU PLEASE TELL ME WHAT'S WRONG? YOU ALWAYS KEEP THINGS FROM ME.
HOW CAN YOU SAY THAT?
WHAT HAVE I KEPT FROM YOU?
AUNT IDA'S DIVORCE...DAD'S HEART MURMUR... GRANDMA DORIS.
WE TALKED ABOUT YOUR GRAND-MOTHER ALL THE TIME.
NO, I MEAN ABOUT HER DISEASE.

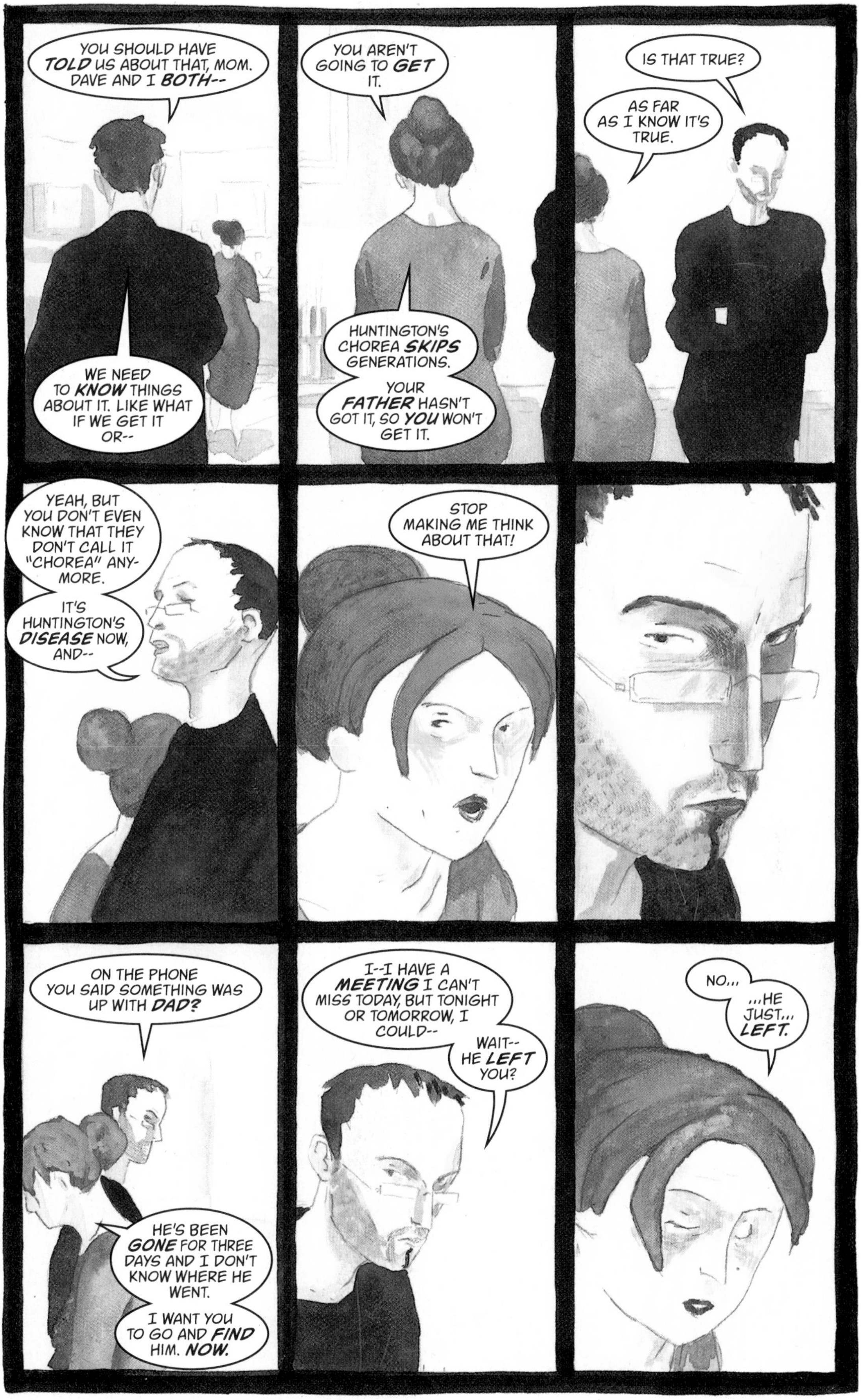
YOU SHOULD HAVE TOLD US ABOUT THAT, MOM. DAVE AND I BOTH--
WE NEED TO KNOW THINGS ABOUT IT. LIKE WHAT IF WE GET IT OR--
YOU AREN'T GOING TO GET IT.
HUNTINGTON'S CHOREA SKIPS GENERATIONS.
YOUR FATHER HASN'T GOT IT, SO YOU WON'T GET IT.
IS THAT TRUE?
AS FAR AS I KNOW IT'S TRUE.
YEAH, BUT YOU DON'T EVEN KNOW THAT THEY DON'T CALL IT "CHOREA" ANY-MORE.
IT'S HUNTINGTON'S DISEASE NOW, AND--
STOP MAKING ME THINK ABOUT THAT!
ON THE PHONE YOU SAID SOMETHING WAS UP WITH DAD?
HE'S BEEN GONE FOR THREE DAYS AND I DON'T KNOW WHERE HE WENT.
I WANT YOU TO GO AND FIND HIM. NOW.
I--I HAVE A MEETING I CAN'T MISS TODAY, BUT TONIGHT OR TOMORROW, I COULD--
WAIT--HE LEFT YOU?
NO...
...HE JUST... LEFT.

LEAVING KRYPTON (Life on another world)

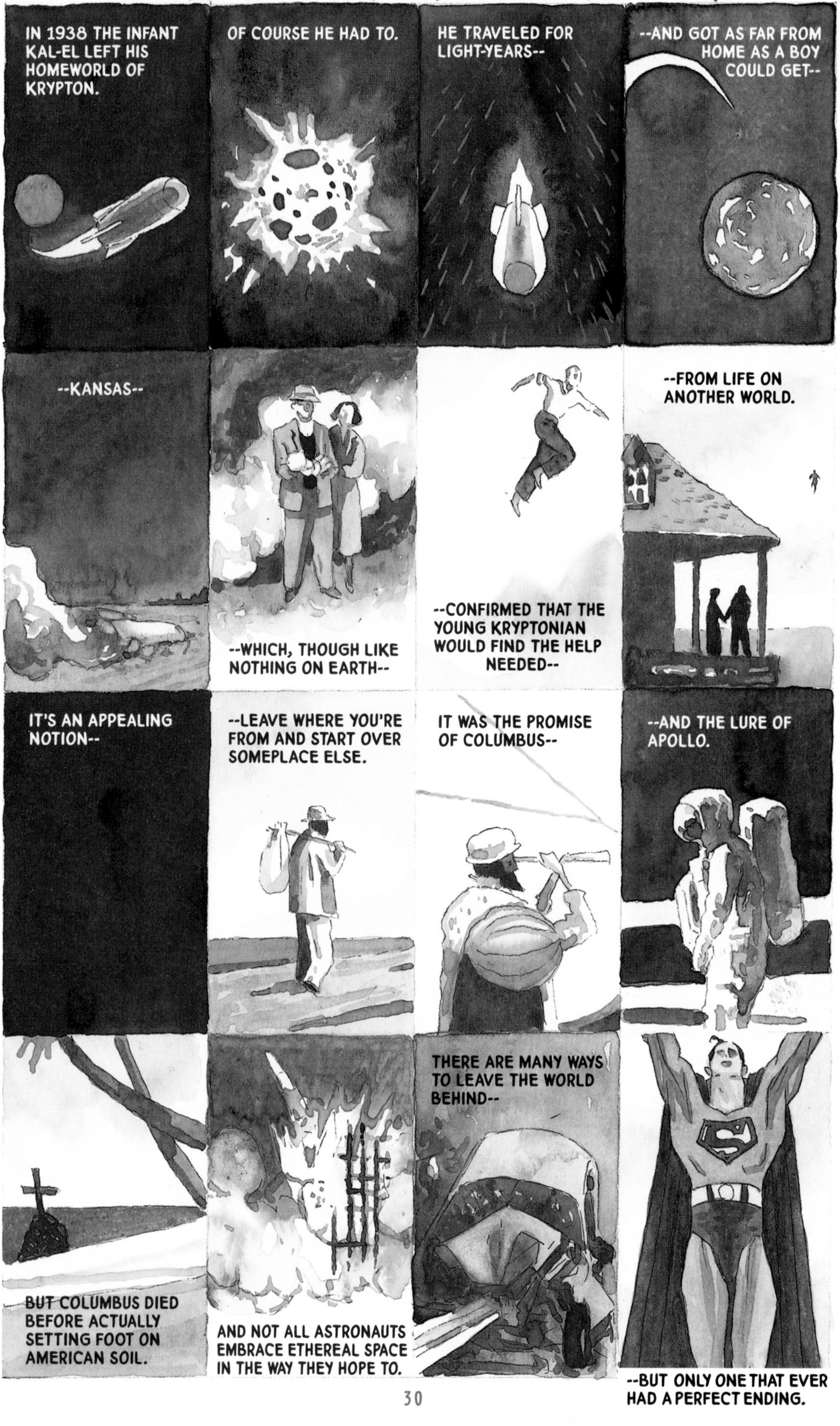
IN 1938 THE INFANT KAL-EL LEFT HIS HOMEWORLD OF KRYPTON.
OF COURSE HE HAD TO.
HE TRAVELED FOR LIGHT-YEARS--
--AND GOT AS FAR FROM HOME AS A BOY COULD GET--
--KANSAS--
--WHICH, THOUGH LIKE NOTHING ON EARTH--
--CONFIRMED THAT THE YOUNG KRYPTONIAN WOULD FIND THE HELP NEEDED--
--FROM LIFE ON ANOTHER WORLD.
IT'S AN APPEALING NOTION--
--LEAVE WHERE YOU'RE FROM AND START OVER SOMEPLACE ELSE.
IT WAS THE PROMISE OF COLUMBUS--
--AND THE LURE OF APOLLO.
BUT COLUMBUS DIED BEFORE ACTUALLY SETTING FOOT ON AMERICAN SOIL.
AND NOT ALL ASTRONAUTS EMBRACE ETHEREAL SPACE IN THE WAY THEY HOPE TO.
THERE ARE MANY WAYS TO LEAVE THE WORLD BEHIND--
--BUT ONLY ONE THAT EVER HAD A PERFECT ENDING.

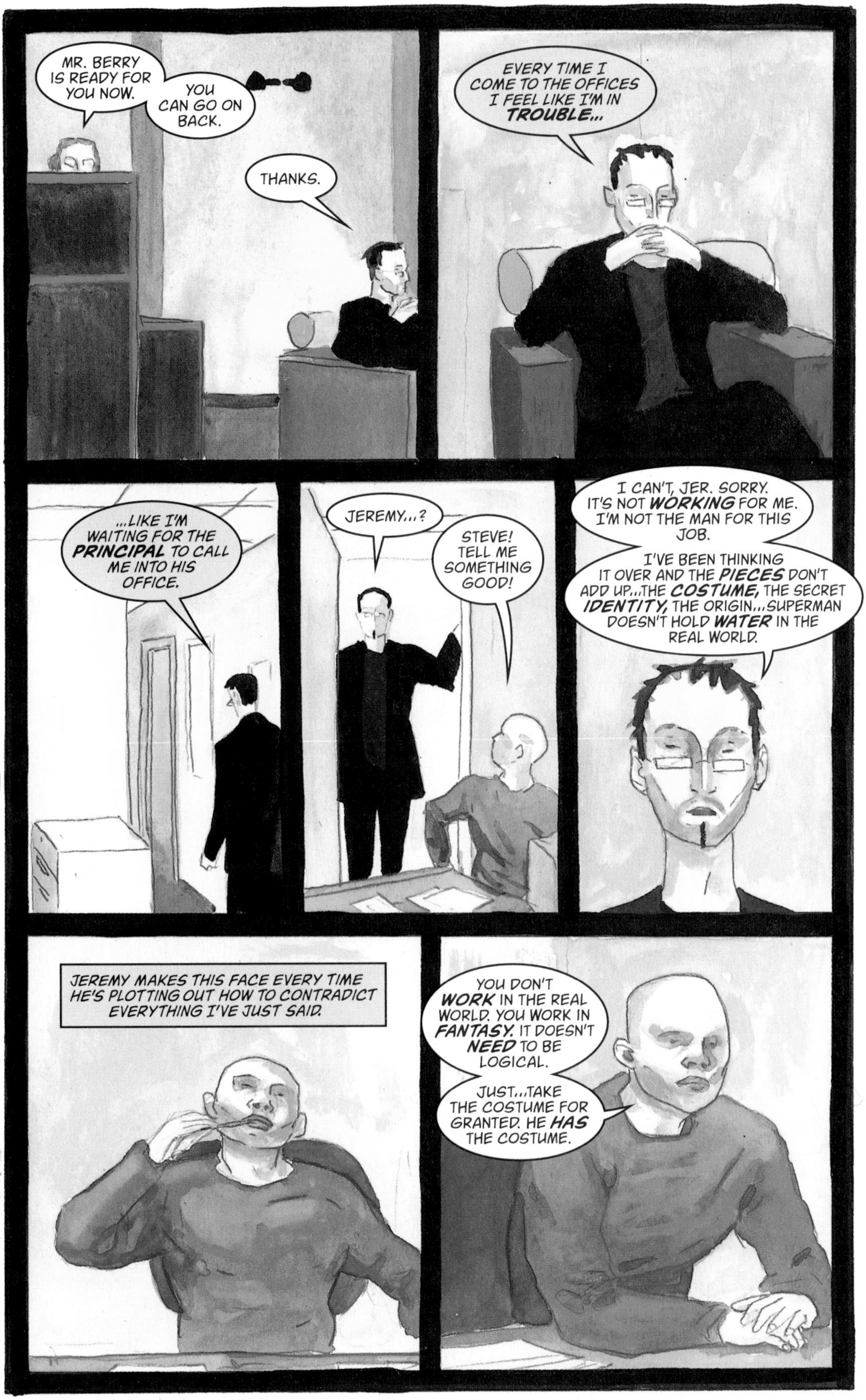

MR. BERRY IS READY FOR YOU NOW.
YOU CAN GO ON BACK.
THANKS.
EVERY TIME I COME TO THE OFFICES I FEEL LIKE I'M IN TROUBLE...
...LIKE I'M WAITING FOR THE PRINCIPAL TO CALL ME INTO HIS OFFICE.
JEREMY...?
STEVE! TELL ME SOMETHING GOOD!
I CAN'T, JER. SORRY. IT'S NOT WORKING FOR ME. I'M NOT THE MAN FOR THIS JOB.
I'VE BEEN THINKING IT OVER AND THE PIECES DON'T ADD UP...THE COSTUME, THE SECRET IDENTITY, THE ORIGIN...SUPERMAN DOESN'T HOLD WATER IN THE REAL WORLD.
JEREMY MAKES THIS FACE EVERY TIME HE'S PLOTTING OUT HOW TO CONTRADICT EVERYTHING I'VE JUST SAID.
YOU DON'T WORK IN THE REAL WORLD. YOU WORK IN FANTASY. IT DOESN'T NEED TO BE LOGICAL.
JUST...TAKE THE COSTUME FOR GRANTED. HE HAS THE COSTUME.

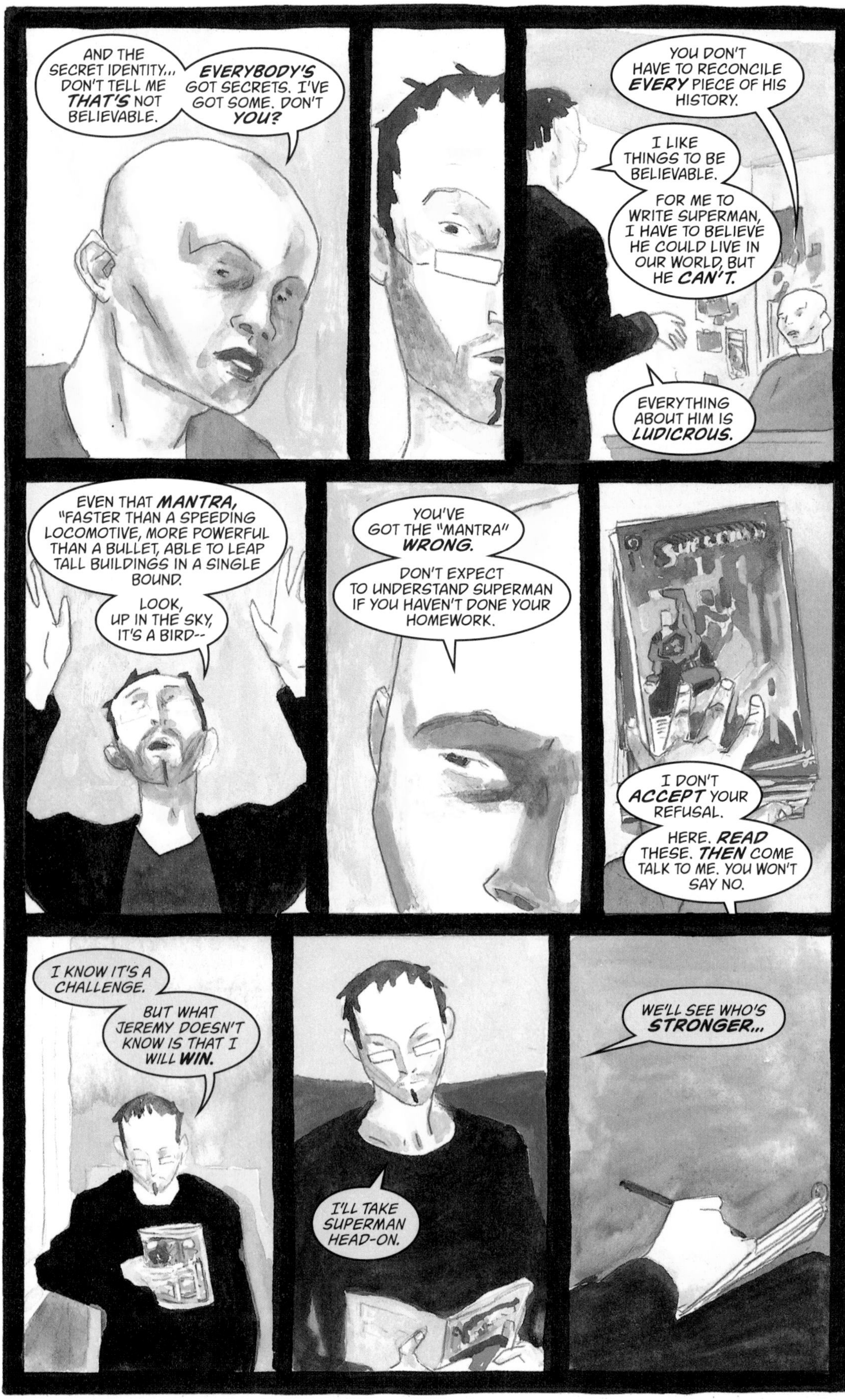
AND THE SECRET IDENTITY... DON'T TELL ME THAT'S NOT BELIEVABLE.
EVERYBODY'S GOT SECRETS. I'VE GOT SOME. DON'T YOU?
YOU DON'T HAVE TO RECONCILE EVERY PIECE OF HIS HISTORY.
I LIKE THINGS TO BE BELIEVABLE.
FOR ME TO WRITE SUPERMAN, I HAVE TO BELIEVE HE COULD LIVE IN OUR WORLD, BUT HE CAN'T.
EVERYTHING ABOUT HIM IS LUDICROUS.
EVEN THAT MANTRA, "FASTER THAN A SPEEDING LOCOMOTIVE, MORE POWERFUL THAN A BULLET, ABLE TO LEAP TALL BUILDINGS IN A SINGLE BOUND.
LOOK, UP IN THE SKY, IT'S A BIRD--
YOU'VE GOT THE "MANTRA" WRONG.
DON'T EXPECT TO UNDERSTAND SUPERMAN IF YOU HAVEN'T DONE YOUR HOMEWORK.
I DON'T ACCEPT YOUR REFUSAL.
HERE. READ THESE. THEN COME TALK TO ME. YOU WON'T SAY NO.
I KNOW IT'S A CHALLENGE.
BUT WHAT JEREMY DOESN'T KNOW IS THAT I WILL WIN.
I'LL TAKE SUPERMAN HEAD-ON.
WE'LL SEE WHO'S STRONGER...

INVULNERABLE

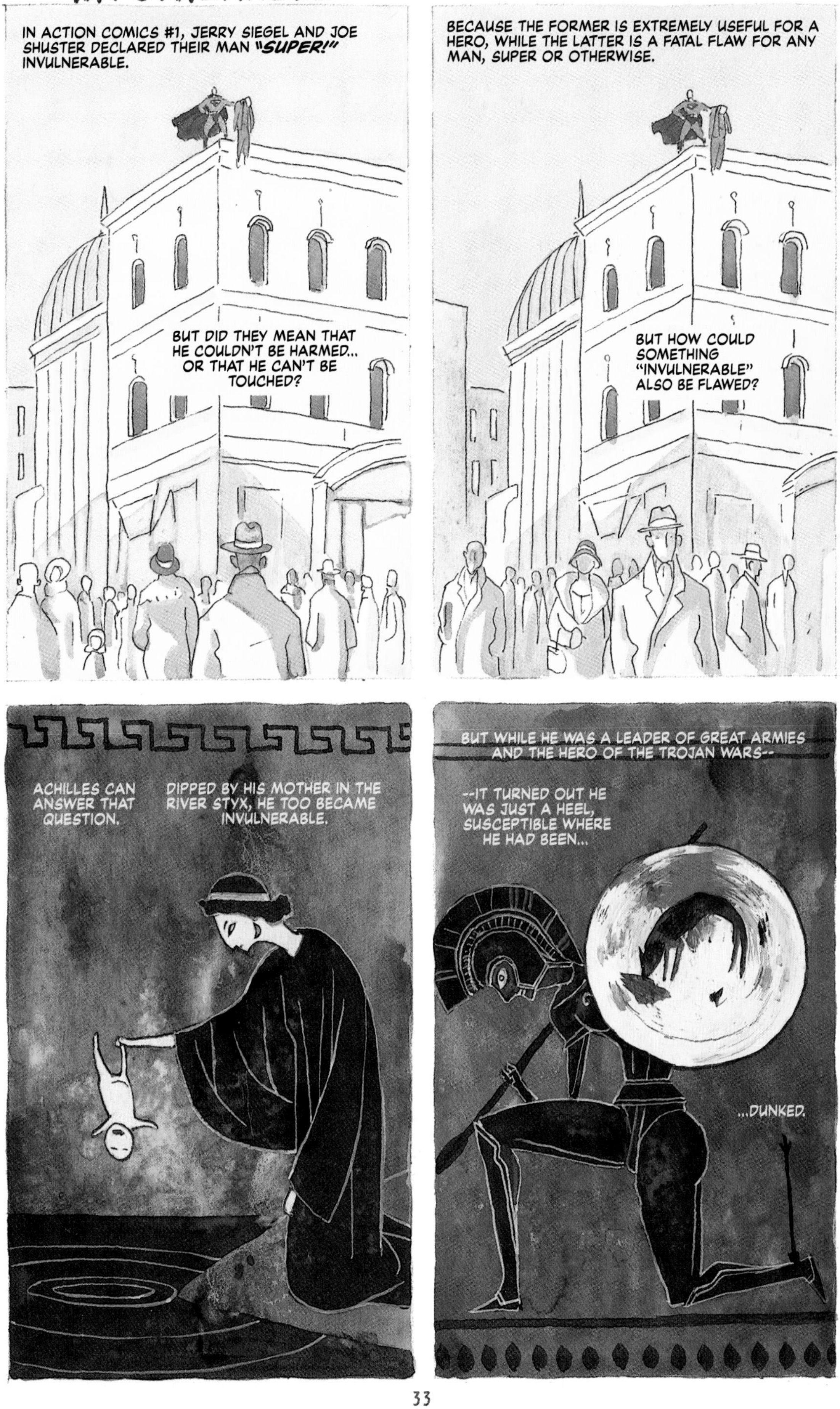

IN ACTION COMICS #1, JERRY SIEGEL AND JOE SHUSTER DECLARED THEIR MAN "SUPER!" INVULNERABLE.
BUT DID THEY MEAN THAT HE COULDN'T BE HARMED... OR THAT HE CAN'T BE TOUCHED?
BECAUSE THE FORMER IS EXTREMELY USEFUL FOR A HERO, WHILE THE LATTER IS A FATAL FLAW FOR ANY MAN, SUPER OR OTHERWISE.
BUT HOW COULD SOMETHING "INVULNERABLE" ALSO BE FLAWED?
ACHILLES CAN ANSWER THAT QUESTION.
DIPPED BY HIS MOTHER IN THE RIVER STYX, HE TOO BECAME INVULNERABLE.
BUT WHILE HE WAS A LEADER OF GREAT ARMIES AND THE HERO OF THE TROJAN WARS--
--IT TURNED OUT HE WAS JUST A HEEL, SUSCEPTIBLE WHERE HE HAD BEEN...
...DUNKED.

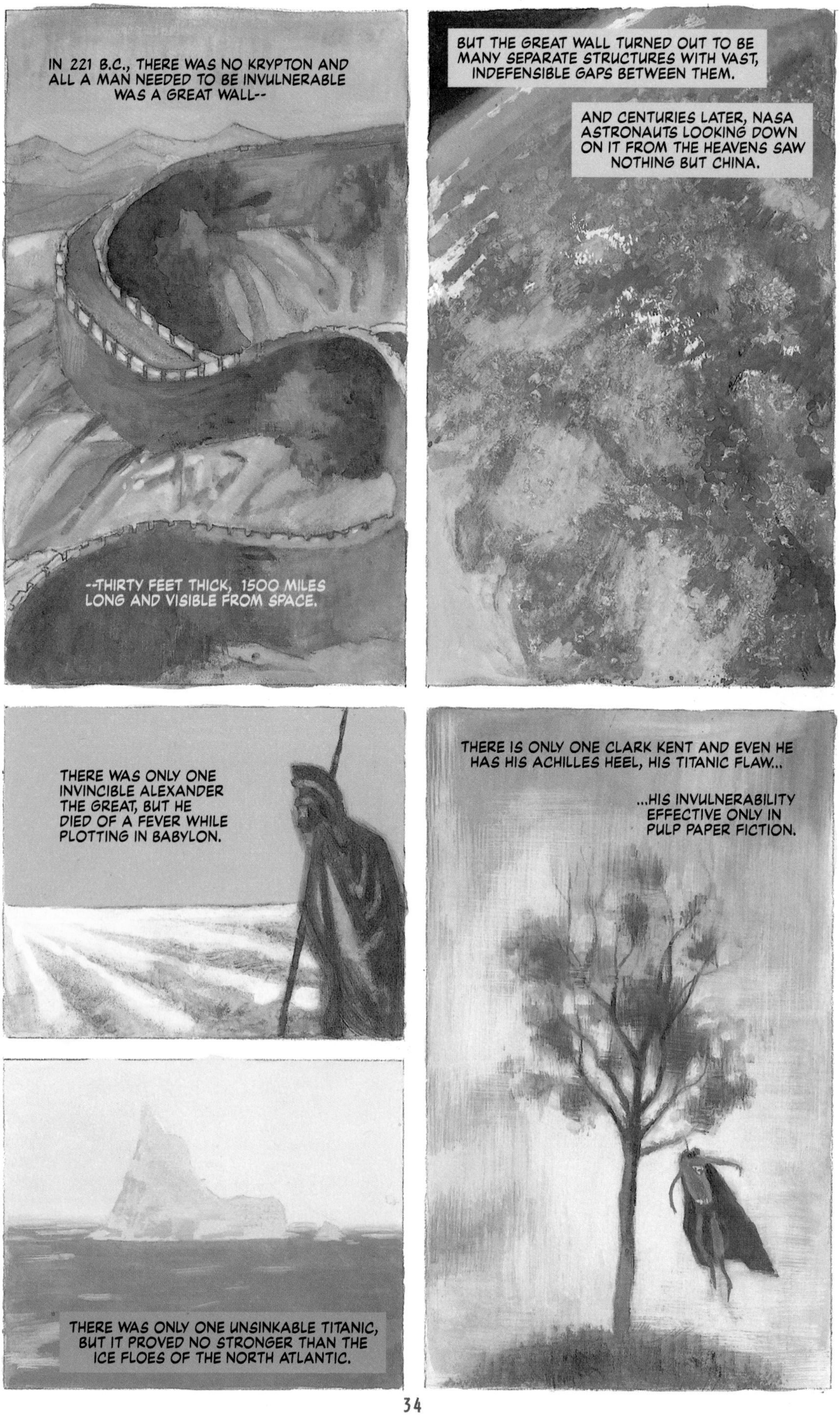
IN 221 B.C., THERE WAS NO KRYPTON AND ALL A MAN NEEDED TO BE INVULNERABLE WAS A GREAT WALL--
--THIRTY FEET THICK, 1500 MILES LONG AND VISIBLE FROM SPACE.
BUT THE GREAT WALL TURNED OUT TO BE MANY SEPARATE STRUCTURES WITH VAST, INDEFENSIBLE GAPS BETWEEN THEM.
AND CENTURIES LATER, NASA ASTRONAUTS LOOKING DOWN ON IT FROM THE HEAVENS SAW NOTHING BUT CHINA.
THERE WAS ONLY ONE INVINCIBLE ALEXANDER THE GREAT, BUT HE DIED OF A FEVER WHILE PLOTTING IN BABYLON.
THERE WAS ONLY ONE UNSINKABLE TITANIC, BUT IT PROVED NO STRONGER THAN THE ICE FLOES OF THE NORTH ATLANTIC.
THERE IS ONLY ONE CLARK KENT AND EVEN HE HAS HIS ACHILLES HEEL, HIS TITANIC FLAW...
...HIS INVULNERABILITY EFFECTIVE ONLY IN PULP PAPER FICTION.

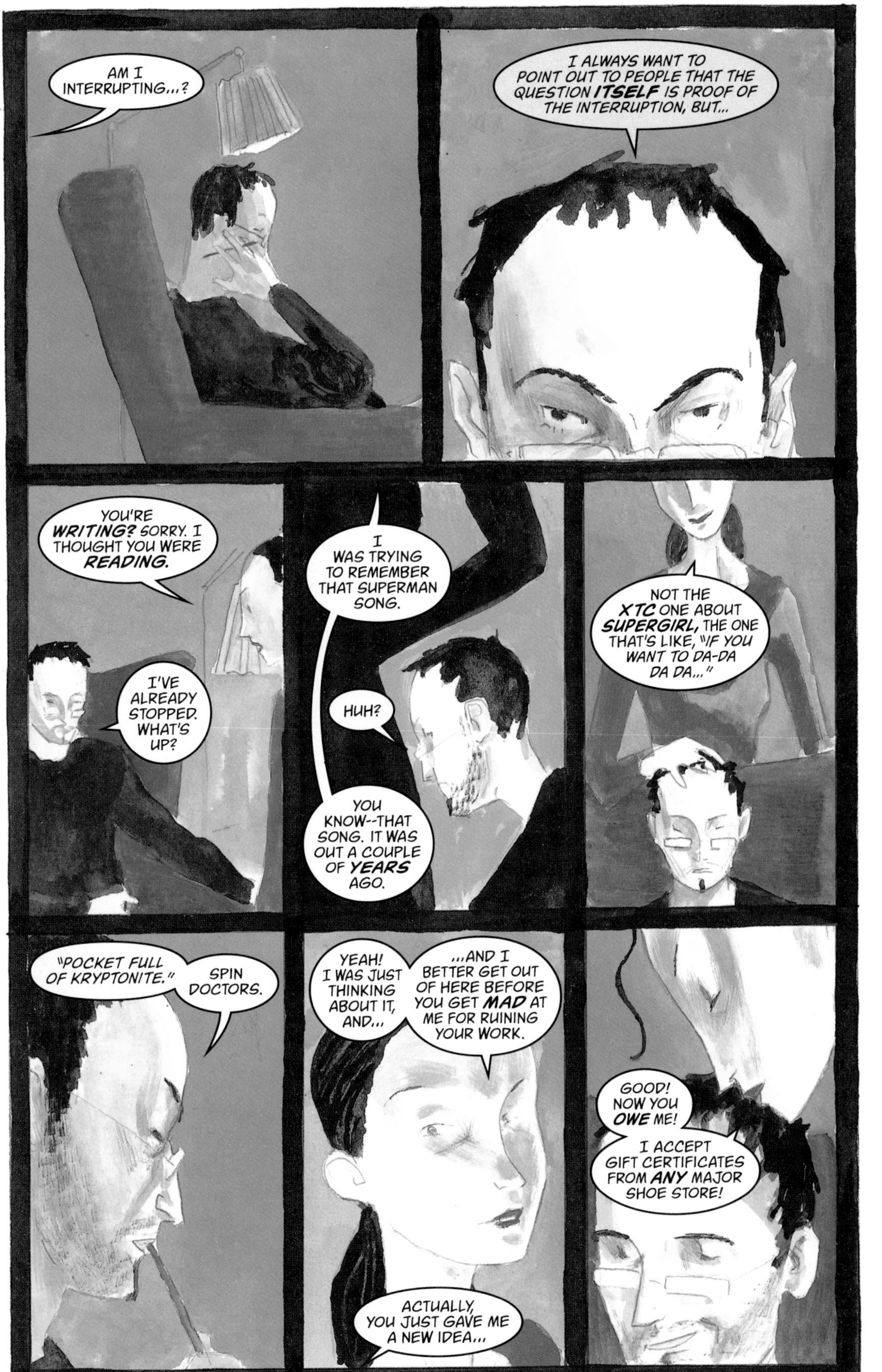
AM I INTERRUPTING...?
I ALWAYS WANT TO POINT OUT TO PEOPLE THAT THE QUESTION ITSELF IS PROOF OF THE INTERRUPTION, BUT...
YOU'RE WRITING? SORRY. I THOUGHT YOU WERE READING.
I'VE ALREADY STOPPED. WHAT'S UP?
I WAS TRYING TO REMEMBER THAT SUPERMAN SONG.
HUH?
YOU KNOW--THAT SONG. IT WAS OUT A COUPLE OF YEARS AGO.
NOT THE XTC ONE ABOUT SUPERGIRL, THE ONE THAT'S LIKE, "IF YOU WANT TO DA-DA DA DA..."
"POCKET FULL OF KRYPTONITE."
SPIN DOCTORS.
YEAH! I WAS JUST THINKING ABOUT IT, AND...
...AND I BETTER GET OUT OF HERE BEFORE YOU GET MAD AT ME FOR RUINING YOUR WORK.
ACTUALLY, YOU JUST GAVE ME A NEW IDEA...
GOOD! NOW YOU OWE ME!
I ACCEPT GIFT CERTIFICATES FROM ANY MAJOR SHOE STORE!

KRYPTONITE

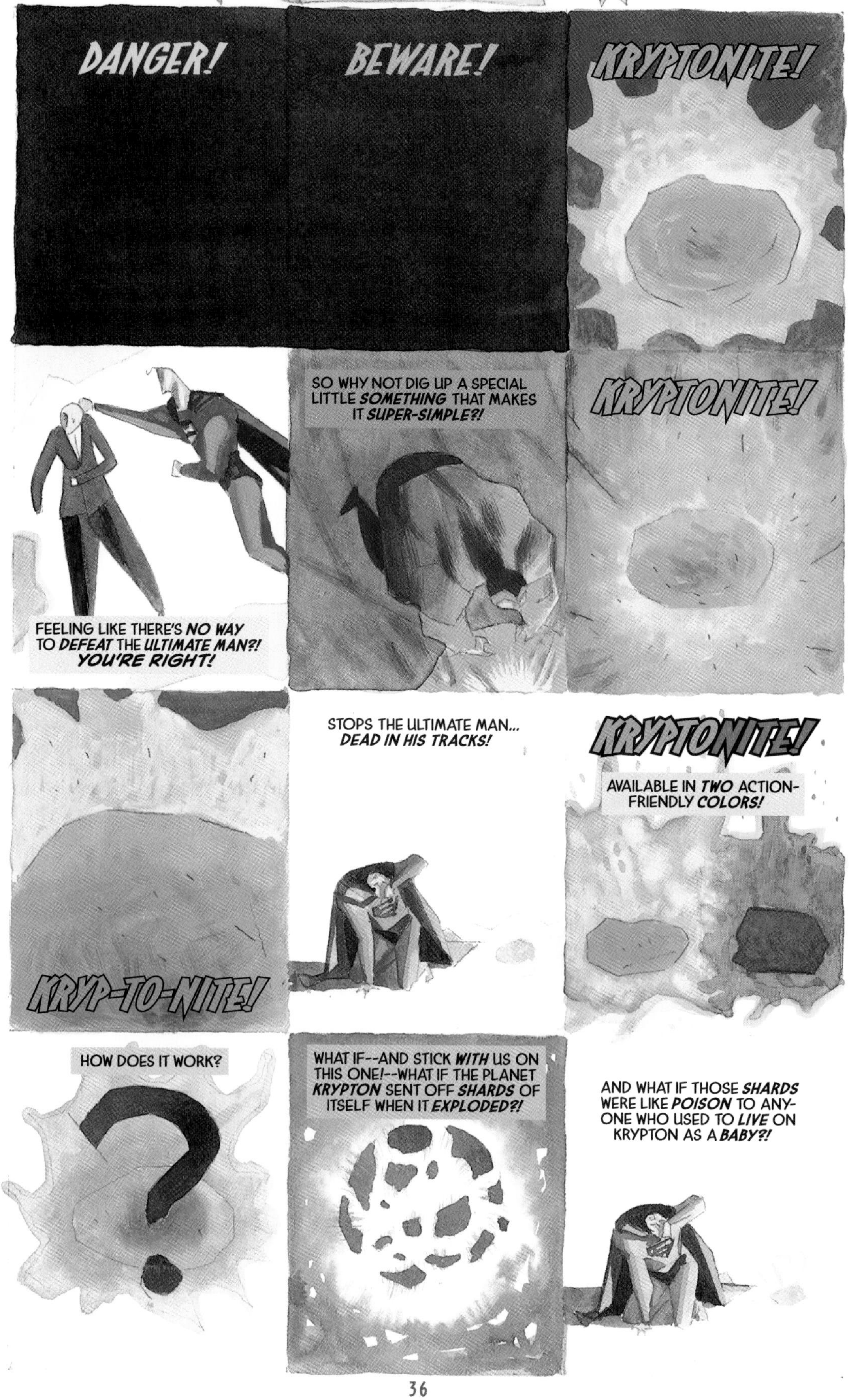

DANGER!
BEWARE!
KRYPTONITE!
FEELING LIKE THERE'S NO WAY TO DEFEAT THE ULTIMATE MAN?! YOU'RE RIGHT!
SO WHY NOT DIG UP A SPECIAL LITTLE SOMETHING THAT MAKES IT SUPER-SIMPLE?!
KRYPTONITE!
KRYP-TO-NITE!
STOPS THE ULTIMATE MAN... DEAD IN HIS TRACKS!
KRYPTONITE!
AVAILABLE IN TWO ACTION-FRIENDLY COLORS!
HOW DOES IT WORK?
WHAT IF--AND STICK WITH US ON THIS ONE!--WHAT IF THE PLANET KRYPTON SENT OFF SHARDS OF ITSELF WHEN IT EXPLODED?!
AND WHAT IF THOSE SHARDS WERE LIKE POISON TO ANYONE WHO USED TO LIVE ON KRYPTON AS A BABY?!

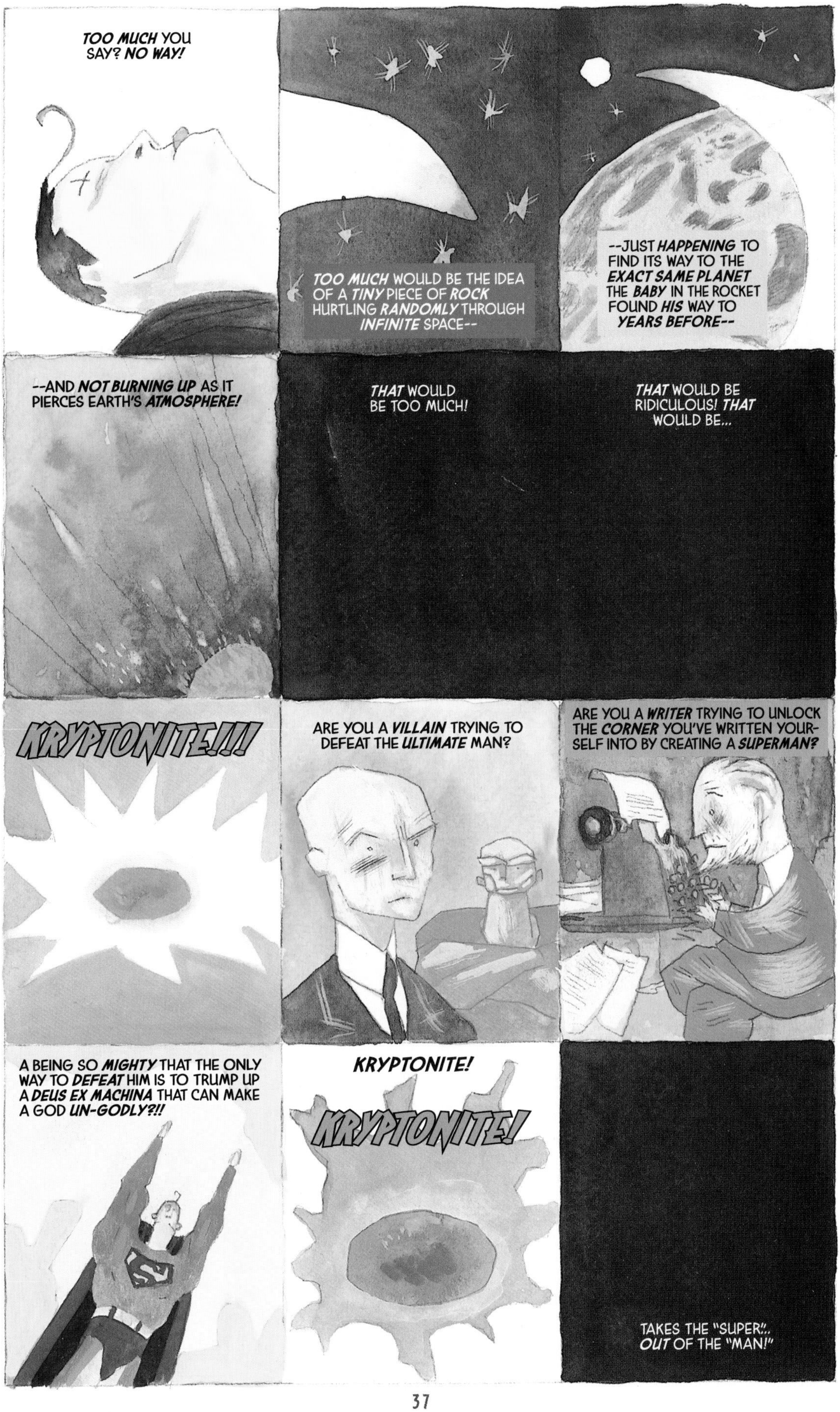

TOO MUCH YOU SAY? NO WAY!
TOO MUCH WOULD BE THE IDEA OF A TINY PIECE OF ROCK HURTLING RANDOMLY THROUGH INFINITE SPACE--
--JUST HAPPENING TO FIND ITS WAY TO THE EXACT SAME PLANET THE BABY IN THE ROCKET FOUND HIS WAY TO YEARS BEFORE--
--AND NOT BURNING UP AS IT PIERCES EARTH'S ATMOSPHERE!
THAT WOULD BE TOO MUCH!
THAT WOULD BE RIDICULOUS! THAT WOULD BE...
KRYPTONITE!!!
ARE YOU A VILLAIN TRYING TO DEFEAT THE ULTIMATE MAN?
ARE YOU A WRITER TRYING TO UNLOCK THE CORNER YOU'VE WRITTEN YOURSELF INTO BY CREATING A SUPERMAN?
A BEING SO MIGHTY THAT THE ONLY WAY TO DEFEAT HIM IS TO TRUMP UP A DEUS EX MACHINA THAT CAN MAKE A GOD UN-GODLY?!!
KRYPTONITE!
KRYPTONITE!
TAKES THE "SUPER"... OUT OF THE "MAN!"

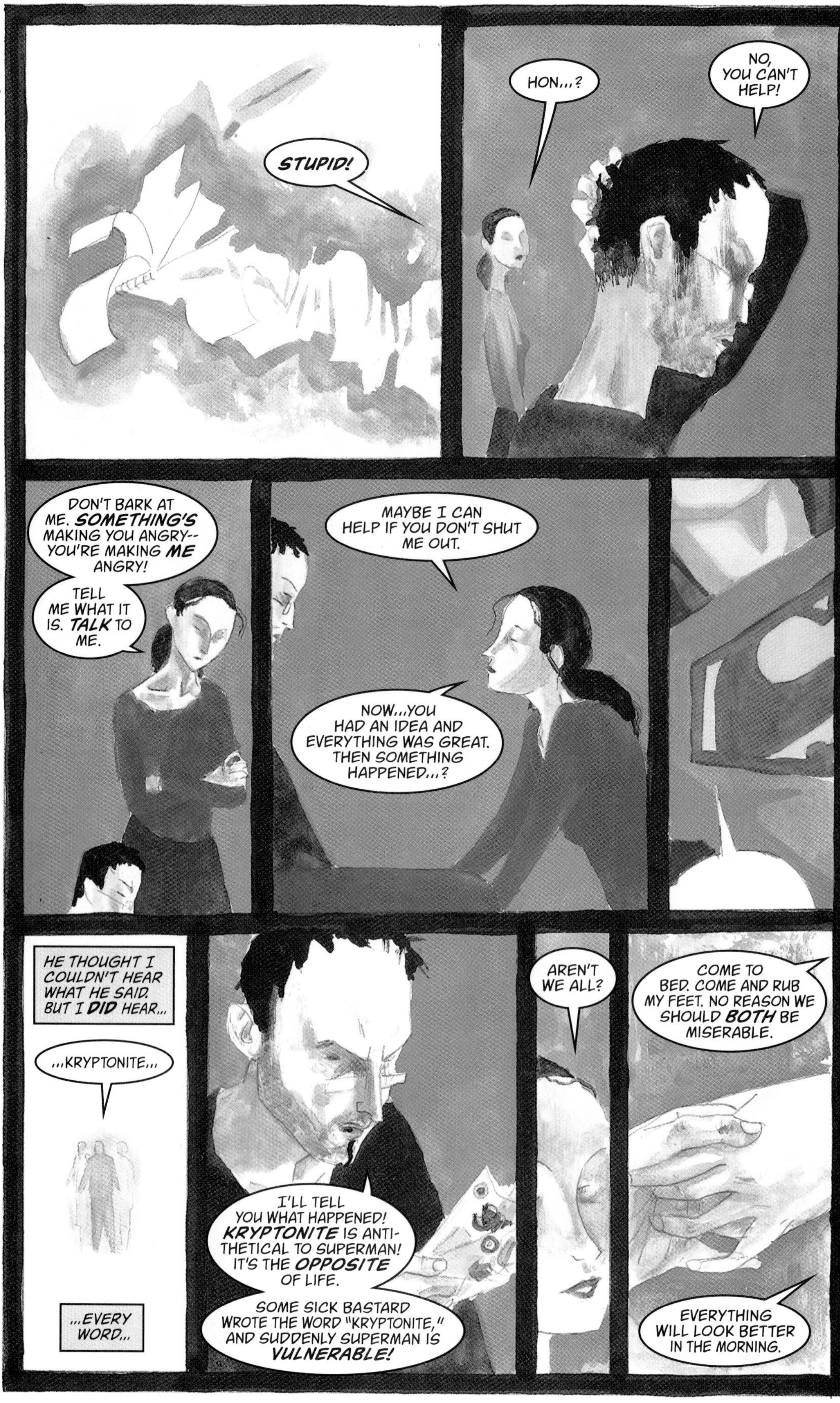
STUPID!
HON...?
NO, YOU CAN'T HELP!
DON'T BARK AT ME. SOMETHING'S MAKING YOU ANGRY-- YOU'RE MAKING ME ANGRY!
TELL ME WHAT IT IS. TALK TO ME.
MAYBE I CAN HELP IF YOU DON'T SHUT ME OUT.
NOW...YOU HAD AN IDEA AND EVERYTHING WAS GREAT. THEN SOMETHING HAPPENED...?
HE THOUGHT I COULDN'T HEAR WHAT HE SAID. BUT I DID HEAR...
...KRYPTONITE...
...EVERY WORD...
I'LL TELL YOU WHAT HAPPENED! KRYPTONITE IS ANTI-THETICAL TO SUPERMAN! IT'S THE OPPOSITE OF LIFE.
SOME SICK BASTARD WROTE THE WORD "KRYPTONITE," AND SUDDENLY SUPERMAN IS VULNERABLE!
AREN'T WE ALL?
COME TO BED. COME AND RUB MY FEET. NO REASON WE SHOULD BOTH BE MISERABLE.
EVERYTHING WILL LOOK BETTER IN THE MORNING.

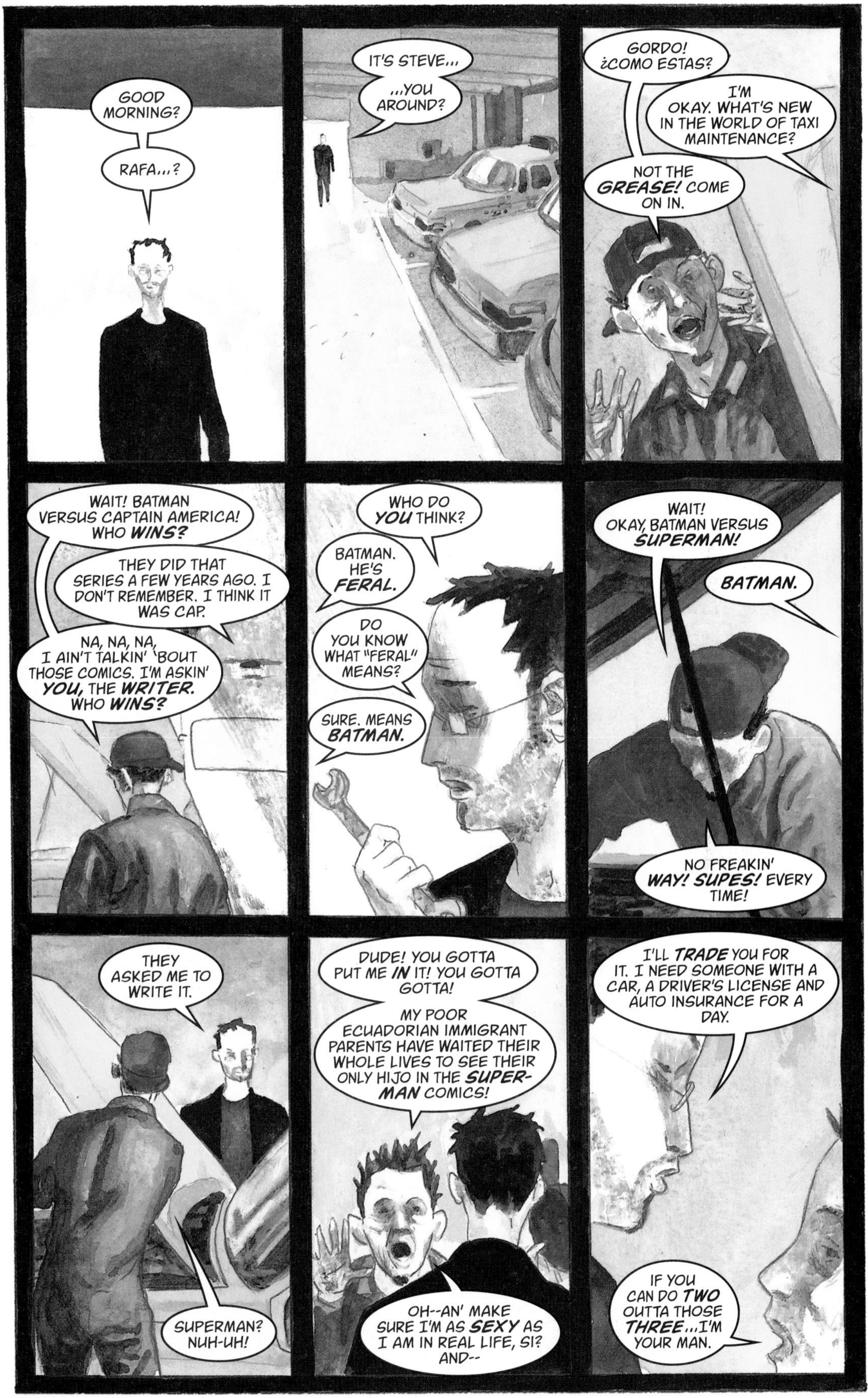
GOOD MORNING?
RAFA...?
IT'S STEVE...
...YOU AROUND?
GORDO! ¿COMO ESTAS?
I'M OKAY. WHAT'S NEW IN THE WORLD OF TAXI MAINTENANCE?
NOT THE GREASE! COME ON IN.
WAIT! BATMAN VERSUS CAPTAIN AMERICA! WHO WINS?
THEY DID THAT SERIES A FEW YEARS AGO. I DON'T REMEMBER. I THINK IT WAS CAP.
NA, NA, NA, I AIN'T TALKIN' 'BOUT THOSE COMICS. I'M ASKIN' YOU, THE WRITER. WHO WINS?
WHO DO YOU THINK?
BATMAN. HE'S FERAL.
DO YOU KNOW WHAT "FERAL" MEANS?
SURE. MEANS BATMAN.
WAIT! OKAY, BATMAN VERSUS SUPERMAN!
BATMAN.
NO FREAKIN' WAY! SUPES! EVERY TIME!
THEY ASKED ME TO WRITE IT.
SUPERMAN? NUH-UH!
DUDE! YOU GOTTA PUT ME IN IT! YOU GOTTA GOTTA!
MY POOR ECUADORIAN IMMIGRANT PARENTS HAVE WAITED THEIR WHOLE LIVES TO SEE THEIR ONLY HIJO IN THE SUPER-MAN COMICS!
OH--AN' MAKE SURE I'M AS SEXY AS I AM IN REAL LIFE, SI? AND--
I'LL TRADE YOU FOR IT. I NEED SOMEONE WITH A CAR, A DRIVER'S LICENSE AND AUTO INSURANCE FOR A DAY.
IF YOU CAN DO TWO OUTTA THOSE THREE...I'M YOUR MAN.

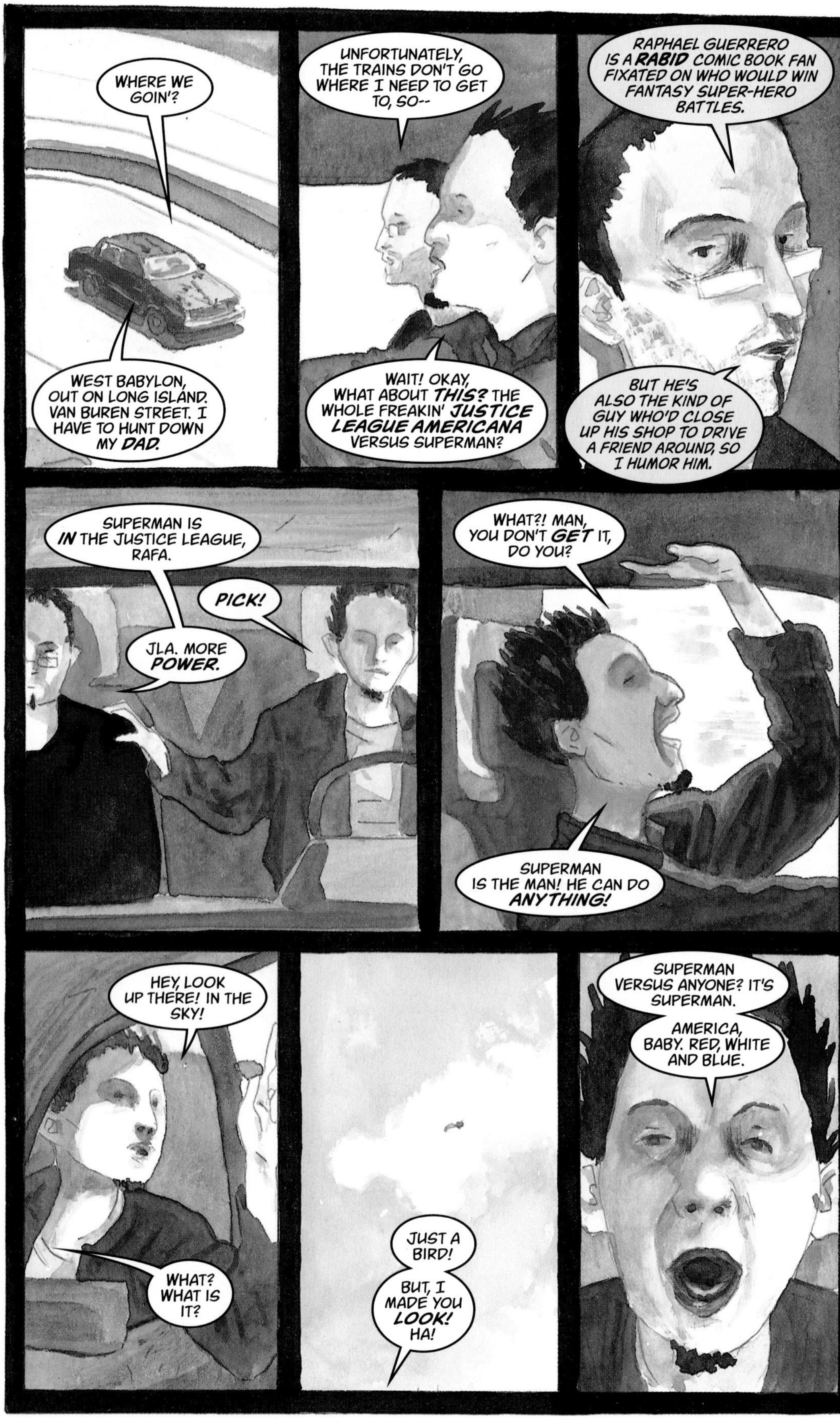
WHERE WE GOIN'?
WEST BABYLON, OUT ON LONG ISLAND. VAN BUREN STREET. I HAVE TO HUNT DOWN MY DAD.
UNFORTUNATELY, THE TRAINS DON'T GO WHERE I NEED TO GET TO, SO--
WAIT! OKAY, WHAT ABOUT THIS? THE WHOLE FREAKIN' JUSTICE LEAGUE AMERICANA VERSUS SUPERMAN?
RAPHAEL GUERRERO IS A RABID COMIC BOOK FAN FIXATED ON WHO WOULD WIN FANTASY SUPER-HERO BATTLES.
BUT HE'S ALSO THE KIND OF GUY WHO'D CLOSE UP HIS SHOP TO DRIVE A FRIEND AROUND, SO I HUMOR HIM.
SUPERMAN IS IN THE JUSTICE LEAGUE, RAFA.
PICK!
JLA. MORE POWER.
WHAT?! MAN, YOU DON'T GET IT, DO YOU?
SUPERMAN IS THE MAN! HE CAN DO ANYTHING!
HEY, LOOK UP THERE! IN THE SKY!
WHAT? WHAT IS IT?
JUST A BIRD!
BUT, I MADE YOU LOOK! HA!
SUPERMAN VERSUS ANYONE? IT'S SUPERMAN.
AMERICA, BABY. RED, WHITE AND BLUE.

RED, YELLOW, BLUE

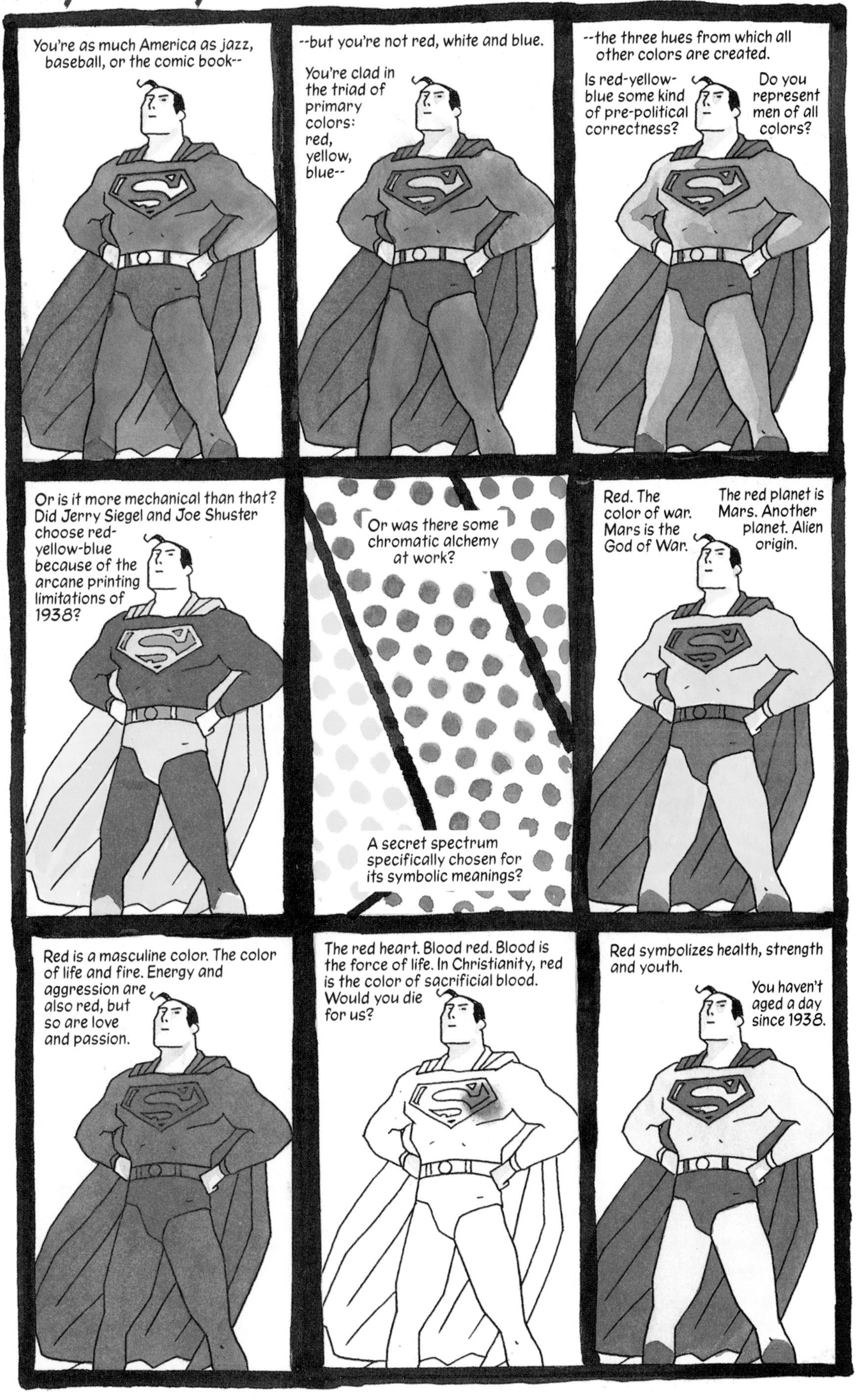

You're as much America as jazz, baseball, or the comic book--
--but you're not red, white and blue.
You're clad in the triad of primary colors: red, yellow, blue--
--the three hues from which all other colors are created.
Is red-yellow-blue some kind of pre-political correctness?
Do you represent men of all colors?
Or is it more mechanical than that? Did Jerry Siegel and Joe Shuster choose red-yellow-blue because of the arcane printing limitations of 1938?
Or was there some chromatic alchemy at work?
A secret spectrum specifically chosen for its symbolic meanings?
Red. The color of war. Mars is the God of War.
The red planet is Mars. Another planet. Alien origin.
Red is a masculine color. The color of life and fire. Energy and aggression are also red, but so are love and passion.
The red heart. Blood red. Blood is the force of life. In Christianity, red is the color of sacrificial blood. Would you die for us?
Red symbolizes health, strength and youth.
You haven't aged a day since 1938.

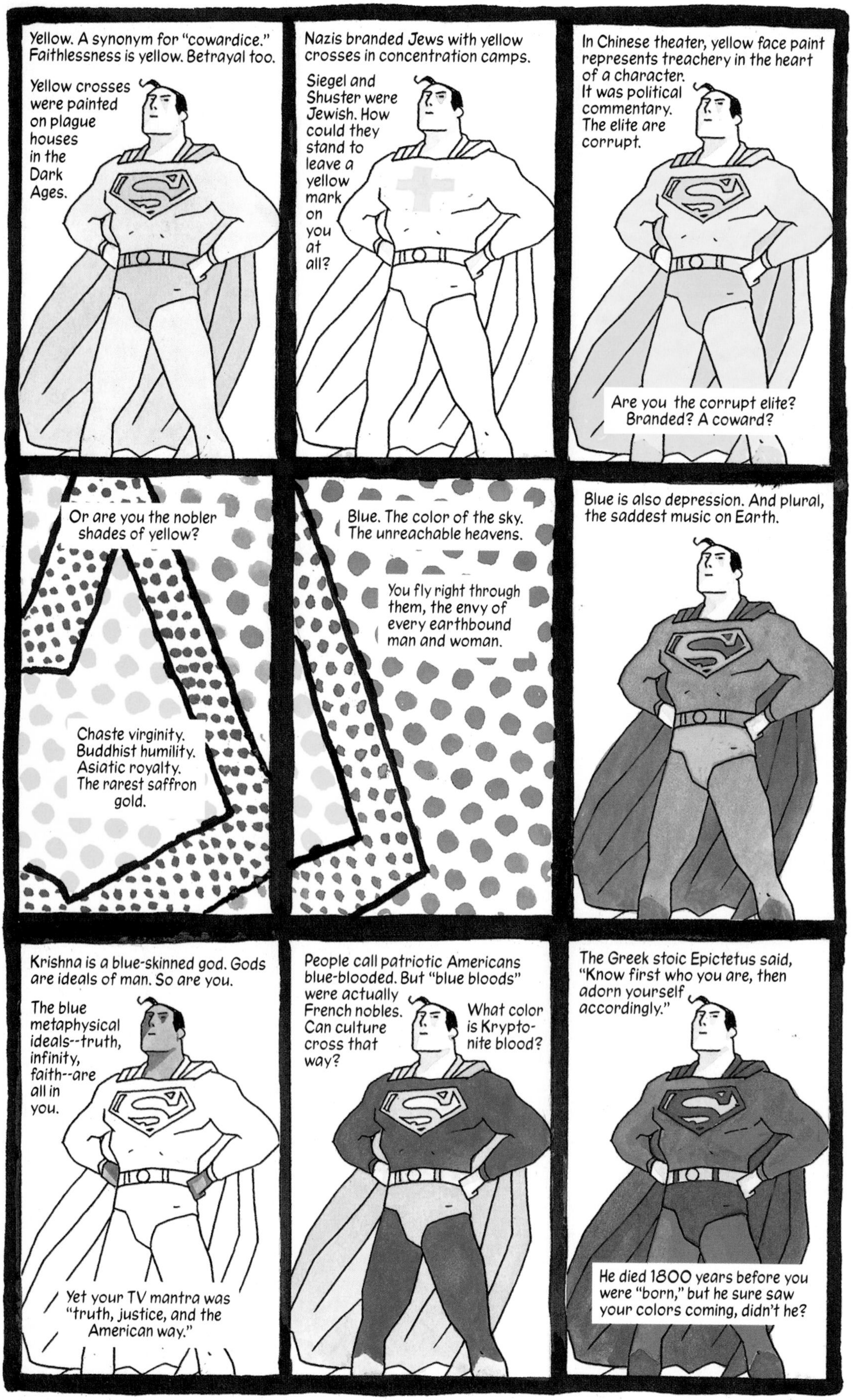
Yellow. A synonym for "cowardice." Faithlessness is yellow. Betrayal too.
Yellow crosses were painted on plague houses in the Dark Ages.
Nazis branded Jews with yellow crosses in concentration camps.
Siegel and Shuster were Jewish. How could they stand to leave a yellow mark on you at all?
In Chinese theater, yellow face paint represents treachery in the heart of a character.
It was political commentary. The elite are corrupt.
Are you the corrupt elite? Branded? A coward?
Or are you the nobler shades of yellow?
Chaste virginity. Buddhist humility. Asiatic royalty. The rarest saffron gold.
Blue. The color of the sky. The unreachable heavens.
You fly right through them, the envy of every earthbound man and woman.
Blue is also depression. And plural, the saddest music on Earth.
Krishna is a blue-skinned god. Gods are ideals of man. So are you.
The blue metaphysical ideals--truth, infinity, faith--are all in you.
Yet your TV mantra was "truth, justice, and the American way."
People call patriotic Americans blue-blooded. But "blue bloods" were actually French nobles. Can culture cross that way?
What color is Krypto-nite blood?
The Greek stoic Epictetus said, "Know first who you are, then adorn yourself accordingly."
He died 1800 years before you were "born," but he sure saw your colors coming, didn't he?

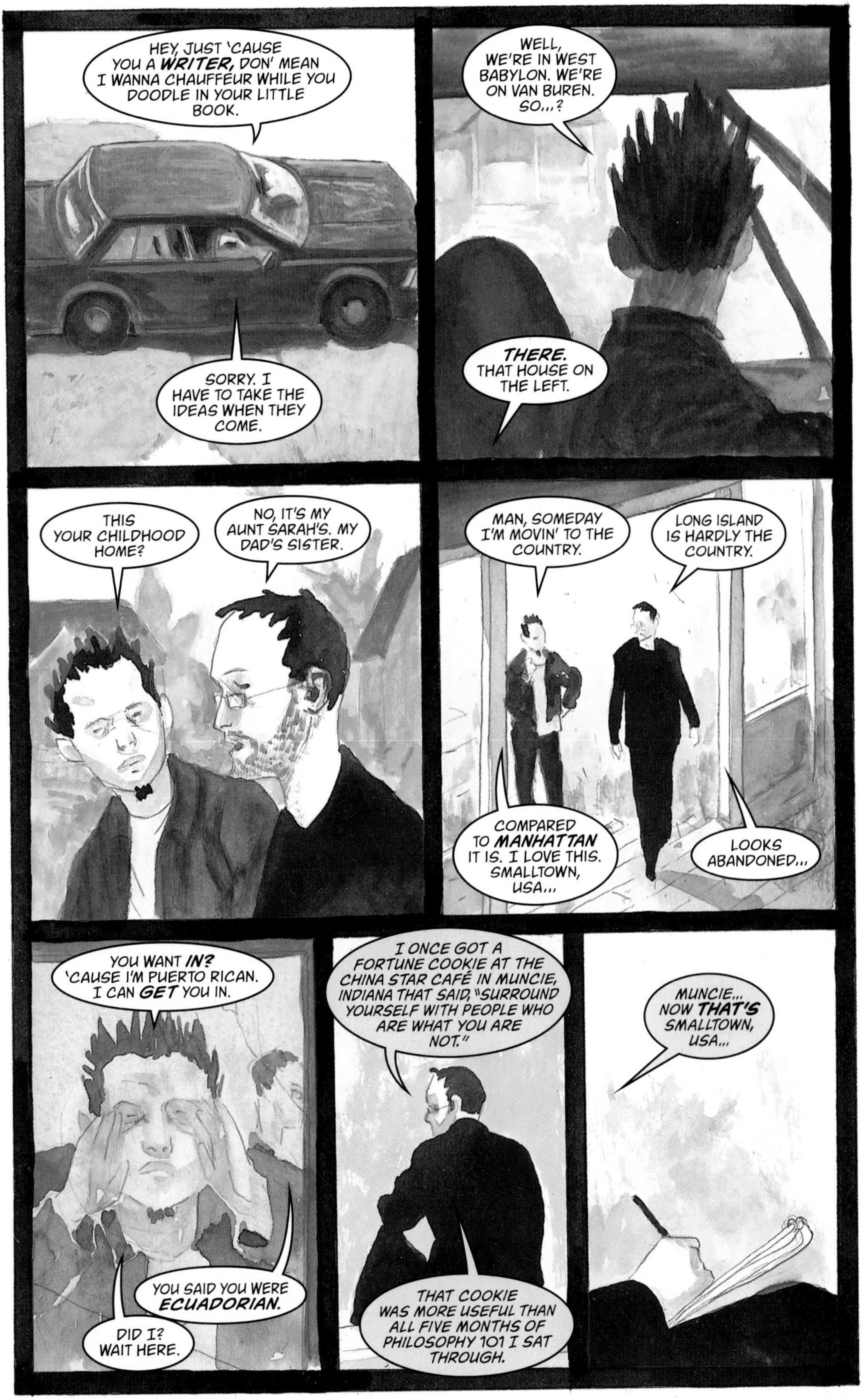
HEY, JUST 'CAUSE YOU A **WRITER,** DON' MEAN I WANNA CHAUFFEUR WHILE YOU DOODLE IN YOUR LITTLE BOOK.
SORRY. I HAVE TO TAKE THE IDEAS WHEN THEY COME.
WELL, WE'RE IN WEST BABYLON. WE'RE ON VAN BUREN. SO...?
THERE. THAT HOUSE ON THE LEFT.
THIS YOUR CHILDHOOD HOME?
NO, IT'S MY AUNT SARAH'S. MY DAD'S SISTER.
MAN, SOMEDAY I'M MOVIN' TO THE COUNTRY.
LONG ISLAND IS HARDLY THE COUNTRY.
COMPARED TO **MANHATTAN** IT IS. I LOVE THIS. SMALLTOWN, USA...
LOOKS ABANDONED...
YOU WANT **IN?** 'CAUSE I'M PUERTO RICAN. I CAN **GET** YOU IN.
YOU SAID YOU WERE **ECUADORIAN.**
DID I? WAIT HERE.
I ONCE GOT A FORTUNE COOKIE AT THE CHINA STAR CAFÉ IN MUNCIE, INDIANA THAT SAID, "SURROUND YOURSELF WITH PEOPLE WHO ARE WHAT YOU ARE NOT."
THAT COOKIE WAS MORE USEFUL THAN ALL FIVE MONTHS OF PHILOSOPHY 101 I SAT THROUGH.
MUNCIE... NOW **THAT'S** SMALLTOWN, USA...

SMALLVILLE

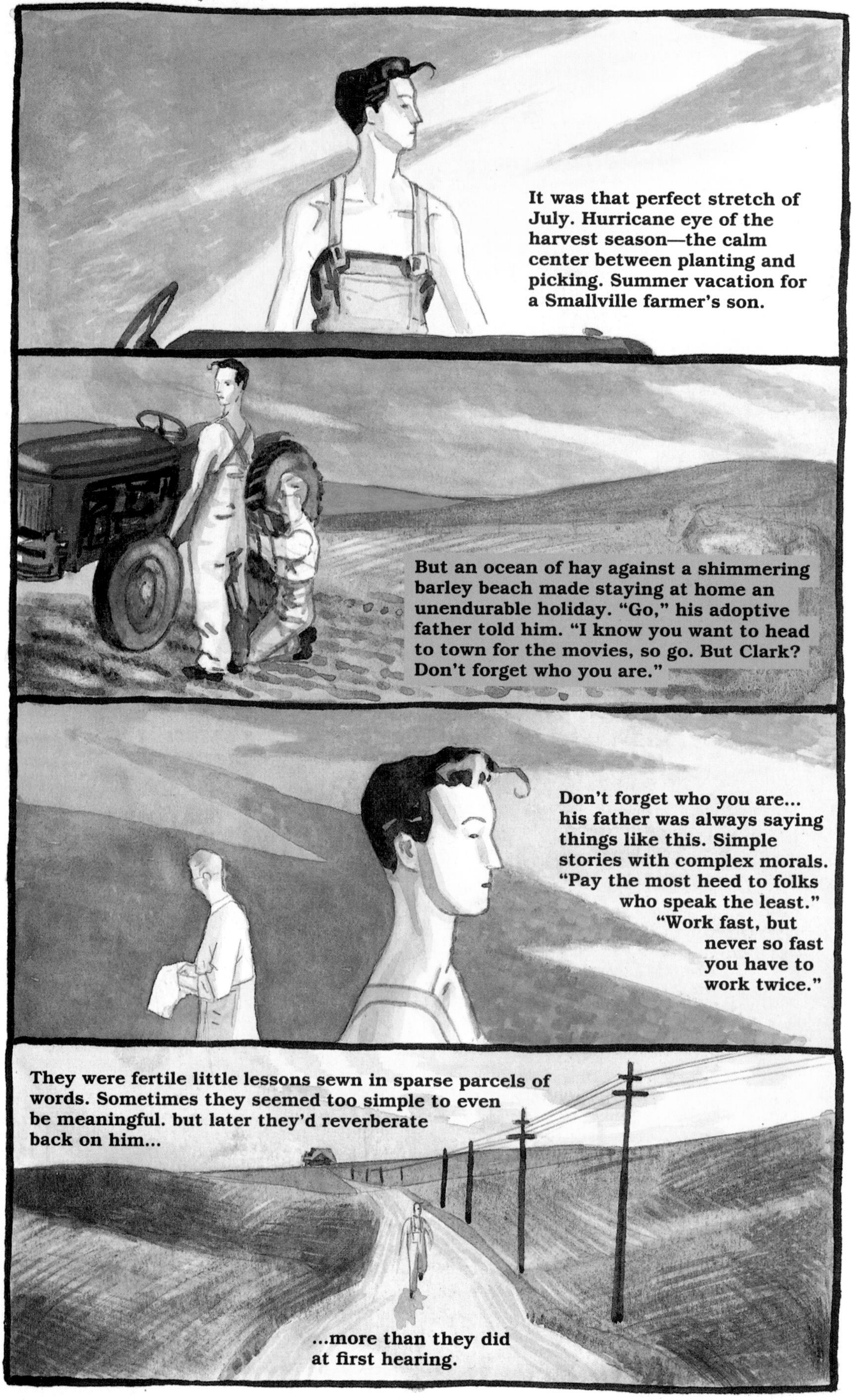

It was that perfect stretch of July. Hurricane eye of the harvest season—the calm center between planting and picking. Summer vacation for a Smallville farmer's son.
But an ocean of hay against a shimmering barley beach made staying at home an unendurable holiday. "Go," his adoptive father told him. "I know you want to head to town for the movies, so go. But Clark? Don't forget who you are."
Don't forget who you are... his father was always saying things like this. Simple stories with complex morals. "Pay the most heed to folks who speak the least." "Work fast, but never so fast you have to work twice."
They were fertile little lessons sewn in sparse parcels of words. Sometimes they seemed too simple to even be meaningful. but later they'd reverberate back on him...
...more than they did at first hearing.

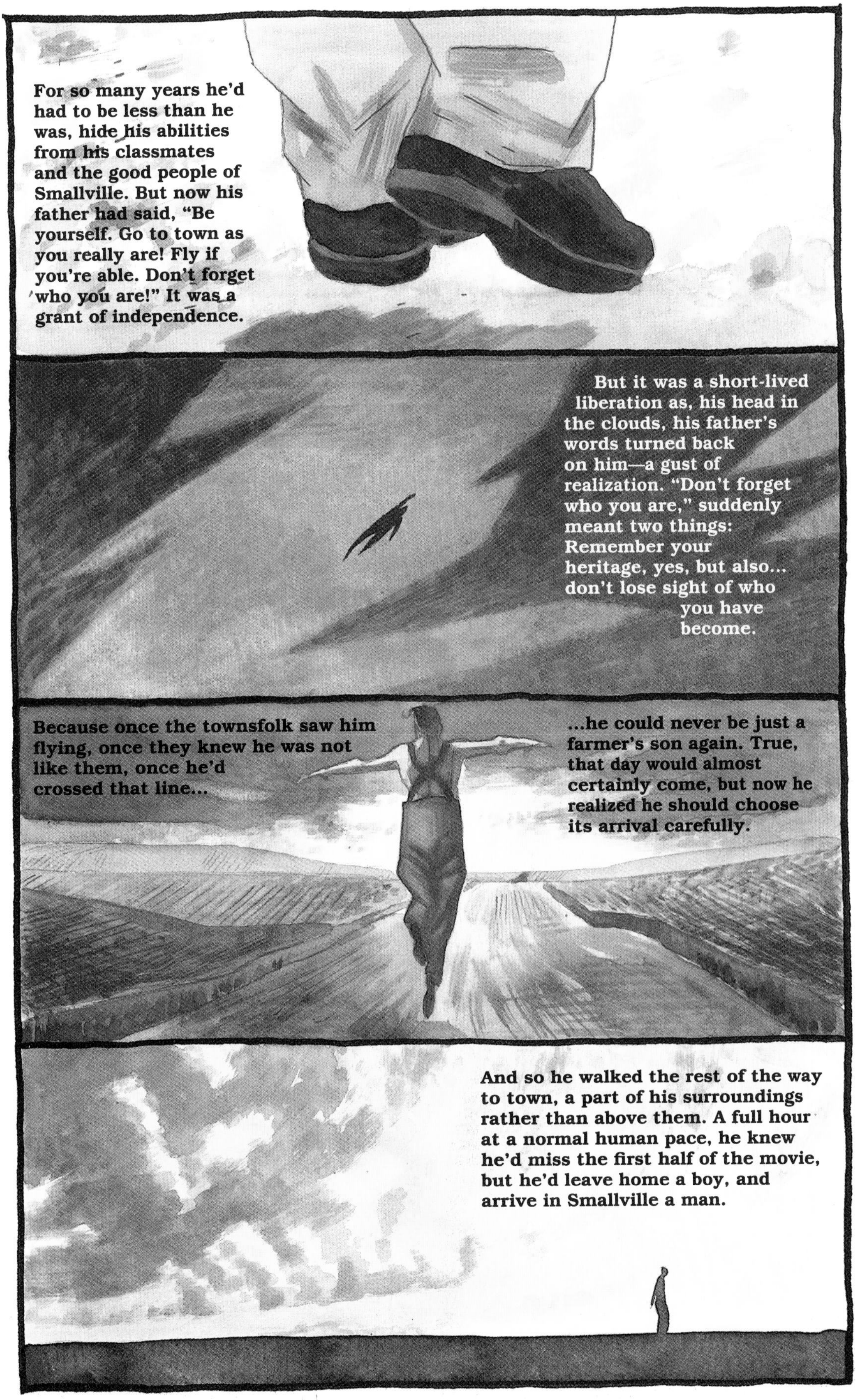
For so many years he'd had to be less than he was, hide his abilities from his classmates and the good people of Smallville. But now his father had said, "Be yourself. Go to town as you really are! Fly if you're able. Don't forget who you are!" It was a grant of independence.
But it was a short-lived liberation as, his head in the clouds, his father's words turned back on him—a gust of realization. "Don't forget who you are," suddenly meant two things: Remember your heritage, yes, but also... don't lose sight of who you have become.
Because once the townsfolk saw him flying, once they knew he was not like them, once he'd crossed that line...
...he could never be just a farmer's son again. True, that day would almost certainly come, but now he realized he should choose its arrival carefully.
And so he walked the rest of the way to town, a part of his surroundings rather than above them. A full hour at a normal human pace, he knew he'd miss the first half of the movie, but he'd leave home a boy, and arrive in Smallville a man.

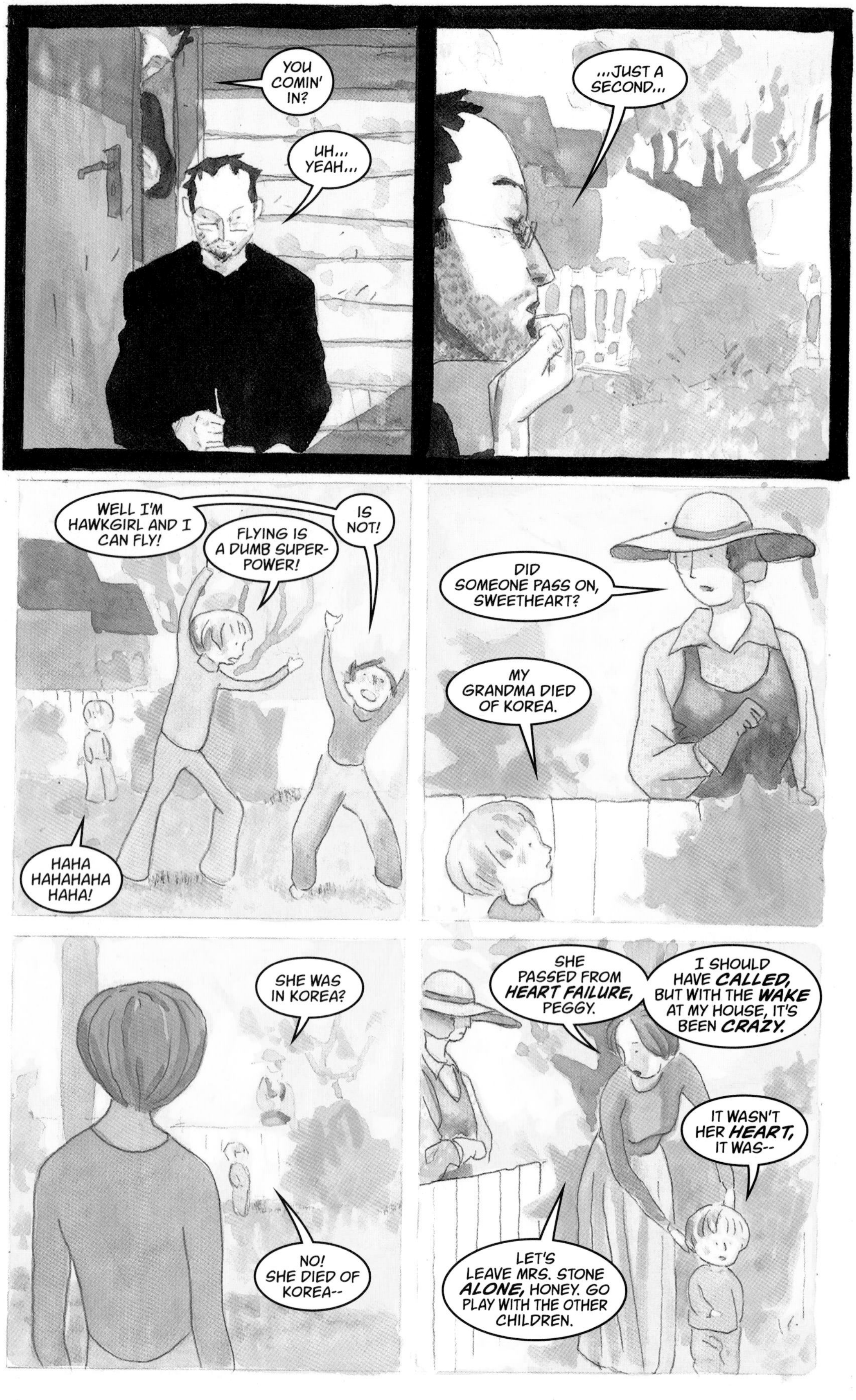
YOU COMIN' IN?
UH... YEAH...
...JUST A SECOND...
WELL I'M HAWKGIRL AND I CAN FLY!
FLYING IS A DUMB SUPER-POWER!
IS NOT!
HAHA HAHAHAHA HAHA!
DID SOMEONE PASS ON, SWEETHEART?
MY GRANDMA DIED OF KOREA.
SHE WAS IN KOREA?
NO! SHE DIED OF KOREA--
SHE PASSED FROM HEART FAILURE, PEGGY.
I SHOULD HAVE CALLED, BUT WITH THE WAKE AT MY HOUSE, IT'S BEEN CRAZY.
IT WASN'T HER HEART, IT WAS--
LET'S LEAVE MRS. STONE ALONE, HONEY. GO PLAY WITH THE OTHER CHILDREN.

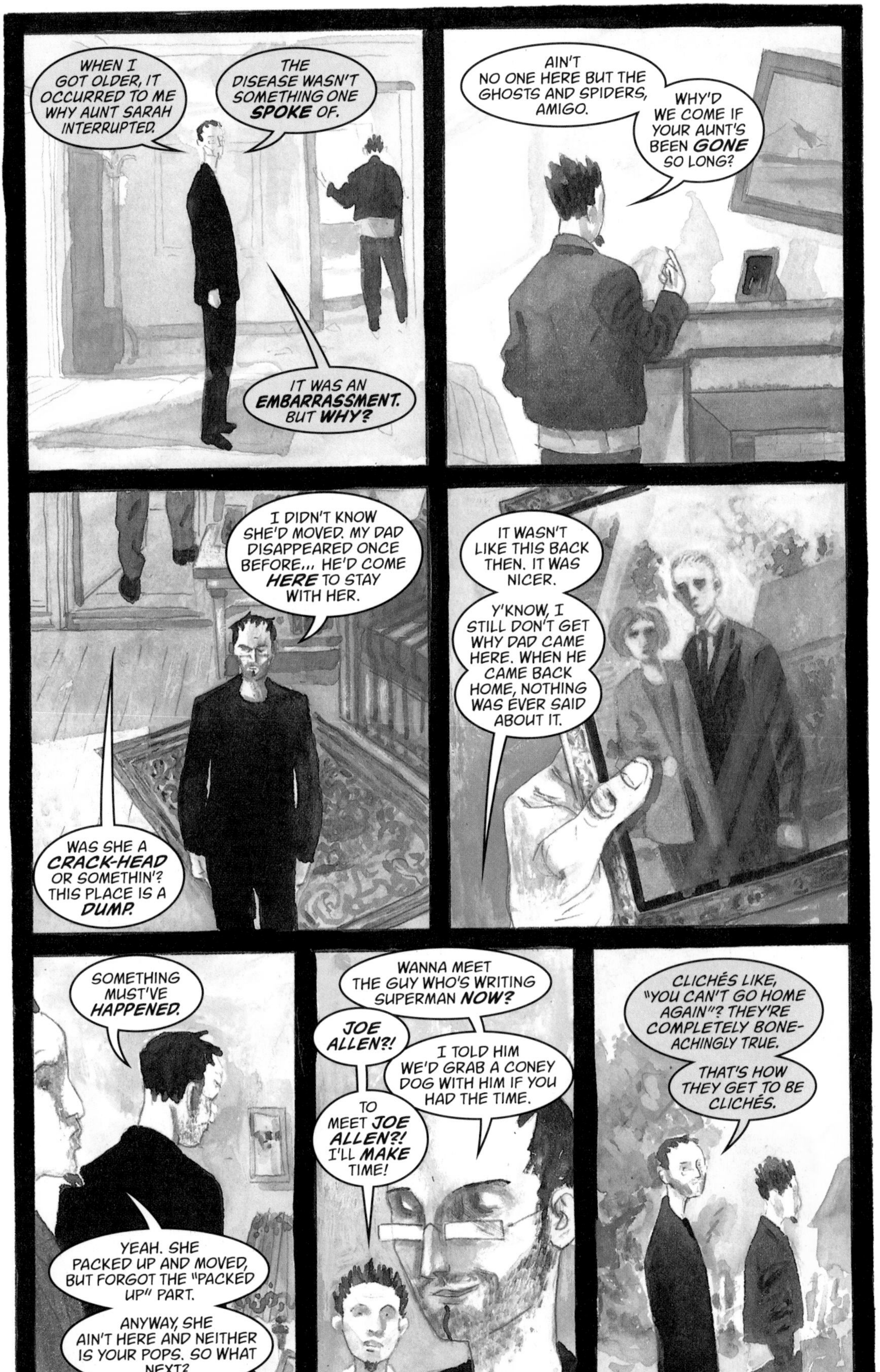
WHEN I GOT OLDER, IT OCCURRED TO ME WHY AUNT SARAH INTERRUPTED.
THE DISEASE WASN'T SOMETHING ONE SPOKE OF.
IT WAS AN EMBARRASSMENT. BUT WHY?
AIN'T NO ONE HERE BUT THE GHOSTS AND SPIDERS, AMIGO.
WHY'D WE COME IF YOUR AUNT'S BEEN GONE SO LONG?
I DIDN'T KNOW SHE'D MOVED. MY DAD DISAPPEARED ONCE BEFORE... HE'D COME HERE TO STAY WITH HER.
WAS SHE A CRACK-HEAD OR SOMETHIN'? THIS PLACE IS A DUMP.
IT WASN'T LIKE THIS BACK THEN. IT WAS NICER.
Y'KNOW, I STILL DON'T GET WHY DAD CAME HERE. WHEN HE CAME BACK HOME, NOTHING WAS EVER SAID ABOUT IT.
SOMETHING MUST'VE HAPPENED.
YEAH. SHE PACKED UP AND MOVED, BUT FORGOT THE "PACKED UP" PART.
ANYWAY, SHE AIN'T HERE AND NEITHER IS YOUR POPS. SO WHAT NEXT?
WANNA MEET THE GUY WHO'S WRITING SUPERMAN NOW?
JOE ALLEN?!
I TOLD HIM WE'D GRAB A CONEY DOG WITH HIM IF YOU HAD THE TIME.
TO MEET JOE ALLEN?! I'LL MAKE TIME!
CLICHÉS LIKE, "YOU CAN'T GO HOME AGAIN"? THEY'RE COMPLETELY BONE-ACHINGLY TRUE.
THAT'S HOW THEY GET TO BE CLICHÉS.

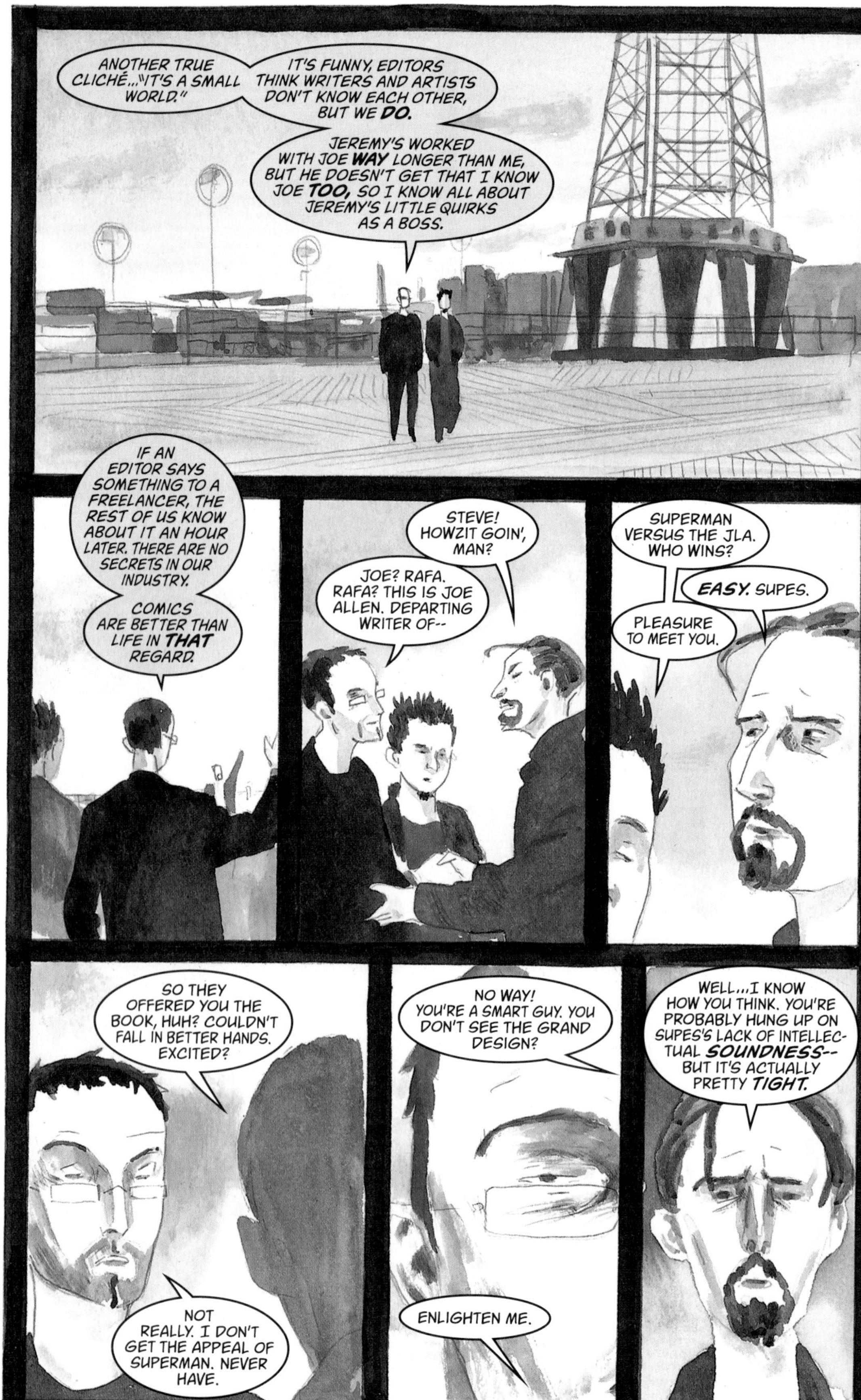
ANOTHER TRUE CLICHÉ..."IT'S A SMALL WORLD."
IT'S FUNNY, EDITORS THINK WRITERS AND ARTISTS DON'T KNOW EACH OTHER, BUT WE DO.
JEREMY'S WORKED WITH JOE WAY LONGER THAN ME, BUT HE DOESN'T GET THAT I KNOW JOE TOO, SO I KNOW ALL ABOUT JEREMY'S LITTLE QUIRKS AS A BOSS.
IF AN EDITOR SAYS SOMETHING TO A FREELANCER, THE REST OF US KNOW ABOUT IT AN HOUR LATER. THERE ARE NO SECRETS IN OUR INDUSTRY.
COMICS ARE BETTER THAN LIFE IN THAT REGARD.
STEVE! HOWZIT GOIN', MAN?
JOE? RAFA. RAFA? THIS IS JOE ALLEN. DEPARTING WRITER OF--
SUPERMAN VERSUS THE JLA. WHO WINS?
EASY. SUPES.
PLEASURE TO MEET YOU.
SO THEY OFFERED YOU THE BOOK, HUH? COULDN'T FALL IN BETTER HANDS. EXCITED?
NOT REALLY. I DON'T GET THE APPEAL OF SUPERMAN. NEVER HAVE.
NO WAY! YOU'RE A SMART GUY. YOU DON'T SEE THE GRAND DESIGN?
ENLIGHTEN ME.
WELL...I KNOW HOW YOU THINK. YOU'RE PROBABLY HUNG UP ON SUPES'S LACK OF INTELLECTUAL SOUNDNESS-- BUT IT'S ACTUALLY PRETTY TIGHT.

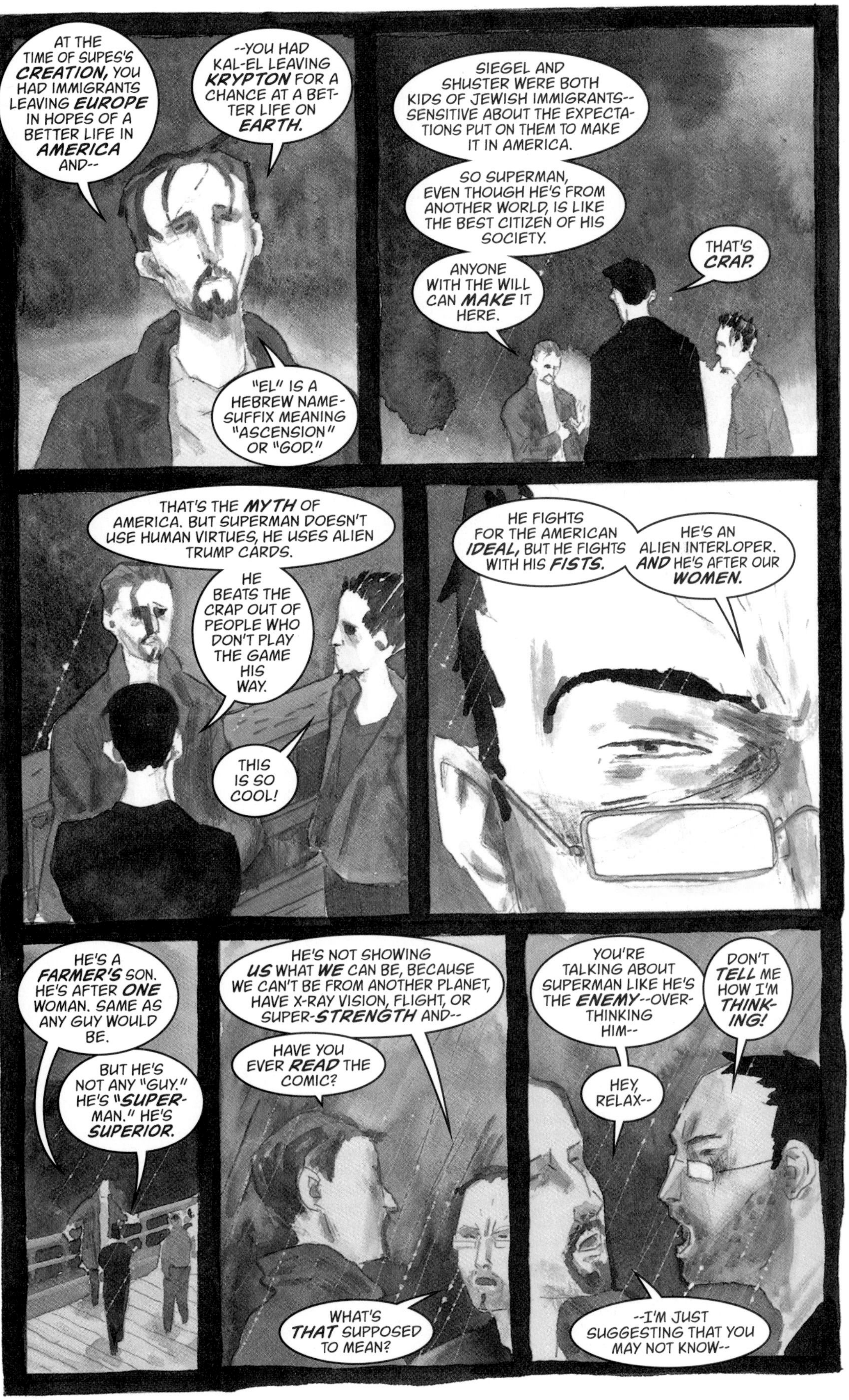
AT THE TIME OF SUPES'S CREATION, YOU HAD IMMIGRANTS LEAVING EUROPE IN HOPES OF A BETTER LIFE IN AMERICA AND--
--YOU HAD KAL-EL LEAVING KRYPTON FOR A CHANCE AT A BETTER LIFE ON EARTH.
"EL" IS A HEBREW NAME-SUFFIX MEANING "ASCENSION" OR "GOD."
SIEGEL AND SHUSTER WERE BOTH KIDS OF JEWISH IMMIGRANTS--SENSITIVE ABOUT THE EXPECTATIONS PUT ON THEM TO MAKE IT IN AMERICA.
SO SUPERMAN, EVEN THOUGH HE'S FROM ANOTHER WORLD, IS LIKE THE BEST CITIZEN OF HIS SOCIETY.
ANYONE WITH THE WILL CAN MAKE IT HERE.
THAT'S CRAP.
THAT'S THE MYTH OF AMERICA. BUT SUPERMAN DOESN'T USE HUMAN VIRTUES, HE USES ALIEN TRUMP CARDS.
HE BEATS THE CRAP OUT OF PEOPLE WHO DON'T PLAY THE GAME HIS WAY.
THIS IS SO COOL!
HE FIGHTS FOR THE AMERICAN IDEAL, BUT HE FIGHTS WITH HIS FISTS.
HE'S AN ALIEN INTERLOPER. AND HE'S AFTER OUR WOMEN.
HE'S A FARMER'S SON. HE'S AFTER ONE WOMAN. SAME AS ANY GUY WOULD BE.
BUT HE'S NOT ANY "GUY." HE'S "SUPER-MAN." HE'S SUPERIOR.
HE'S NOT SHOWING US WHAT WE CAN BE, BECAUSE WE CAN'T BE FROM ANOTHER PLANET, HAVE X-RAY VISION, FLIGHT, OR SUPER-STRENGTH AND--
HAVE YOU EVER READ THE COMIC?
WHAT'S THAT SUPPOSED TO MEAN?
YOU'RE TALKING ABOUT SUPERMAN LIKE HE'S THE ENEMY--OVER-THINKING HIM--
DON'T TELL ME HOW I'M THINKING!
HEY, RELAX--
--I'M JUST SUGGESTING THAT YOU MAY NOT KNOW--

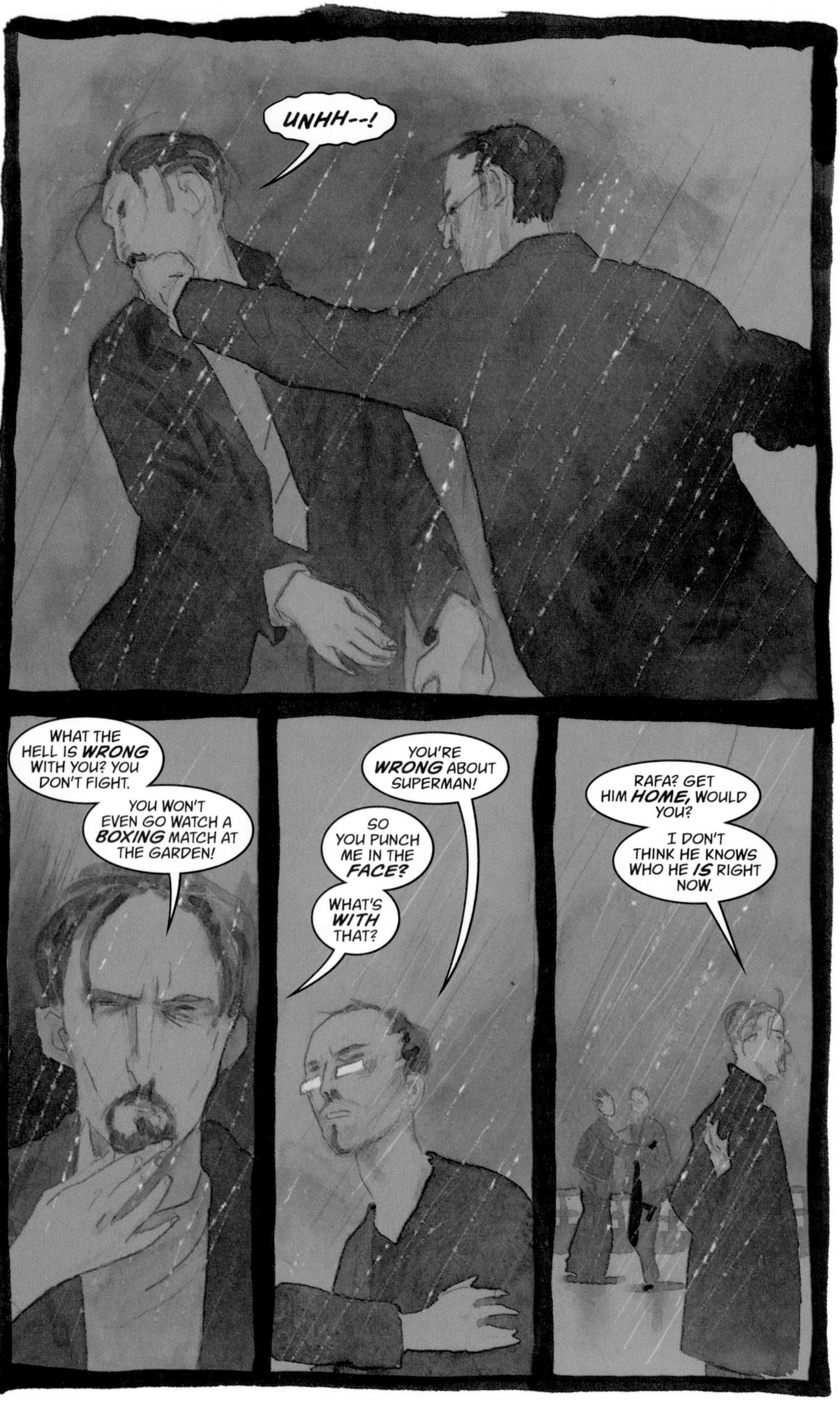
UNHH--!
WHAT THE HELL IS **WRONG** WITH YOU? YOU DON'T FIGHT.
YOU WON'T EVEN GO WATCH A **BOXING** MATCH AT THE GARDEN!
YOU'RE **WRONG** ABOUT SUPERMAN!
SO YOU PUNCH ME IN THE **FACE?**
WHAT'S **WITH** THAT?
RAFA? GET HIM **HOME,** WOULD YOU?
I DON'T THINK HE KNOWS WHO HE **IS** RIGHT NOW.

SECRET IDENTITY

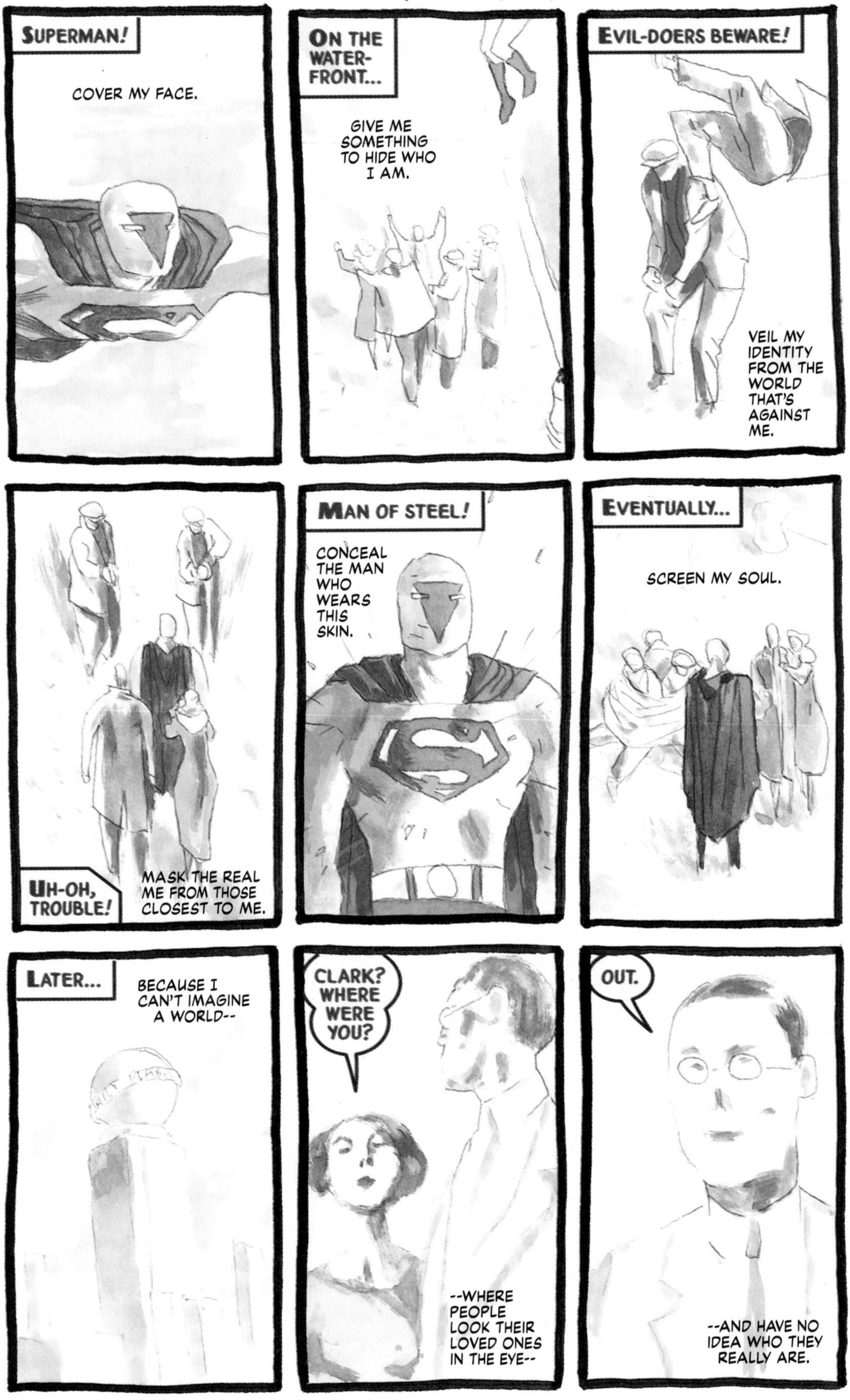

SUPERMAN!
COVER MY FACE.
ON THE WATER-FRONT...
GIVE ME SOMETHING TO HIDE WHO I AM.
EVIL-DOERS BEWARE!
VEIL MY IDENTITY FROM THE WORLD THAT'S AGAINST ME.
UH-OH, TROUBLE!
MASK THE REAL ME FROM THOSE CLOSEST TO ME.
MAN OF STEEL!
CONCEAL THE MAN WHO WEARS THIS SKIN.
EVENTUALLY...
SCREEN MY SOUL.
LATER...
BECAUSE I CAN'T IMAGINE A WORLD--
CLARK? WHERE WERE YOU?
--WHERE PEOPLE LOOK THEIR LOVED ONES IN THE EYE--
OUT.
--AND HAVE NO IDEA WHO THEY REALLY ARE.

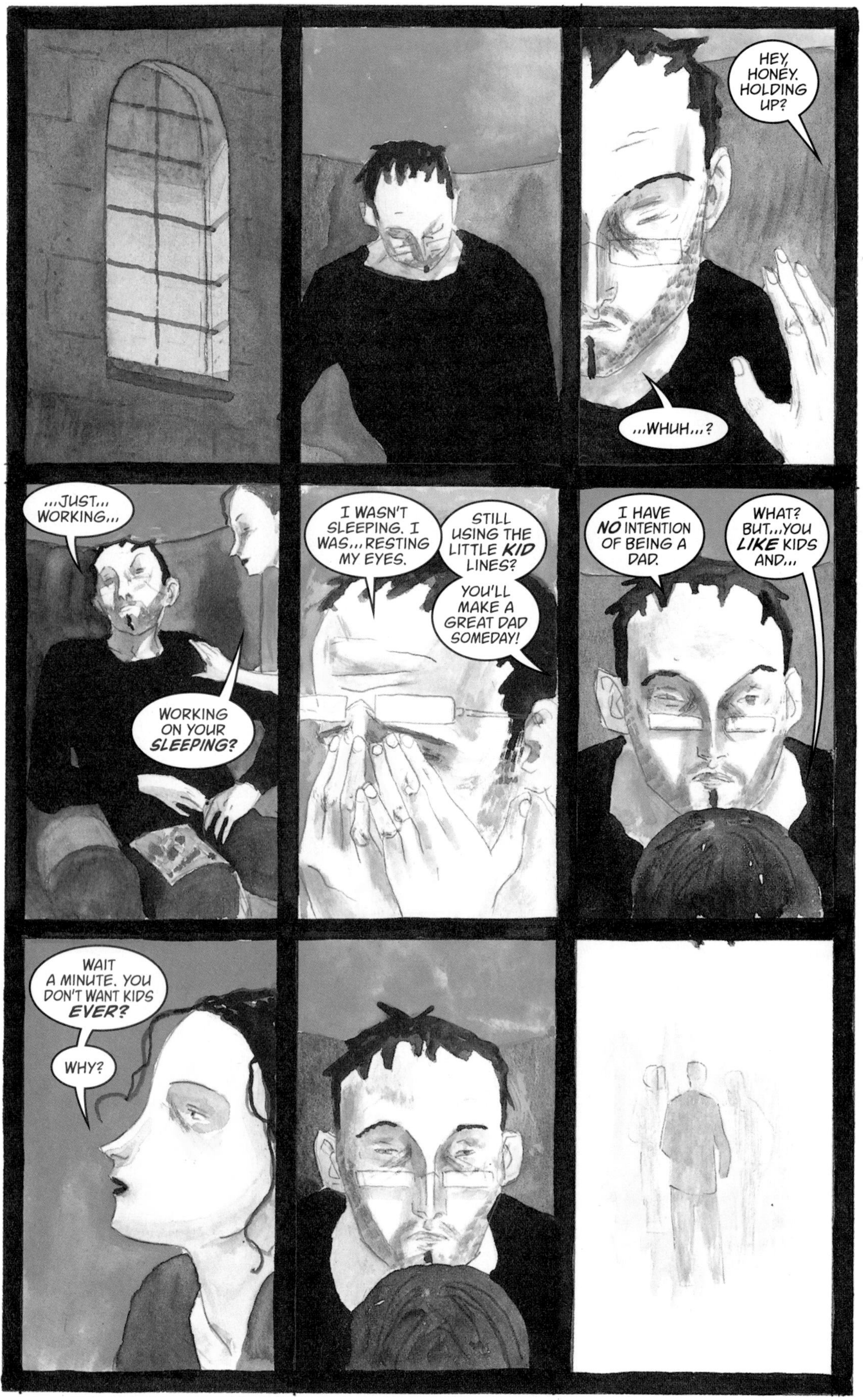
HEY, HONEY. HOLDING UP?
...WHUH...?
...JUST... WORKING...
WORKING ON YOUR SLEEPING?
I WASN'T SLEEPING. I WAS... RESTING MY EYES.
STILL USING THE LITTLE KID LINES?
YOU'LL MAKE A GREAT DAD SOMEDAY!
I HAVE NO INTENTION OF BEING A DAD.
WHAT? BUT... YOU LIKE KIDS AND...
WAIT A MINUTE. YOU DON'T WANT KIDS EVER?
WHY?

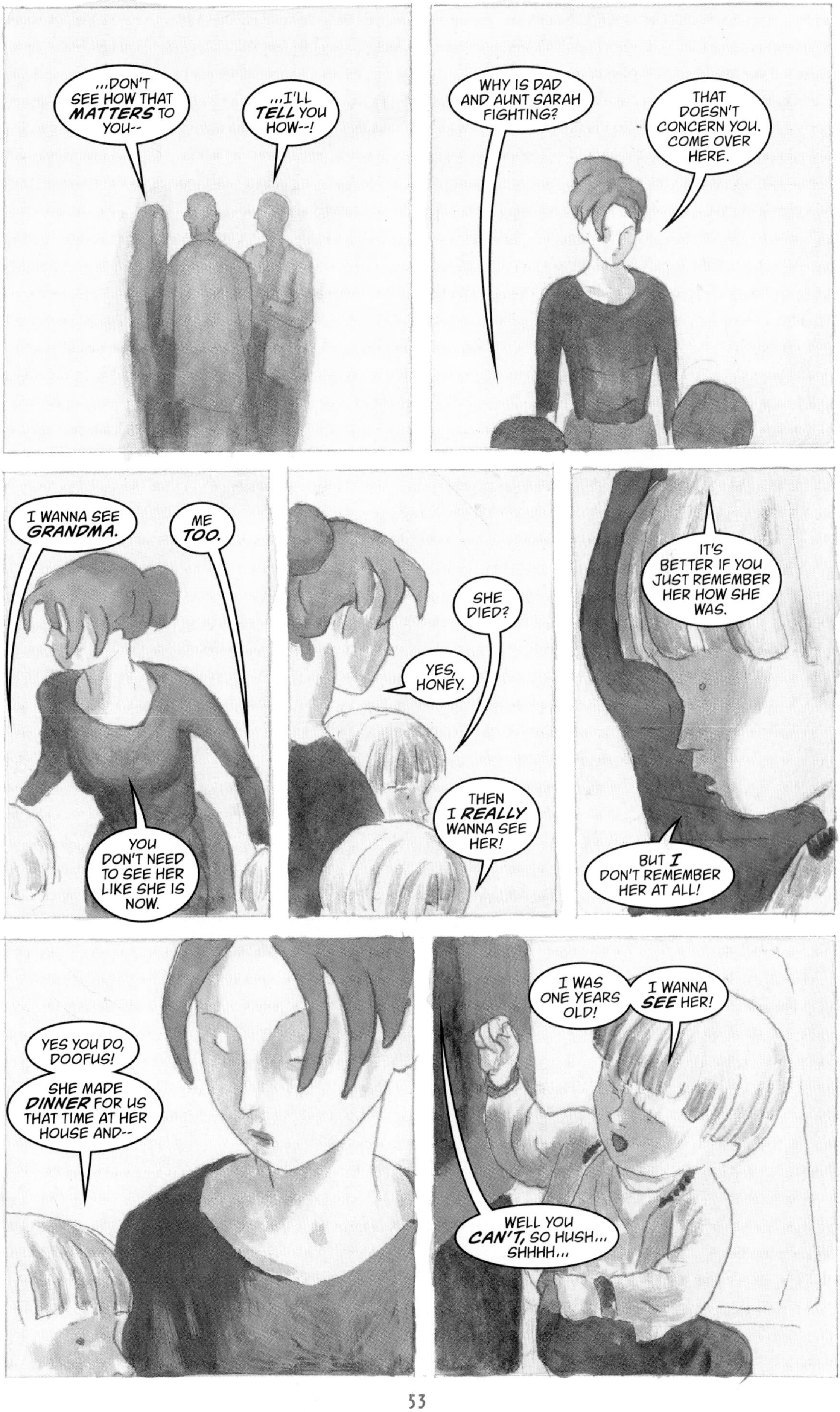

...DON'T SEE HOW THAT MATTERS TO YOU--
...I'LL TELL YOU HOW--!
WHY IS DAD AND AUNT SARAH FIGHTING?
THAT DOESN'T CONCERN YOU. COME OVER HERE.
I WANNA SEE GRANDMA.
ME TOO.
YOU DON'T NEED TO SEE HER LIKE SHE IS NOW.
SHE DIED?
YES, HONEY.
THEN I REALLY WANNA SEE HER!
IT'S BETTER IF YOU JUST REMEMBER HER HOW SHE WAS.
BUT I DON'T REMEMBER HER AT ALL!
YES YOU DO, DOOFUS!
SHE MADE DINNER FOR US THAT TIME AT HER HOUSE AND--
I WAS ONE YEARS OLD!
I WANNA SEE HER!
WELL YOU CAN'T, SO HUSH... SHHHH...

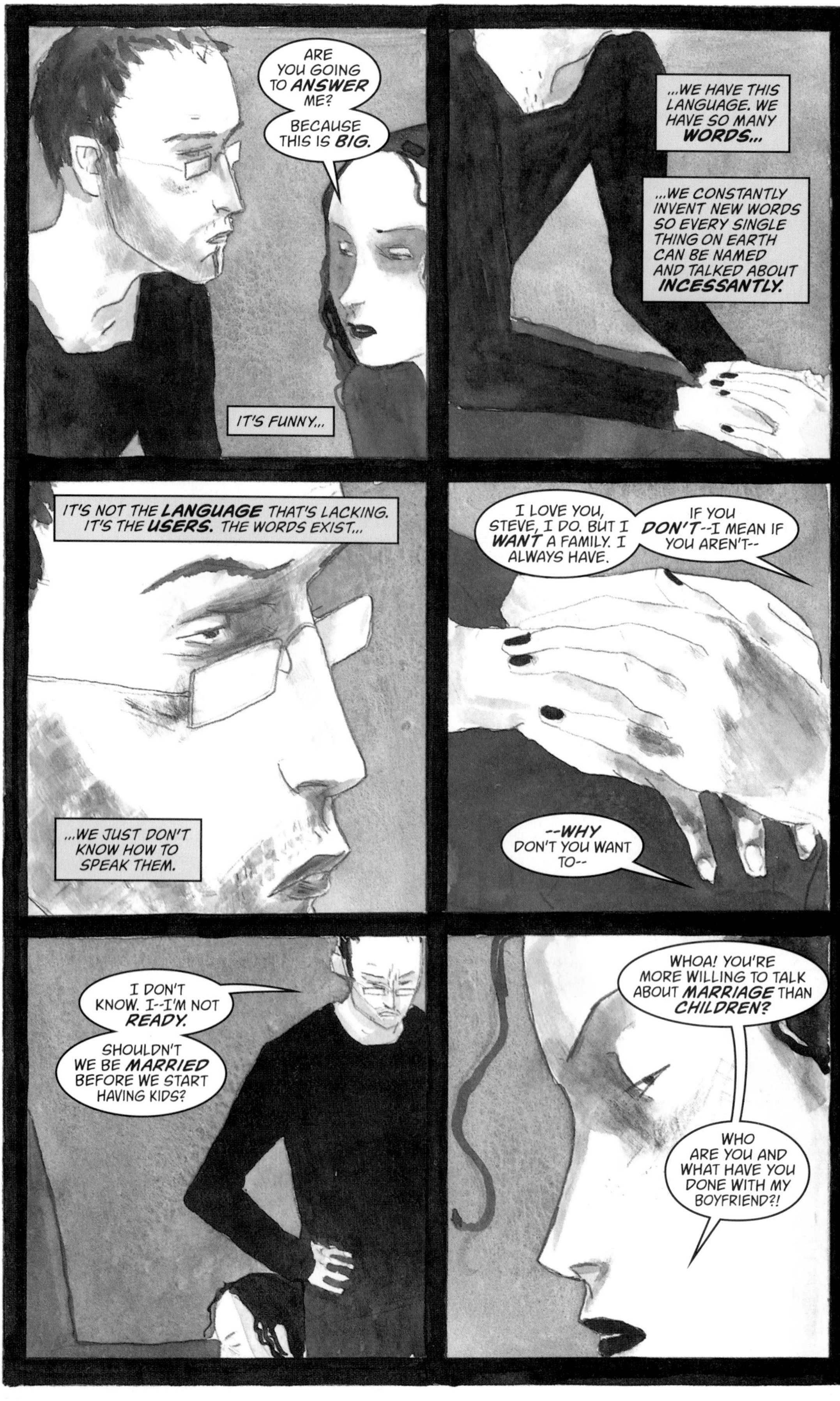

ARE YOU GOING TO **ANSWER** ME?
BECAUSE THIS IS **BIG.**
IT'S FUNNY...
...WE HAVE THIS LANGUAGE. WE HAVE SO MANY **WORDS...**
...WE CONSTANTLY INVENT NEW WORDS SO EVERY SINGLE THING ON EARTH CAN BE NAMED AND TALKED ABOUT **INCESSANTLY.**
IT'S NOT THE **LANGUAGE** THAT'S LACKING. IT'S THE **USERS.** THE WORDS EXIST...
...WE JUST DON'T KNOW HOW TO SPEAK THEM.
I LOVE YOU, STEVE, I DO. BUT I **WANT** A FAMILY. I ALWAYS HAVE.
IF YOU **DON'T**--I MEAN IF YOU AREN'T--
--WHY DON'T YOU WANT TO--
I DON'T KNOW. I--I'M NOT **READY.**
SHOULDN'T WE BE **MARRIED** BEFORE WE START HAVING KIDS?
WHOA! YOU'RE MORE WILLING TO TALK ABOUT **MARRIAGE** THAN **CHILDREN?**
WHO ARE YOU AND WHAT HAVE YOU DONE WITH MY BOYFRIEND?!

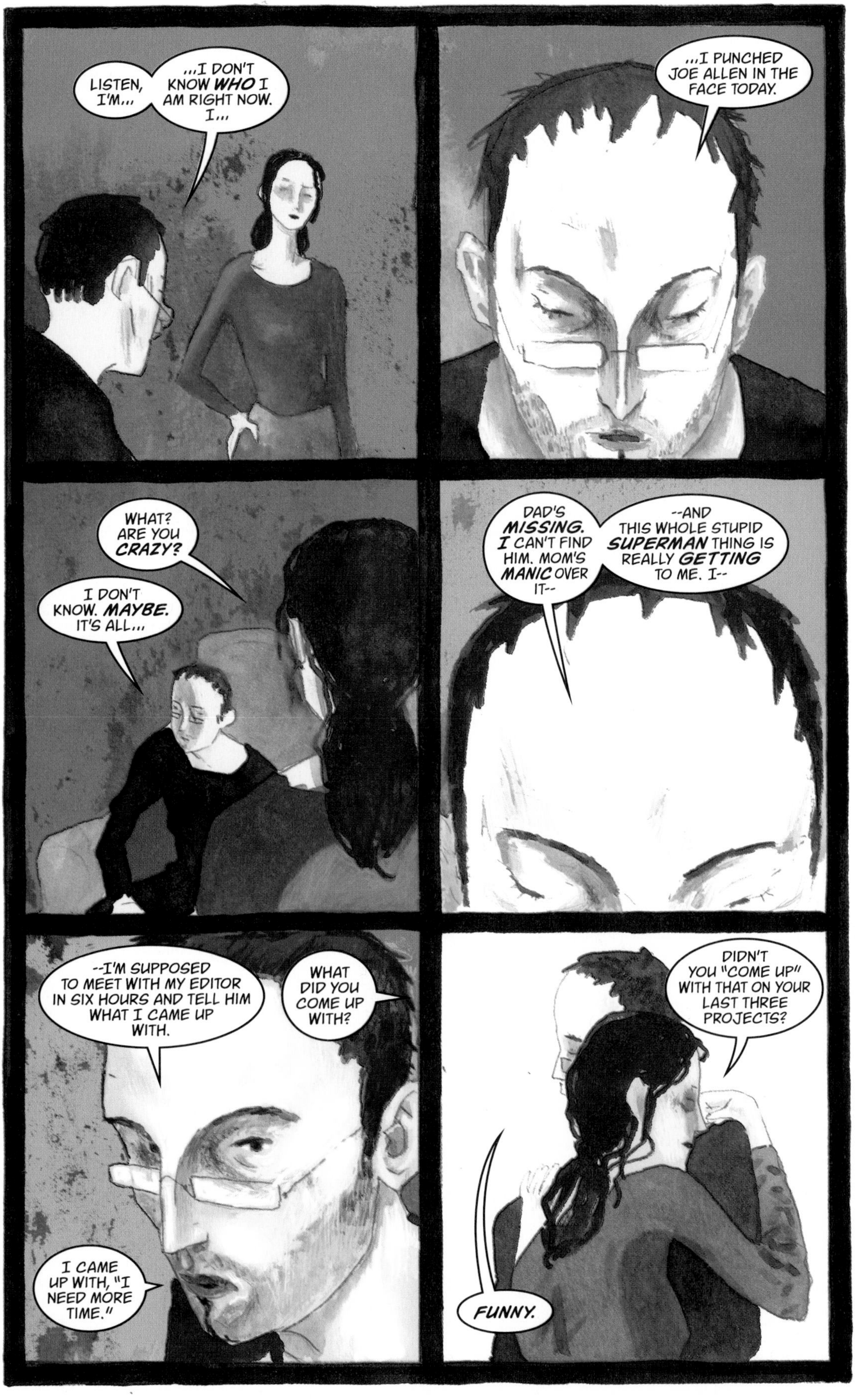
LISTEN, I'M...
...I DON'T KNOW WHO I AM RIGHT NOW. I...
...I PUNCHED JOE ALLEN IN THE FACE TODAY.
WHAT? ARE YOU CRAZY?
I DON'T KNOW. MAYBE. IT'S ALL...
DAD'S MISSING. I CAN'T FIND HIM. MOM'S MANIC OVER IT--
--AND THIS WHOLE STUPID SUPERMAN THING IS REALLY GETTING TO ME. I--
--I'M SUPPOSED TO MEET WITH MY EDITOR IN SIX HOURS AND TELL HIM WHAT I CAME UP WITH.
WHAT DID YOU COME UP WITH?
I CAME UP WITH, "I NEED MORE TIME."
DIDN'T YOU "COME UP" WITH THAT ON YOUR LAST THREE PROJECTS?
FUNNY.

...HEY, MA, IT'S ME...

...ANY WORD FROM DAD YET?

WHAT'S THAT *NOISE?*

MY KEYBOARD. I'M RESEARCHING STUFF ON THE INTERNET FOR A STORY I'M WORKING ON...

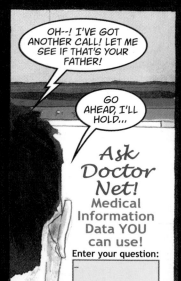

OH--! I'VE GOT ANOTHER CALL! LET ME SEE IF THAT'S YOUR FATHER!

GO AHEAD, I'LL HOLD...

Ask Doctor Net!
Medical Information Data YOU can use!
Enter your question:

Ask Doctor Net!
Medical Information Data YOU can use!
Enter your question:

What are the early symptoms of Huntington's Disease?_

SEARCH

Wait one moment while Doctor Net finds the answer to your question...

TAP
TAP
TAP
TAP

Doctor Net says...

Early symptoms of Huntington's Disease are depression and involuntary movement.

TAP
TAP
TAP
TAP

TAP ⋇

IT WASN'T HIM.

HEY, LISTEN, DO YOU KNOW WHERE AUNT SARAH IS? HER HOUSE IS *ABANDONED.*

I HAVE NO IDEA. YOUR FATHER HASN'T SPOKEN TO HER SINCE THE TIME HE STAYED THERE YEARS AGO.

TRY NOT TO WORRY. I'LL LOOK FOR HIM SOME MORE AFTER I TAKE CARE OF SOME BUSINESS. EVERY-THING'LL BE FINE.

THAT'S THE SAME THING YOUR FATHER ALWAYS *SAID.*

"SAYS," MA. USE THE RIGHT WORD.

HE'S NOT *DEAD.* IT'S *"SAYS."*

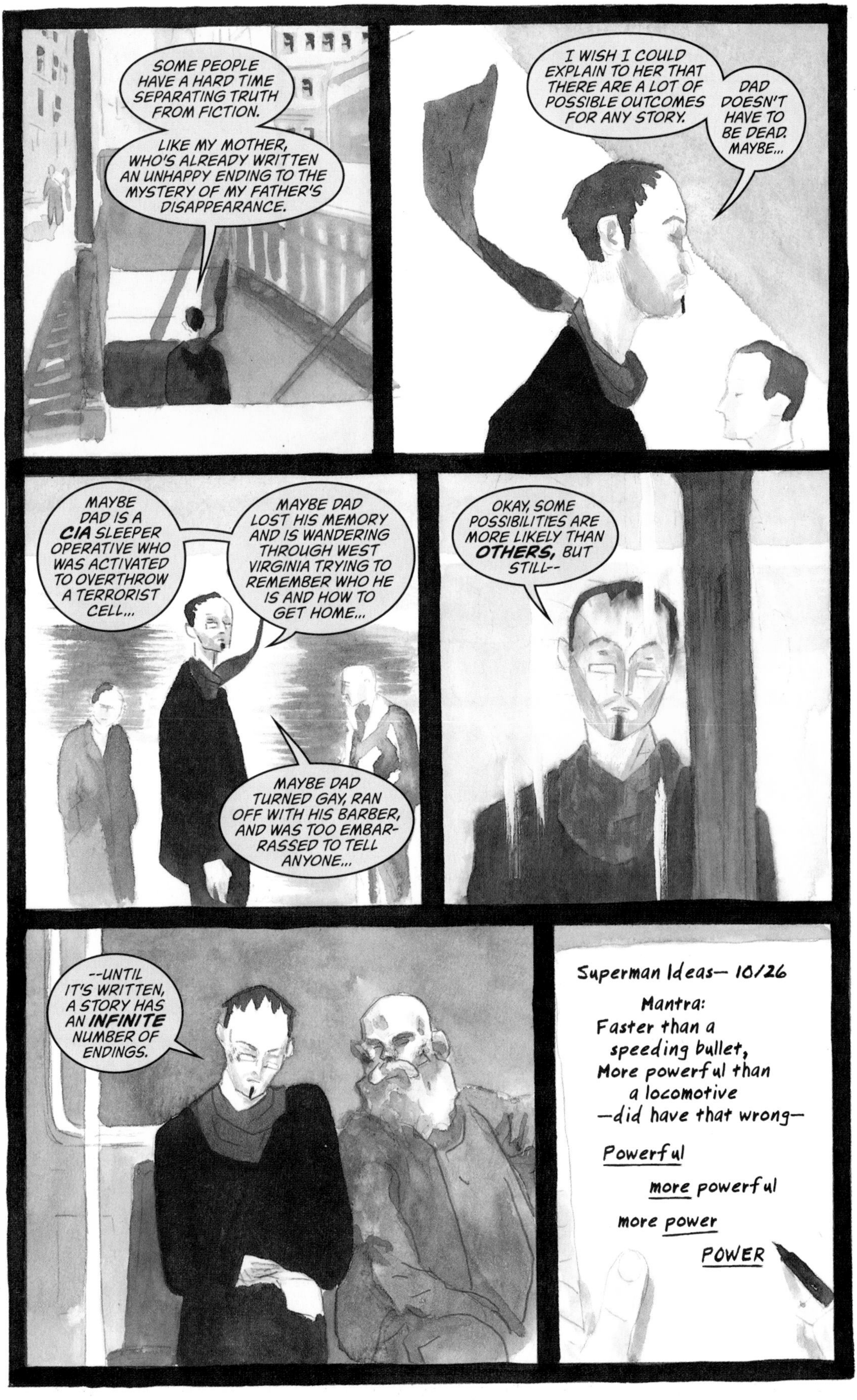
SOME PEOPLE HAVE A HARD TIME SEPARATING TRUTH FROM FICTION.
LIKE MY MOTHER, WHO'S ALREADY WRITTEN AN UNHAPPY ENDING TO THE MYSTERY OF MY FATHER'S DISAPPEARANCE.
I WISH I COULD EXPLAIN TO HER THAT THERE ARE A LOT OF POSSIBLE OUTCOMES FOR ANY STORY.
DAD DOESN'T HAVE TO BE DEAD. MAYBE...
MAYBE DAD IS A CIA SLEEPER OPERATIVE WHO WAS ACTIVATED TO OVERTHROW A TERRORIST CELL...
MAYBE DAD LOST HIS MEMORY AND IS WANDERING THROUGH WEST VIRGINIA TRYING TO REMEMBER WHO HE IS AND HOW TO GET HOME...
MAYBE DAD TURNED GAY, RAN OFF WITH HIS BARBER, AND WAS TOO EMBARRASSED TO TELL ANYONE...
OKAY, SOME POSSIBILITIES ARE MORE LIKELY THAN OTHERS, BUT STILL--
--UNTIL IT'S WRITTEN, A STORY HAS AN INFINITE NUMBER OF ENDINGS.
Superman Ideas— 10/26
Mantra:
Faster than a speeding bullet,
More powerful than a locomotive
—did have that wrong—
Powerful
more powerful
more power
POWER

POWER

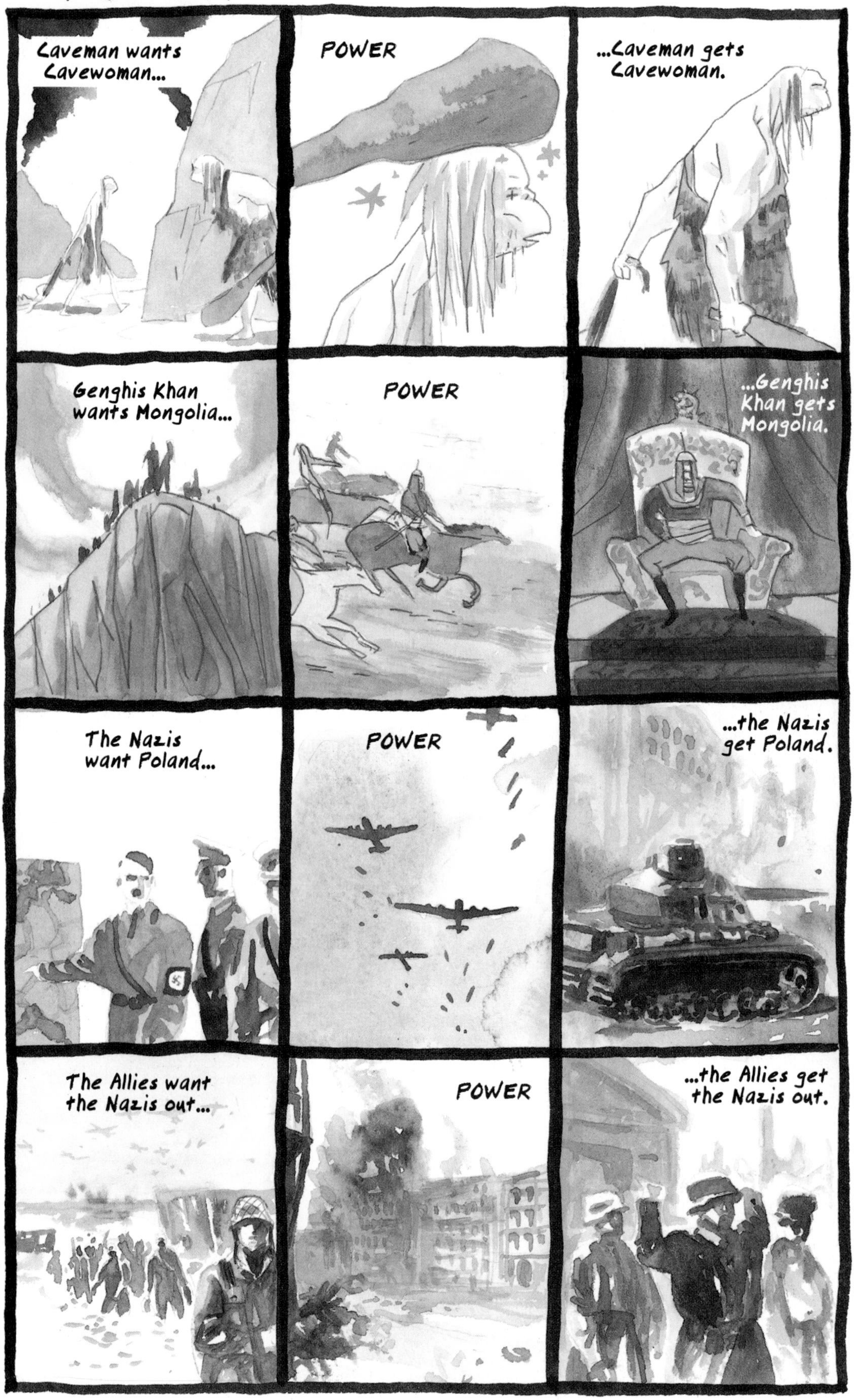

Caveman wants Cavewoman...
POWER
...Caveman gets Cavewoman.
Genghis Khan wants Mongolia...
POWER
...Genghis Khan gets Mongolia.
The Nazis want Poland...
POWER
...the Nazis get Poland.
The Allies want the Nazis out...
POWER
...the Allies get the Nazis out.

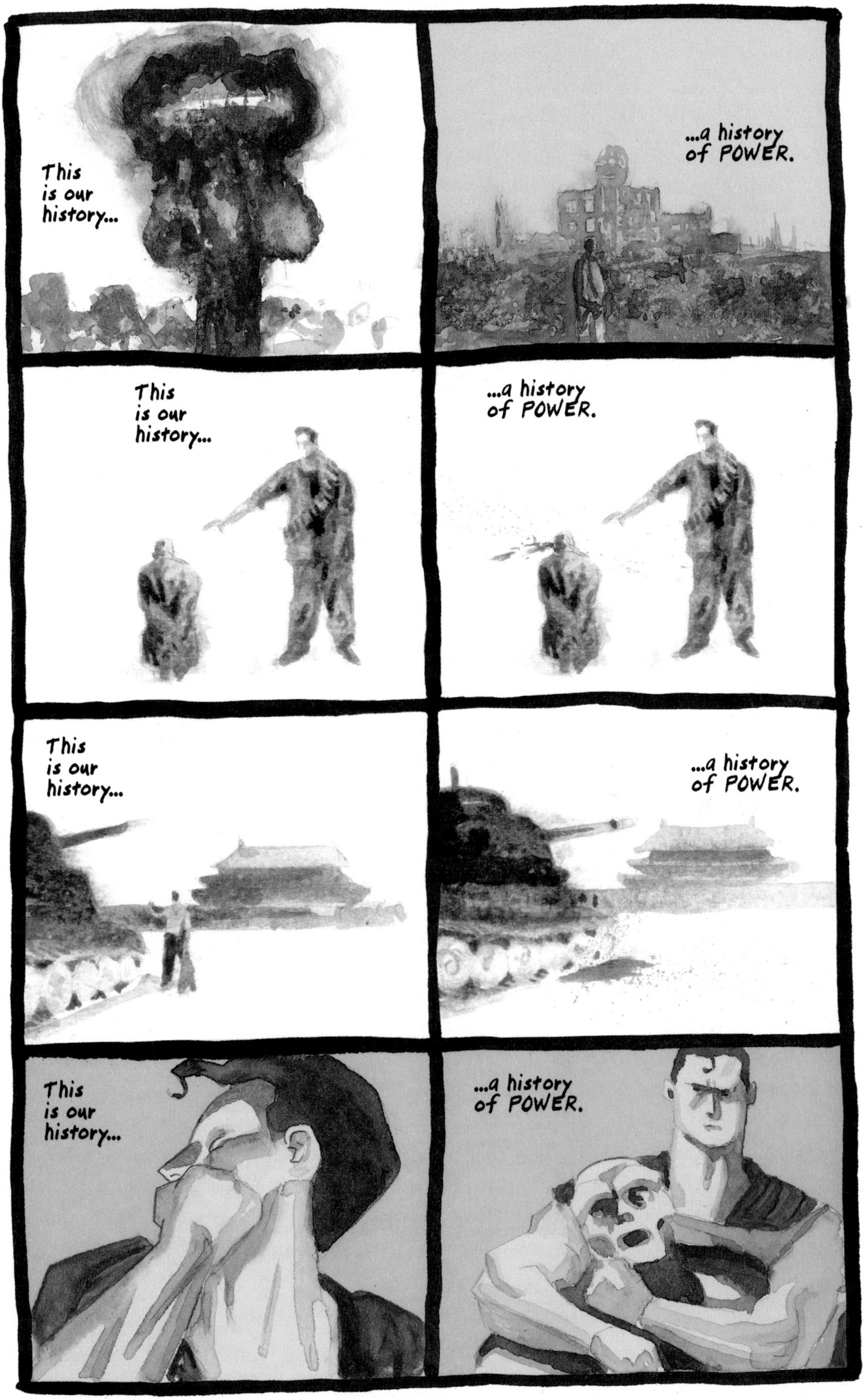
This is our history...
...a history of POWER.
This is our history...
...a history of POWER.
This is our history...
...a history of POWER.
This is our history...
...a history of POWER.

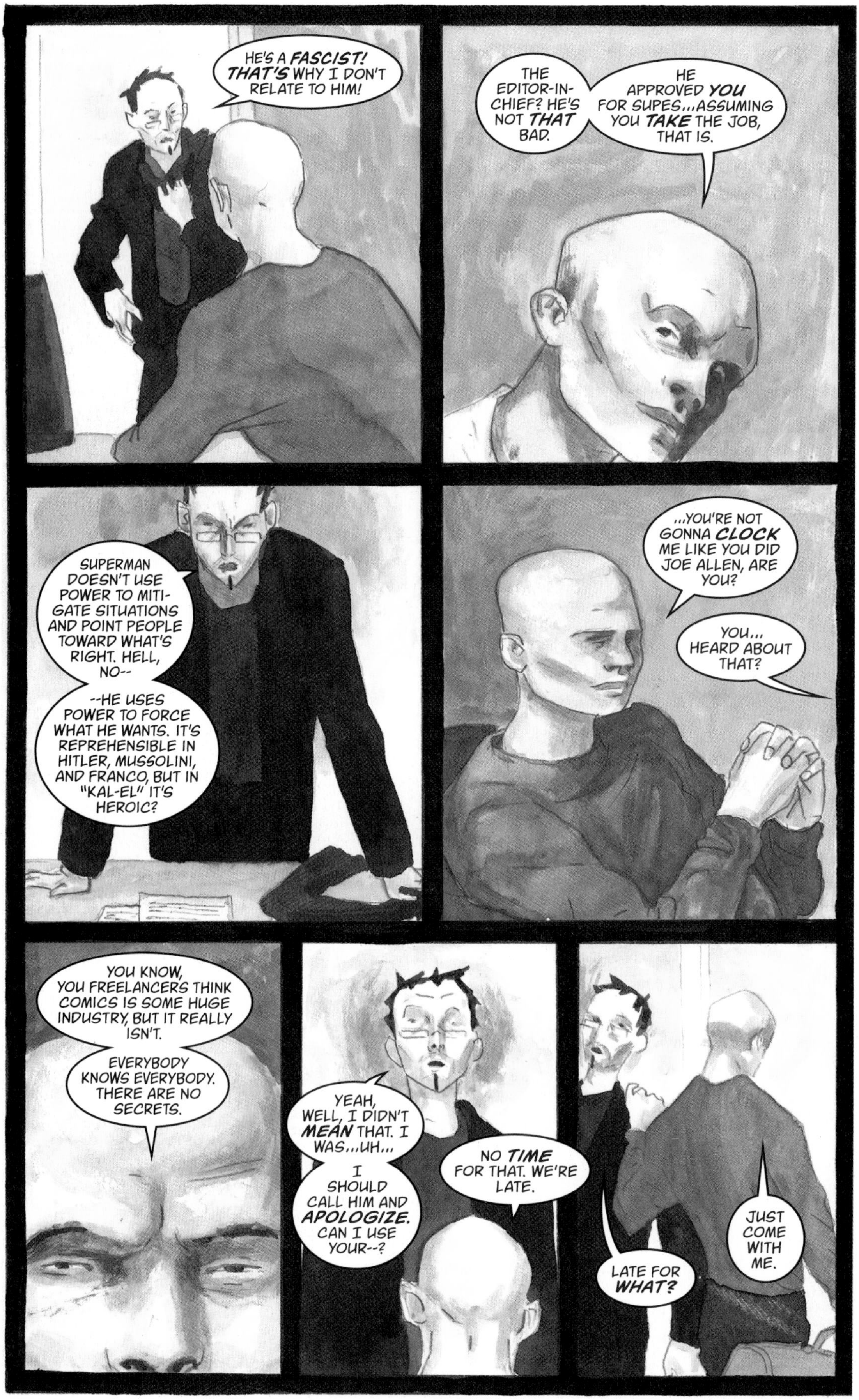
HE'S A FASCIST! THAT'S WHY I DON'T RELATE TO HIM!
THE EDITOR-IN-CHIEF? HE'S NOT THAT BAD.
HE APPROVED YOU FOR SUPES...ASSUMING YOU TAKE THE JOB, THAT IS.
SUPERMAN DOESN'T USE POWER TO MITI-GATE SITUATIONS AND POINT PEOPLE TOWARD WHAT'S RIGHT. HELL, NO--
--HE USES POWER TO FORCE WHAT HE WANTS. IT'S REPREHENSIBLE IN HITLER, MUSSOLINI, AND FRANCO, BUT IN "KAL-EL" IT'S HEROIC?
...YOU'RE NOT GONNA CLOCK ME LIKE YOU DID JOE ALLEN, ARE YOU?
YOU... HEARD ABOUT THAT?
YOU KNOW, YOU FREELANCERS THINK COMICS IS SOME HUGE INDUSTRY, BUT IT REALLY ISN'T.
EVERYBODY KNOWS EVERYBODY. THERE ARE NO SECRETS.
YEAH, WELL, I DIDN'T MEAN THAT. I WAS...UH...
I SHOULD CALL HIM AND APOLOGIZE. CAN I USE YOUR--?
NO TIME FOR THAT. WE'RE LATE.
LATE FOR WHAT?
JUST COME WITH ME.

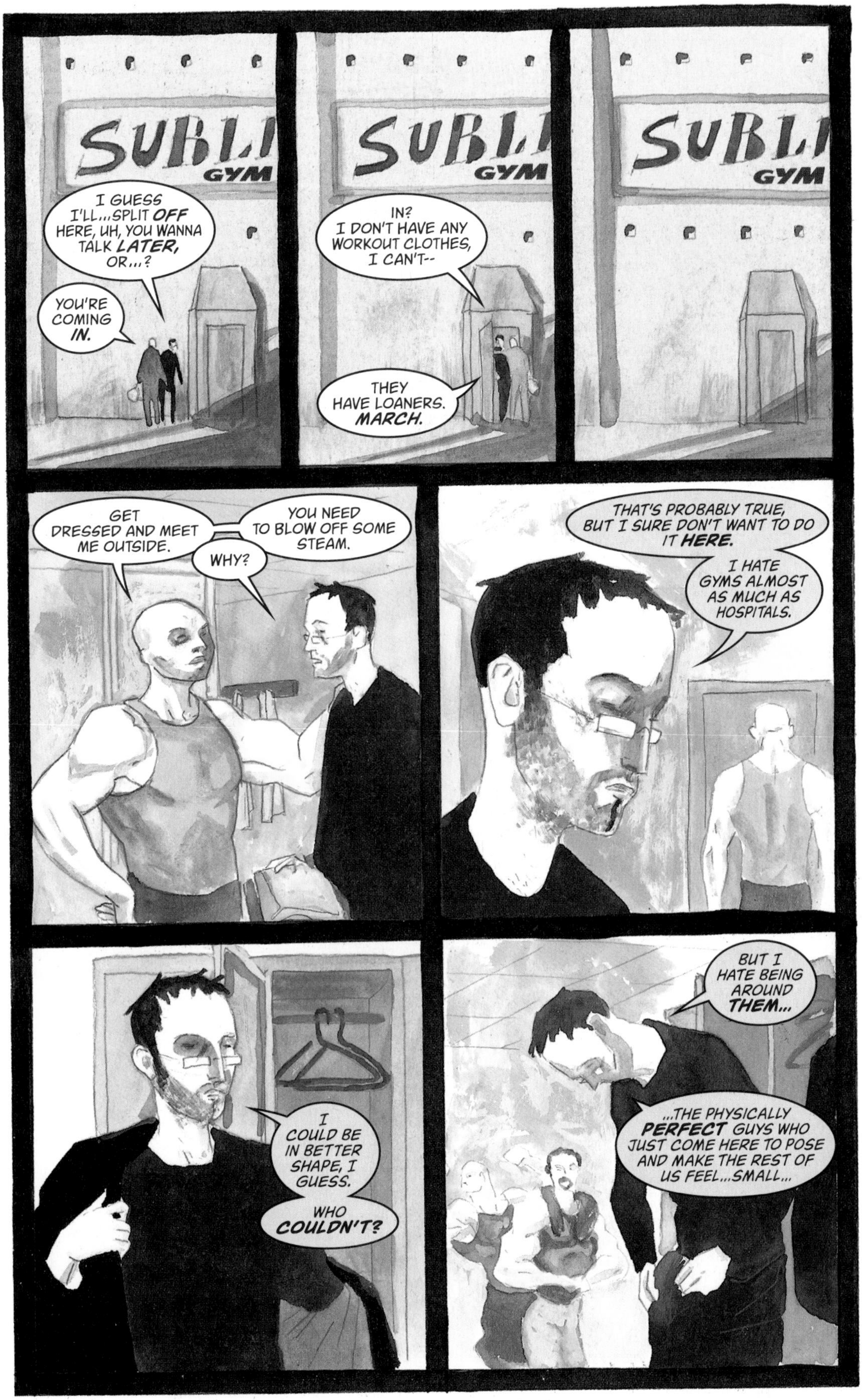
SUBLI
GYM
I GUESS I'LL...SPLIT OFF HERE, UH, YOU WANNA TALK LATER, OR...?
YOU'RE COMING IN.
SUBLI
GYM
IN? I DON'T HAVE ANY WORKOUT CLOTHES, I CAN'T--
THEY HAVE LOANERS. MARCH.
SUBLI
GYM
GET DRESSED AND MEET ME OUTSIDE.
WHY?
YOU NEED TO BLOW OFF SOME STEAM.
THAT'S PROBABLY TRUE, BUT I SURE DON'T WANT TO DO IT HERE.
I HATE GYMS ALMOST AS MUCH AS HOSPITALS.
I COULD BE IN BETTER SHAPE, I GUESS.
WHO COULDN'T?
BUT I HATE BEING AROUND THEM...
...THE PHYSICALLY PERFECT GUYS WHO JUST COME HERE TO POSE AND MAKE THE REST OF US FEEL...SMALL...

PERFECT

IN ALL MY YEARS I NEVER SEEN ANYTHING LIKE THIS...

WHAT YOU GOT HERE IS PERFECT PROPORTIONS IF YOU DON'T MIND MY SAYING SO! TURN LEFT...

NOT THAT I'M GETTING FRESH OR NOTHING! PLEASE! HA!

NO, NO, NO, MY WIFE ETTA, AFTER 38 YEARS, SHE'S STILL MORE THAN I CAN HANDLE! YESSIREE!

MET HER AT A U.S.O. DANCE. BACK IN THE DAY, SHE HAD A PERFECT BODY HER OWN SELF!

BUT DON'T LET HER CATCH ME TALKING TRASH OR SHE'LL HAVE MY HIDE! HA!

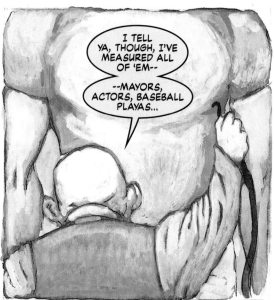

I TELL YA, THOUGH, I'VE MEASURED ALL OF 'EM--

--MAYORS, ACTORS, BASEBALL PLAYAS...

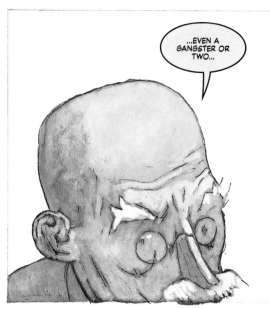

...EVEN A GANGSTER OR TWO...

...BUT YOU-- YOU'RE THE ONLY ONE I EVER SEEN LIKE THIS.

LOOK AT THIS STOMACH! LIKE STEEL PLATE! TURN AROUND PLEASE.

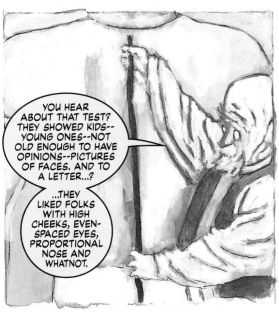

YOU HEAR ABOUT THAT TEST? THEY SHOWED KIDS--YOUNG ONES--NOT OLD ENOUGH TO HAVE OPINIONS--PICTURES OF FACES. AND TO A LETTER...?

...THEY LIKED FOLKS WITH HIGH CHEEKS, EVEN-SPACED EYES, PROPORTIONAL NOSE AND WHATNOT.

SEE? IT AIN'T *TV* MAKIN' US LOOK FOR THE PERFECT BODY.

IT'S INSTINCT! CAN YOU BELIEVE THAT?

AND I DON'T ONLY KNOW FROM CLOTHES, NEITHER. NO, SIR.

I TOOK ART CLASSES!

THOUGHT I'D BE A PAINTER. PORTRAITS AND THE LIKE.

EVEN SAW THAT MICHELANGELO DAVID STATUE THINGY. I TELL YOU, HE HAD NOTHIN' ON YOU!

BUT...I TURNED OUT TO BE JUST A TAILOR.

THOUGH THAT DON'T MEAN I CAN'T MAKE MY CLOTHES MY ART. AM I RIGHT?

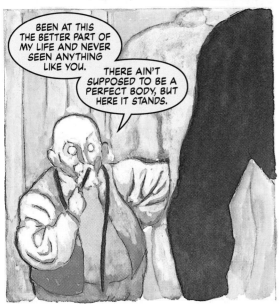

BEEN AT THIS THE BETTER PART OF MY LIFE AND NEVER SEEN ANYTHING LIKE YOU.

THERE AIN'T SUPPOSED TO BE A PERFECT BODY, BUT HERE IT STANDS.

ANYHOW, I GOT MY NUMBERS, SO I'LL GET THE SUIT CUT.

YOU CAN STOP IN NEXT THURSDAY FOR A FIT CHECK, MR. KENT.

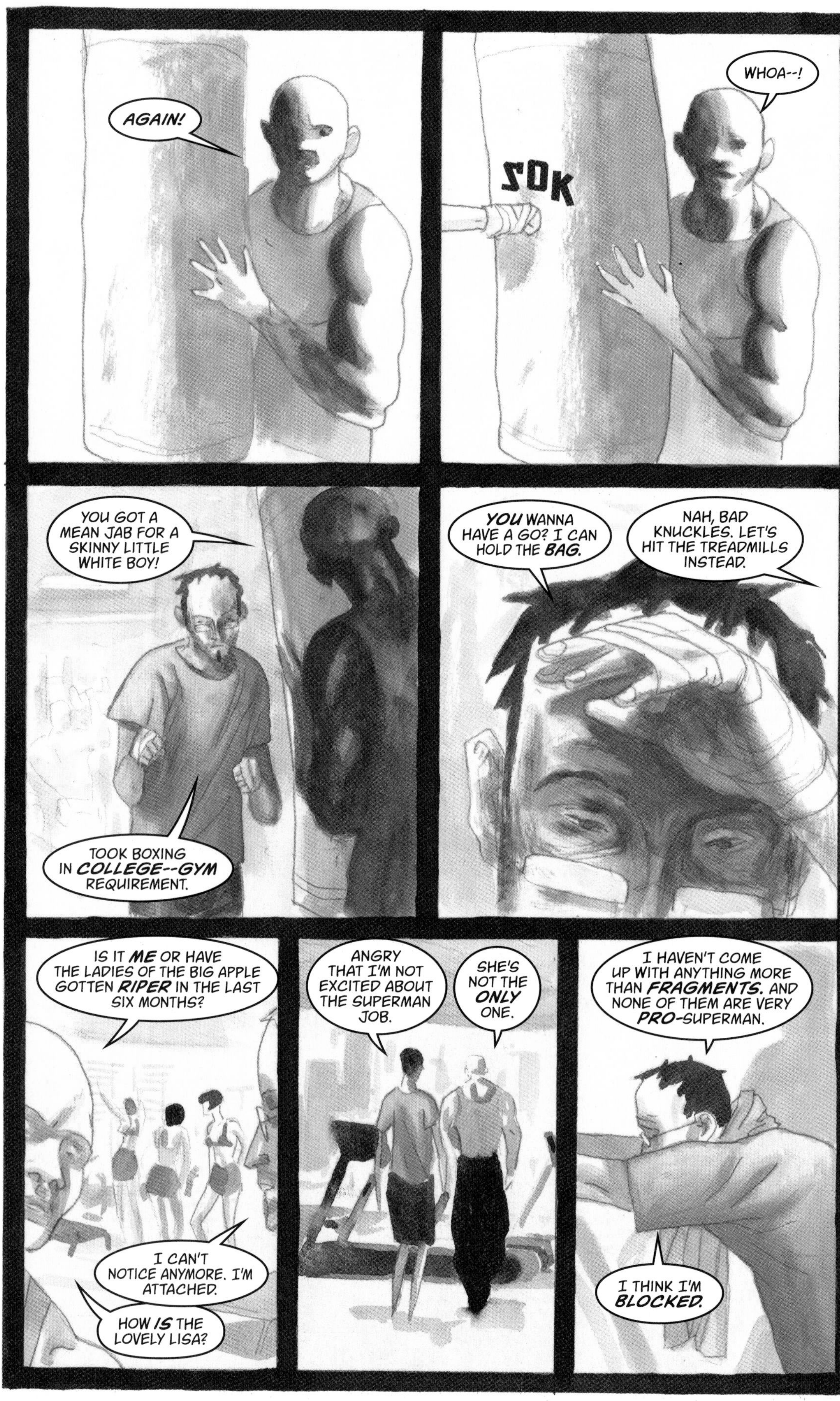
AGAIN!
WHOA--!
SOK
YOU GOT A MEAN JAB FOR A SKINNY LITTLE WHITE BOY!
TOOK BOXING IN COLLEGE--GYM REQUIREMENT.
YOU WANNA HAVE A GO? I CAN HOLD THE BAG.
NAH, BAD KNUCKLES. LET'S HIT THE TREADMILLS INSTEAD.
IS IT ME OR HAVE THE LADIES OF THE BIG APPLE GOTTEN RIPER IN THE LAST SIX MONTHS?
I CAN'T NOTICE ANYMORE. I'M ATTACHED.
HOW IS THE LOVELY LISA?
ANGRY THAT I'M NOT EXCITED ABOUT THE SUPERMAN JOB.
SHE'S NOT THE ONLY ONE.
I HAVEN'T COME UP WITH ANYTHING MORE THAN FRAGMENTS. AND NONE OF THEM ARE VERY PRO-SUPERMAN.
I THINK I'M BLOCKED.

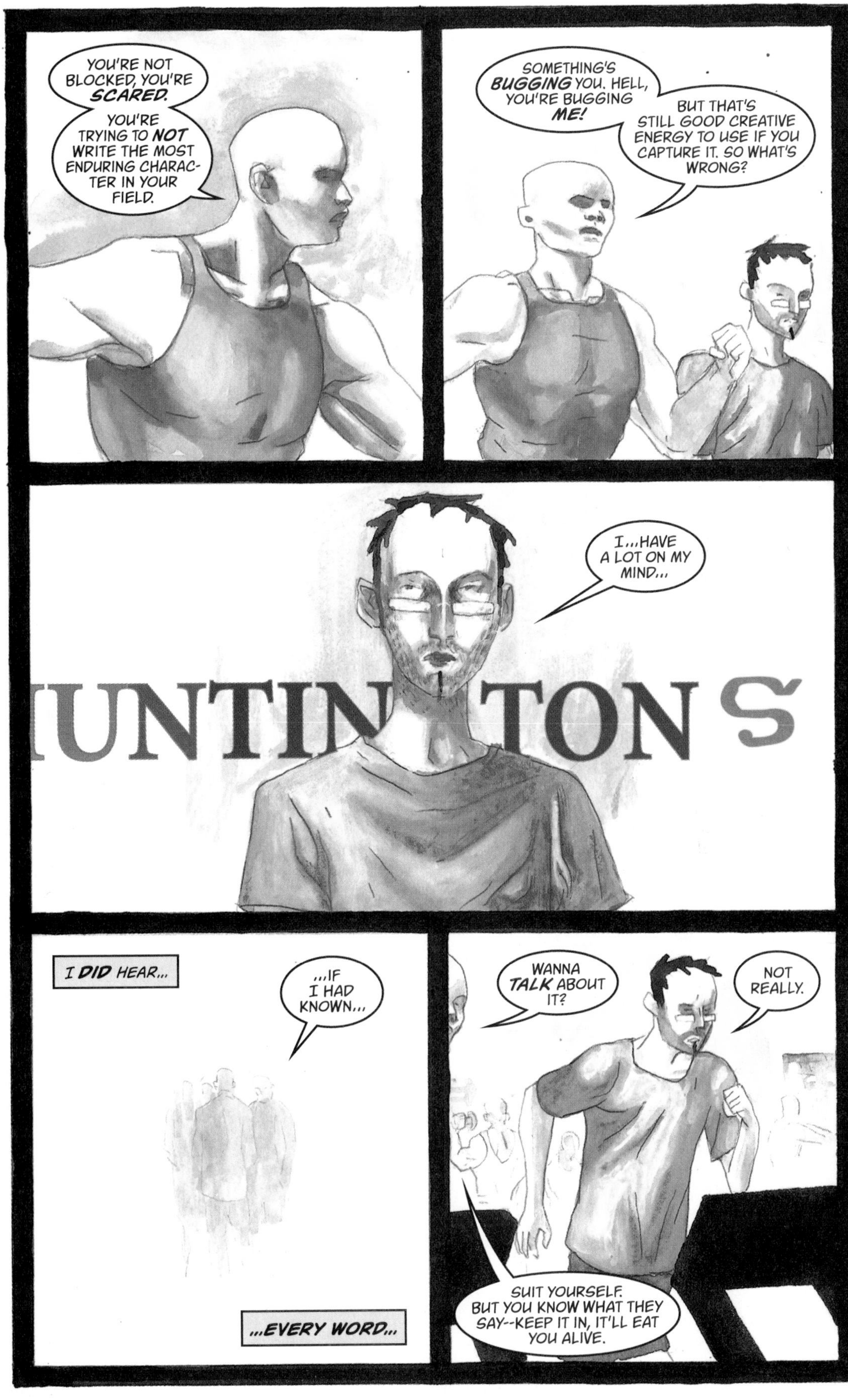
YOU'RE NOT BLOCKED, YOU'RE SCARED.
YOU'RE TRYING TO NOT WRITE THE MOST ENDURING CHARACTER IN YOUR FIELD.
SOMETHING'S BUGGING YOU. HELL, YOU'RE BUGGING ME!
BUT THAT'S STILL GOOD CREATIVE ENERGY TO USE IF YOU CAPTURE IT. SO WHAT'S WRONG?
I...HAVE A LOT ON MY MIND...
UNTIN TON S
I DID HEAR...
...IF I HAD KNOWN...
...EVERY WORD...
WANNA TALK ABOUT IT?
NOT REALLY.
SUIT YOURSELF. BUT YOU KNOW WHAT THEY SAY--KEEP IT IN, IT'LL EAT YOU ALIVE.

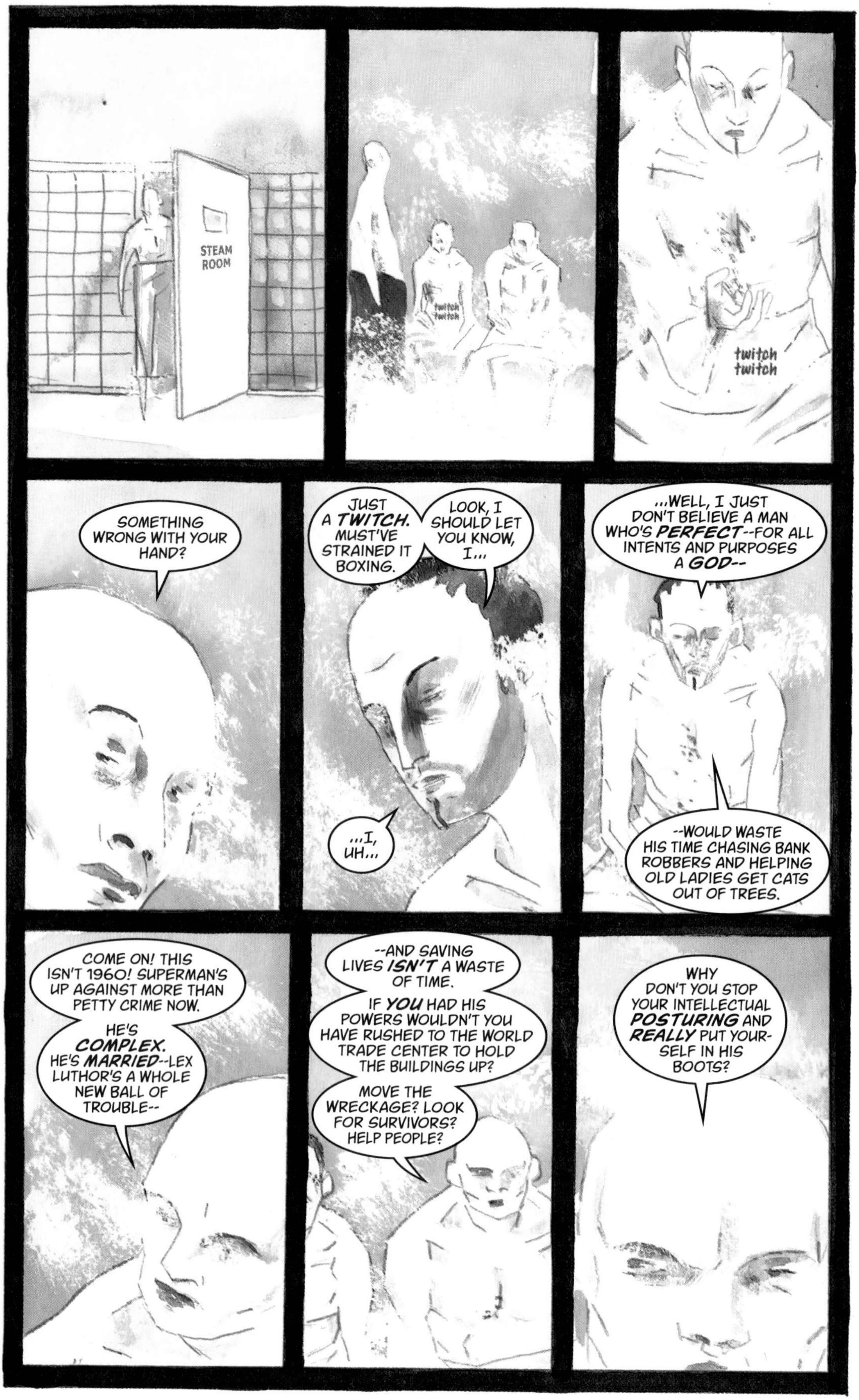

STEAM ROOM
twitch twitch
twitch twitch
SOMETHING WRONG WITH YOUR HAND?
JUST A TWITCH. MUST'VE STRAINED IT BOXING.
LOOK, I SHOULD LET YOU KNOW, I...
...I, UH...
...WELL, I JUST DON'T BELIEVE A MAN WHO'S PERFECT--FOR ALL INTENTS AND PURPOSES A GOD--
--WOULD WASTE HIS TIME CHASING BANK ROBBERS AND HELPING OLD LADIES GET CATS OUT OF TREES.
COME ON! THIS ISN'T 1960! SUPERMAN'S UP AGAINST MORE THAN PETTY CRIME NOW.
HE'S COMPLEX. HE'S MARRIED--LEX LUTHOR'S A WHOLE NEW BALL OF TROUBLE--
--AND SAVING LIVES ISN'T A WASTE OF TIME.
IF YOU HAD HIS POWERS WOULDN'T YOU HAVE RUSHED TO THE WORLD TRADE CENTER TO HOLD THE BUILDINGS UP?
MOVE THE WRECKAGE? LOOK FOR SURVIVORS? HELP PEOPLE?
WHY DON'T YOU STOP YOUR INTELLECTUAL POSTURING AND REALLY PUT YOUR-SELF IN HIS BOOTS?

HIDDEN

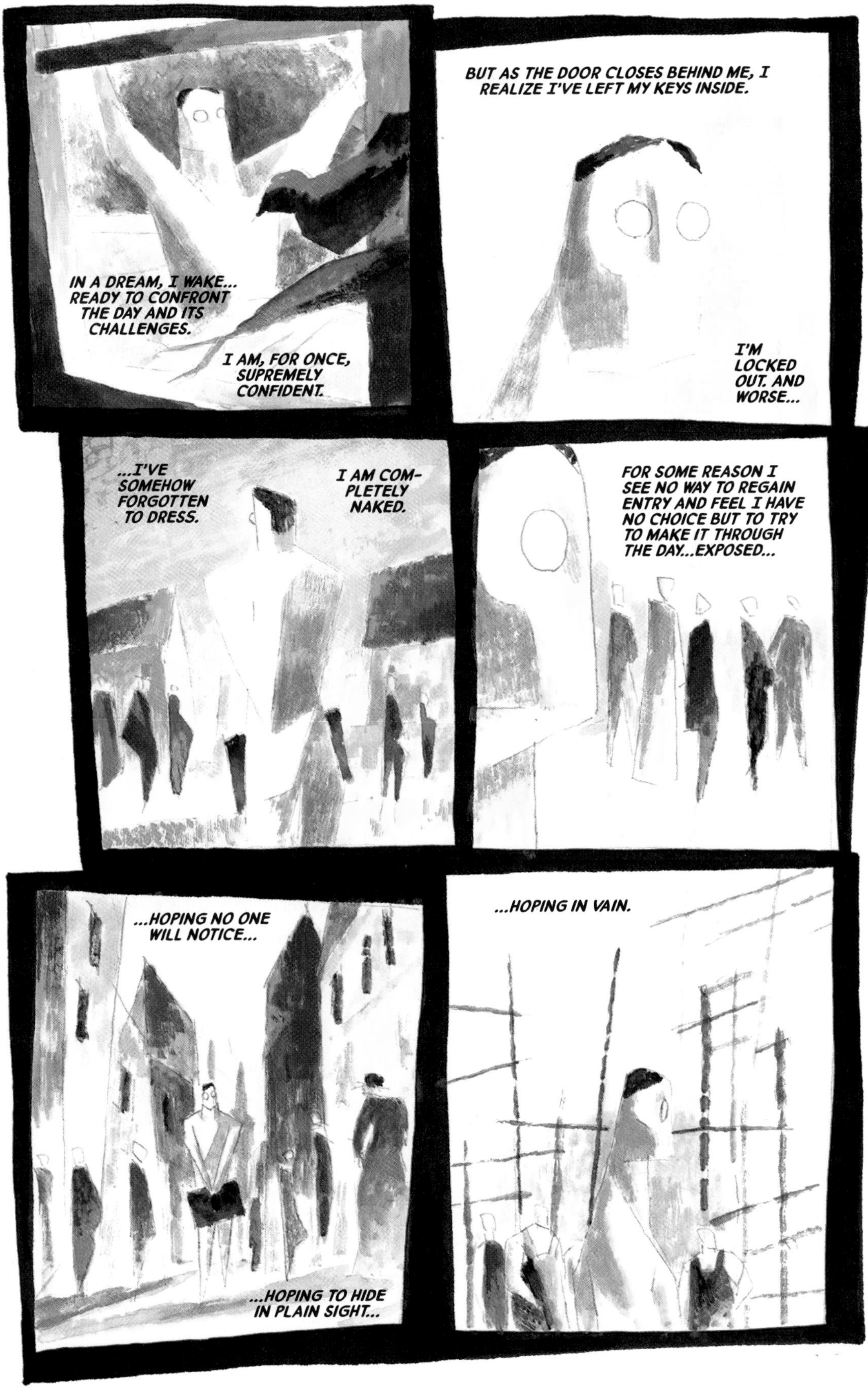
IN A DREAM, I WAKE... READY TO CONFRONT THE DAY AND ITS CHALLENGES.
I AM, FOR ONCE, SUPREMELY CONFIDENT.
BUT AS THE DOOR CLOSES BEHIND ME, I REALIZE I'VE LEFT MY KEYS INSIDE.
I'M LOCKED OUT. AND WORSE...
...I'VE SOMEHOW FORGOTTEN TO DRESS.
I AM COMPLETELY NAKED.
FOR SOME REASON I SEE NO WAY TO REGAIN ENTRY AND FEEL I HAVE NO CHOICE BUT TO TRY TO MAKE IT THROUGH THE DAY...EXPOSED...
...HOPING NO ONE WILL NOTICE...
...HOPING TO HIDE IN PLAIN SIGHT...
...HOPING IN VAIN.

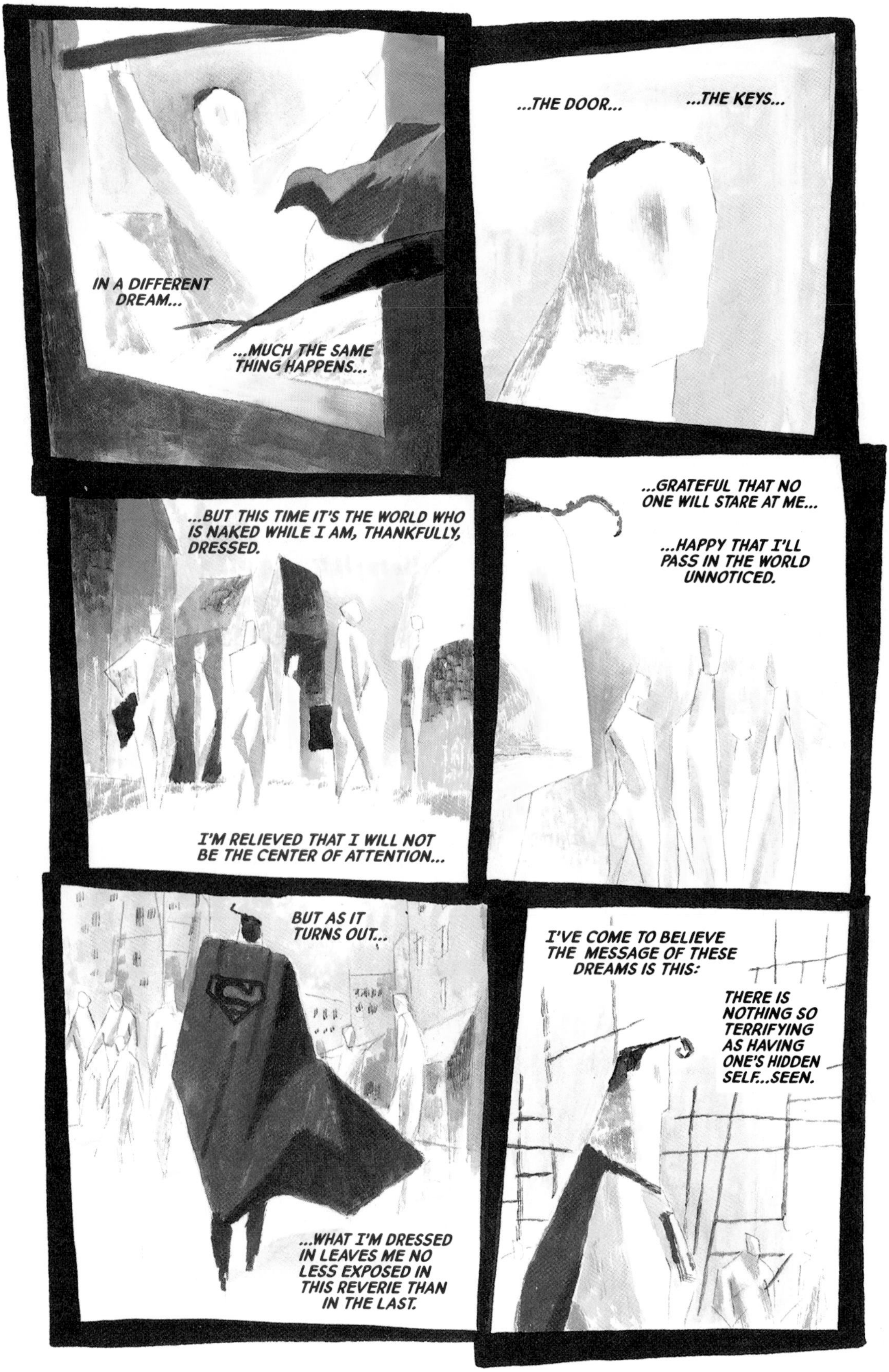
IN A DIFFERENT DREAM...
...MUCH THE SAME THING HAPPENS...
...THE DOOR...
...THE KEYS...
...BUT THIS TIME IT'S THE WORLD WHO IS NAKED WHILE I AM, THANKFULLY, DRESSED.
I'M RELIEVED THAT I WILL NOT BE THE CENTER OF ATTENTION...
...GRATEFUL THAT NO ONE WILL STARE AT ME...
...HAPPY THAT I'LL PASS IN THE WORLD UNNOTICED.
BUT AS IT TURNS OUT...
...WHAT I'M DRESSED IN LEAVES ME NO LESS EXPOSED IN THIS REVERIE THAN IN THE LAST.
I'VE COME TO BELIEVE THE MESSAGE OF THESE DREAMS IS THIS:
THERE IS NOTHING SO TERRIFYING AS HAVING ONE'S HIDDEN SELF...SEEN.

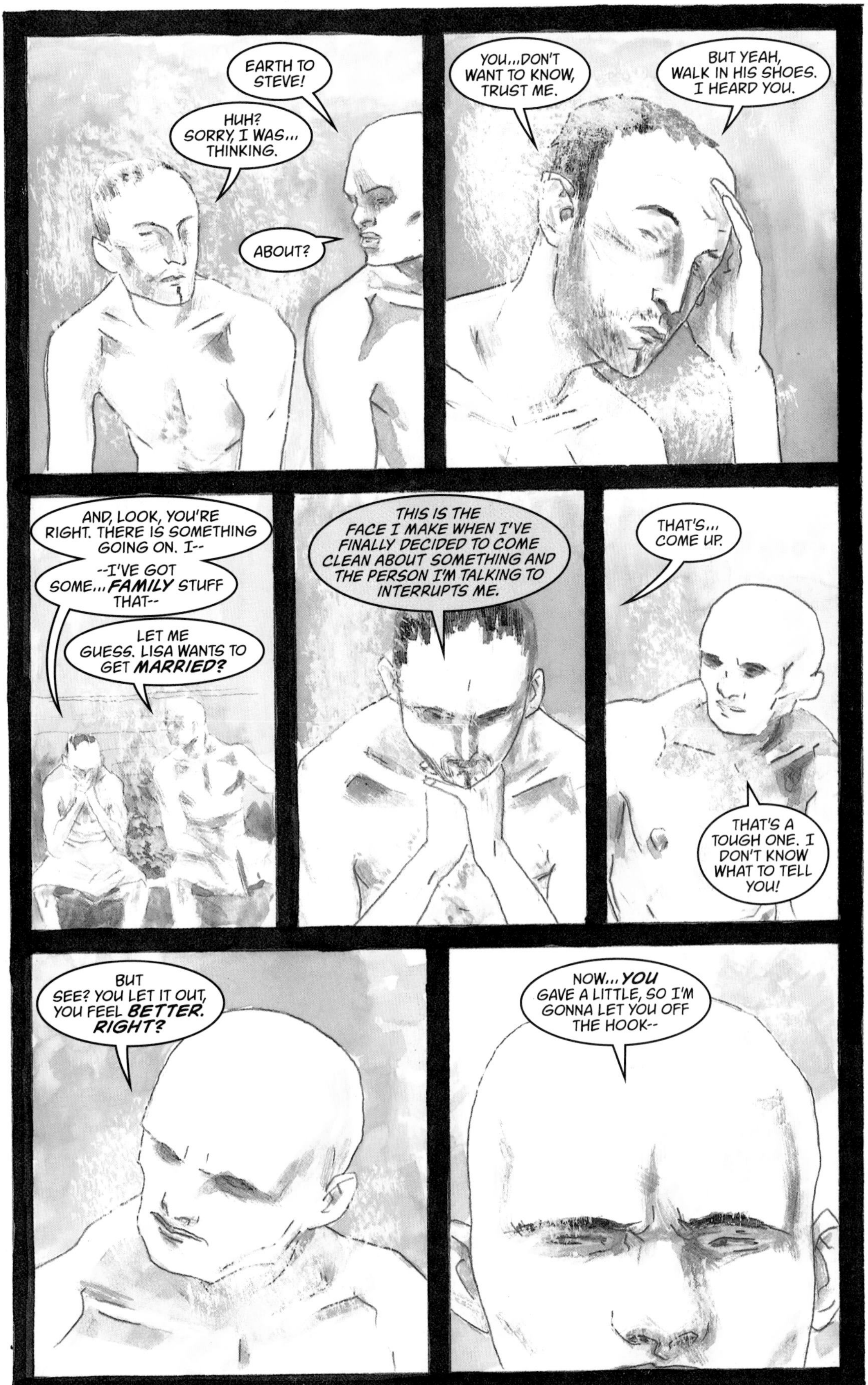
EARTH TO STEVE!
HUH? SORRY, I WAS... THINKING.
ABOUT?
YOU...DON'T WANT TO KNOW, TRUST ME.
BUT YEAH, WALK IN HIS SHOES. I HEARD YOU.
AND, LOOK, YOU'RE RIGHT. THERE IS SOMETHING GOING ON. I--
--I'VE GOT SOME...**FAMILY** STUFF THAT--
LET ME GUESS. LISA WANTS TO GET **MARRIED?**
THIS IS THE FACE I MAKE WHEN I'VE FINALLY DECIDED TO COME CLEAN ABOUT SOMETHING AND THE PERSON I'M TALKING TO INTERRUPTS ME.
THAT'S... COME UP.
THAT'S A TOUGH ONE. I DON'T KNOW WHAT TO TELL YOU!
BUT SEE? YOU LET IT OUT, YOU FEEL **BETTER. RIGHT?**
NOW...**YOU** GAVE A LITTLE, SO I'M GONNA LET YOU OFF THE HOOK--

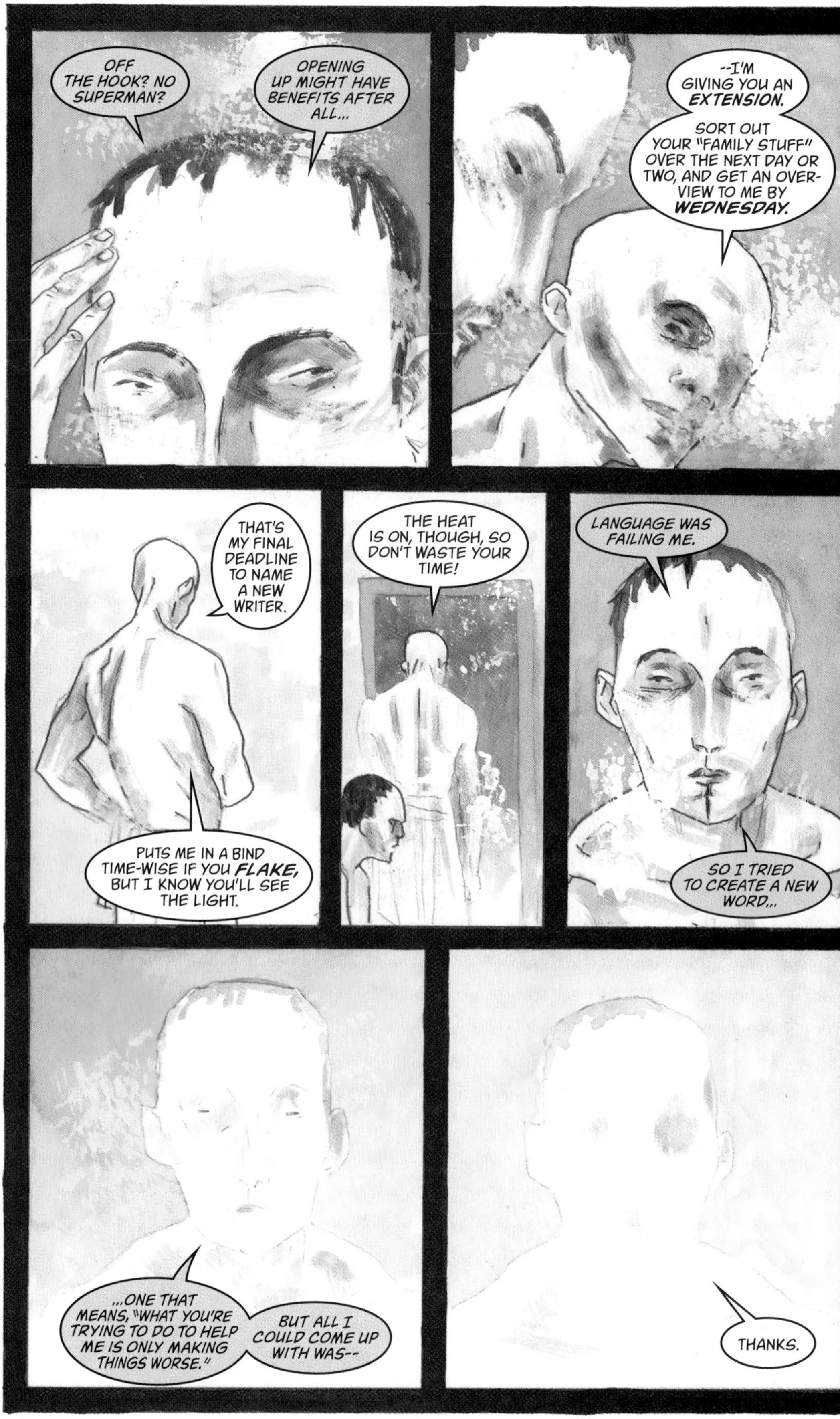
OFF THE HOOK? NO SUPERMAN?
OPENING UP MIGHT HAVE BENEFITS AFTER ALL...
--I'M GIVING YOU AN EXTENSION.
SORT OUT YOUR "FAMILY STUFF" OVER THE NEXT DAY OR TWO, AND GET AN OVER-VIEW TO ME BY WEDNESDAY.
THAT'S MY FINAL DEADLINE TO NAME A NEW WRITER.
PUTS ME IN A BIND TIME-WISE IF YOU FLAKE, BUT I KNOW YOU'LL SEE THE LIGHT.
THE HEAT IS ON, THOUGH, SO DON'T WASTE YOUR TIME!
LANGUAGE WAS FAILING ME.
SO I TRIED TO CREATE A NEW WORD...
...ONE THAT MEANS, "WHAT YOU'RE TRYING TO DO TO HELP ME IS ONLY MAKING THINGS WORSE."
BUT ALL I COULD COME UP WITH WAS--
THANKS.

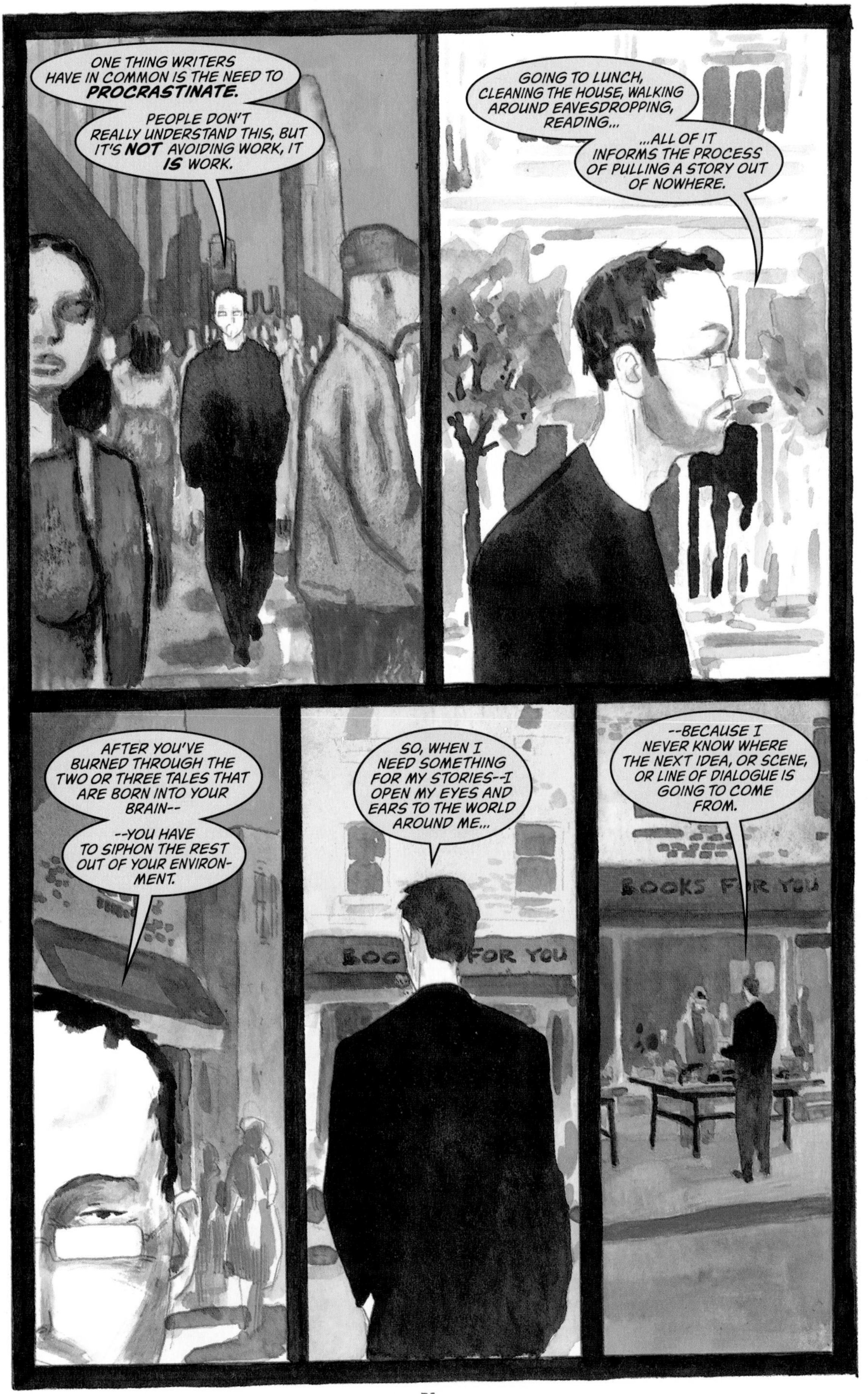
ONE THING WRITERS HAVE IN COMMON IS THE NEED TO **PROCRASTINATE.**
PEOPLE DON'T REALLY UNDERSTAND THIS, BUT IT'S **NOT** AVOIDING WORK, IT **IS** WORK.
GOING TO LUNCH, CLEANING THE HOUSE, WALKING AROUND EAVESDROPPING, READING...
...ALL OF IT INFORMS THE PROCESS OF PULLING A STORY OUT OF NOWHERE.
AFTER YOU'VE BURNED THROUGH THE TWO OR THREE TALES THAT ARE BORN INTO YOUR BRAIN--
--YOU HAVE TO SIPHON THE REST OUT OF YOUR ENVIRON-MENT.
SO, WHEN I NEED SOMETHING FOR MY STORIES--I OPEN MY EYES AND EARS TO THE WORLD AROUND ME...
BOO FOR YOU
--BECAUSE I NEVER KNOW WHERE THE NEXT IDEA, OR SCENE, OR LINE OF DIALOGUE IS GOING TO COME FROM.
BOOKS FOR YOU

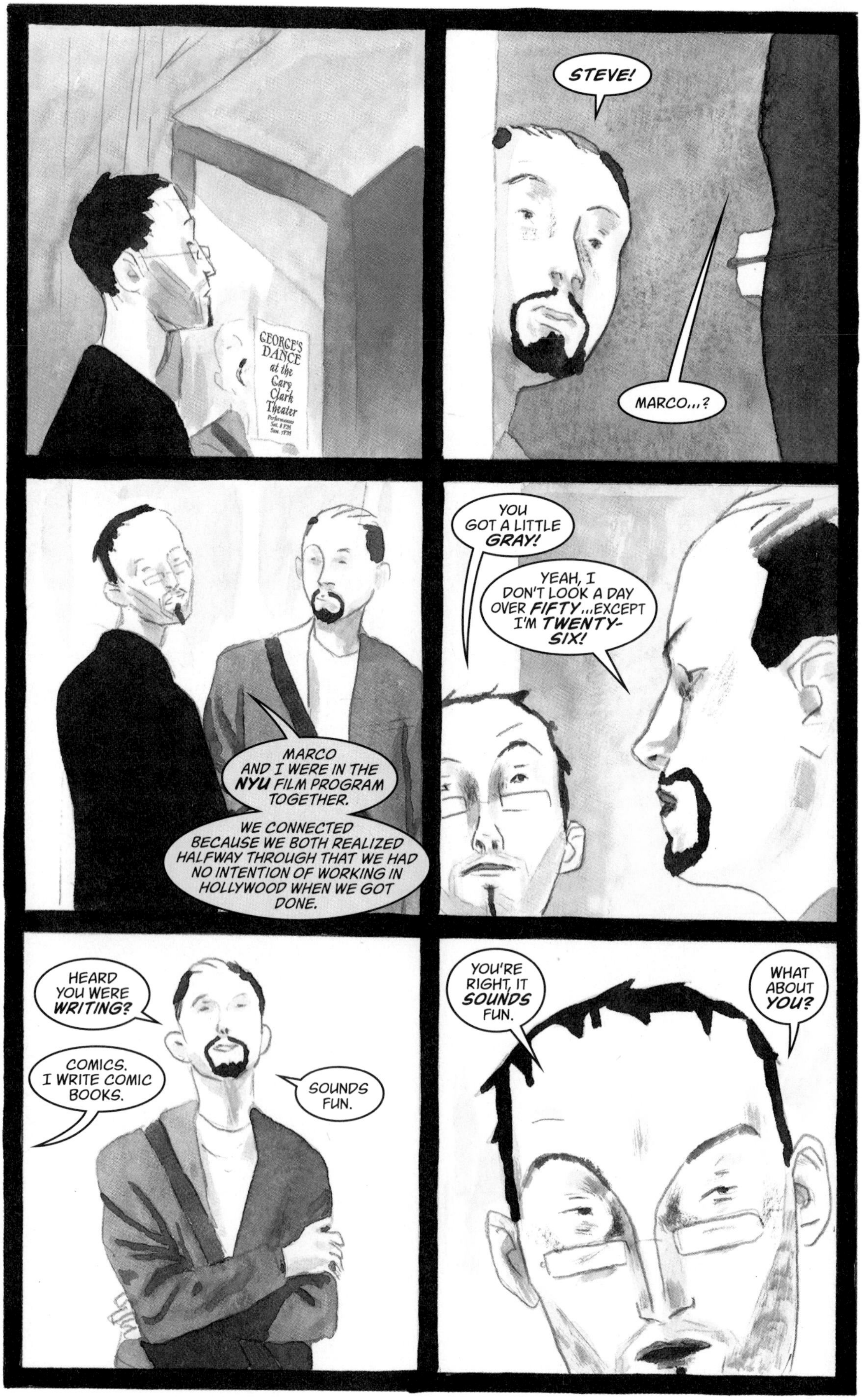
GEORGE'S DANCE at the Gary Clark Theater
STEVE!
MARCO...?
MARCO AND I WERE IN THE NYU FILM PROGRAM TOGETHER.
WE CONNECTED BECAUSE WE BOTH REALIZED HALFWAY THROUGH THAT WE HAD NO INTENTION OF WORKING IN HOLLYWOOD WHEN WE GOT DONE.
YOU GOT A LITTLE GRAY!
YEAH, I DON'T LOOK A DAY OVER FIFTY...EXCEPT I'M TWENTY-SIX!
HEARD YOU WERE WRITING?
COMICS. I WRITE COMIC BOOKS.
SOUNDS FUN.
YOU'RE RIGHT, IT SOUNDS FUN.
WHAT ABOUT YOU?

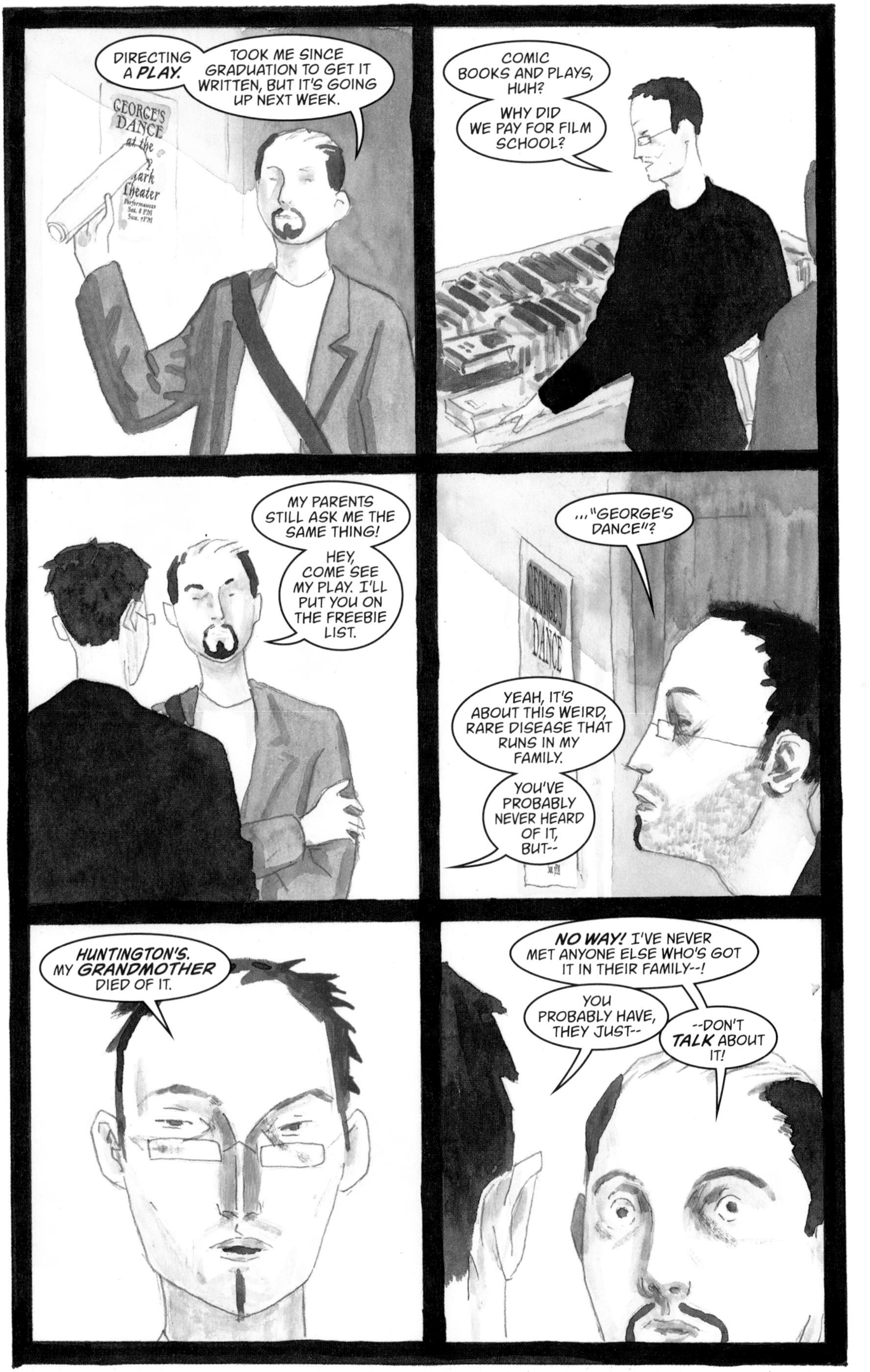

DIRECTING A PLAY.
TOOK ME SINCE GRADUATION TO GET IT WRITTEN, BUT IT'S GOING UP NEXT WEEK.
GEORGE'S DANCE
COMIC BOOKS AND PLAYS, HUH?
WHY DID WE PAY FOR FILM SCHOOL?
MY PARENTS STILL ASK ME THE SAME THING!
HEY, COME SEE MY PLAY. I'LL PUT YOU ON THE FREEBIE LIST.
..."GEORGE'S DANCE"?
GEORGE'S DANCE
YEAH, IT'S ABOUT THIS WEIRD, RARE DISEASE THAT RUNS IN MY FAMILY.
YOU'VE PROBABLY NEVER HEARD OF IT, BUT--
HUNTINGTON'S. MY GRANDMOTHER DIED OF IT.
NO WAY! I'VE NEVER MET ANYONE ELSE WHO'S GOT IT IN THEIR FAMILY--!
YOU PROBABLY HAVE, THEY JUST--
--DON'T TALK ABOUT IT!

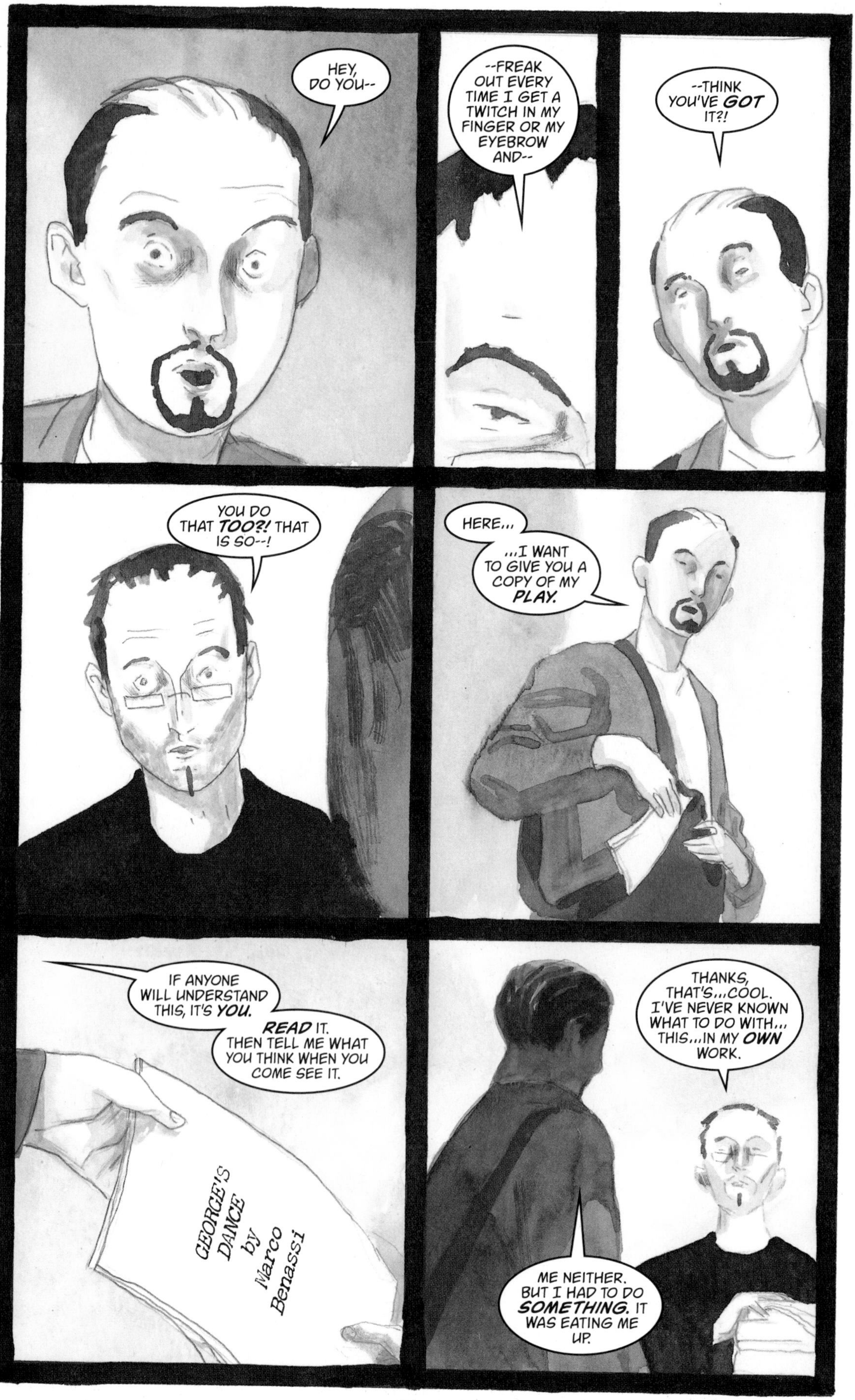
HEY, DO YOU--
--FREAK OUT EVERY TIME I GET A TWITCH IN MY FINGER OR MY EYEBROW AND--
--THINK YOU'VE GOT IT?!
YOU DO THAT TOO?! THAT IS SO--!
HERE...
...I WANT TO GIVE YOU A COPY OF MY PLAY.
IF ANYONE WILL UNDERSTAND THIS, IT'S YOU.
READ IT. THEN TELL ME WHAT YOU THINK WHEN YOU COME SEE IT.
GEORGE'S DANCE by Marco Benassi
THANKS, THAT'S...COOL. I'VE NEVER KNOWN WHAT TO DO WITH... THIS...IN MY OWN WORK.
ME NEITHER. BUT I HAD TO DO SOMETHING. IT WAS EATING ME UP.

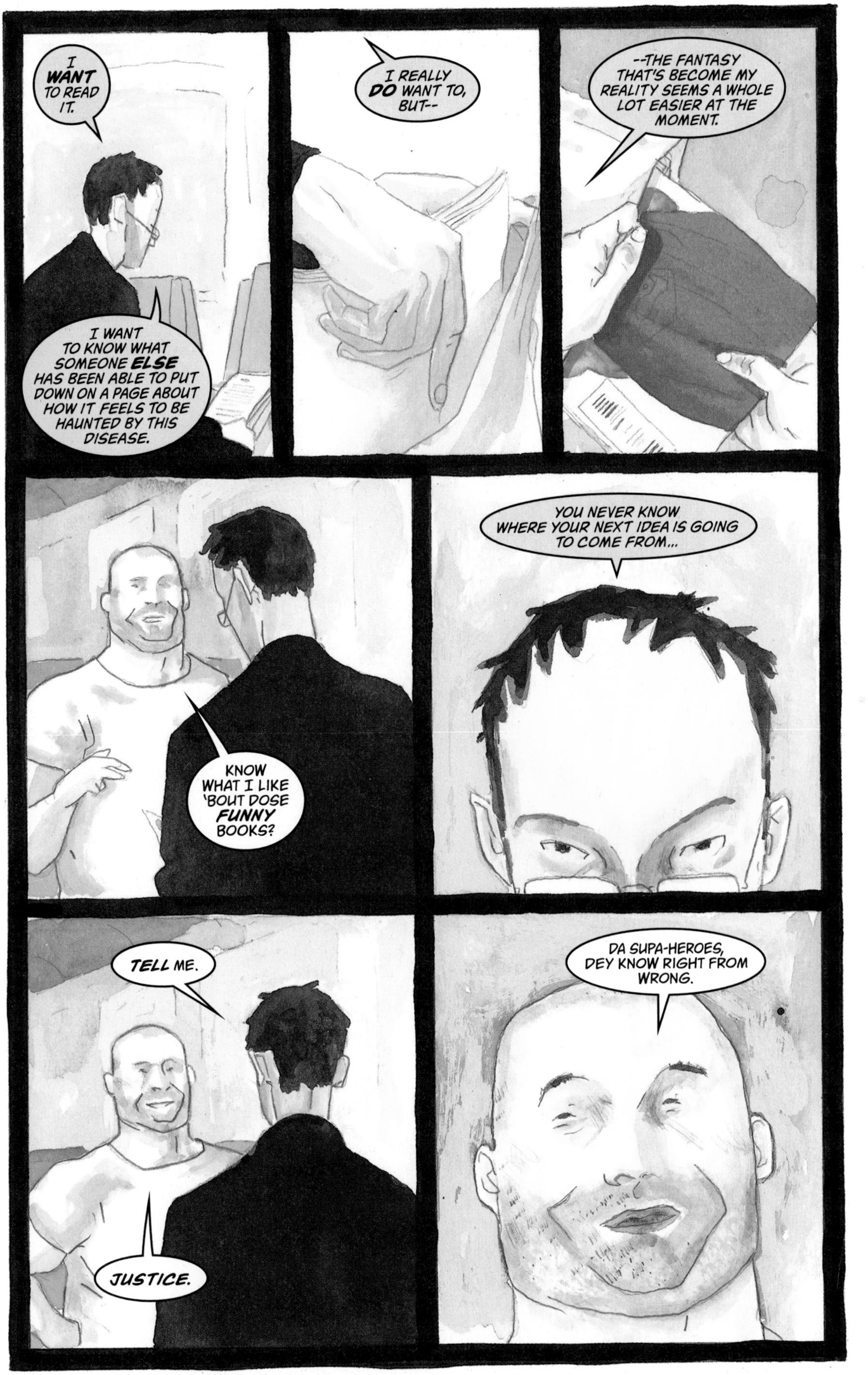
I WANT TO READ IT.
I WANT TO KNOW WHAT SOMEONE ELSE HAS BEEN ABLE TO PUT DOWN ON A PAGE ABOUT HOW IT FEELS TO BE HAUNTED BY THIS DISEASE.
I REALLY DO WANT TO, BUT--
--THE FANTASY THAT'S BECOME MY REALITY SEEMS A WHOLE LOT EASIER AT THE MOMENT.
KNOW WHAT I LIKE 'BOUT DOSE FUNNY BOOKS?
YOU NEVER KNOW WHERE YOUR NEXT IDEA IS GOING TO COME FROM...
TELL ME.
JUSTICE.
DA SUPA-HEROES, DEY KNOW RIGHT FROM WRONG.

JUSTICE

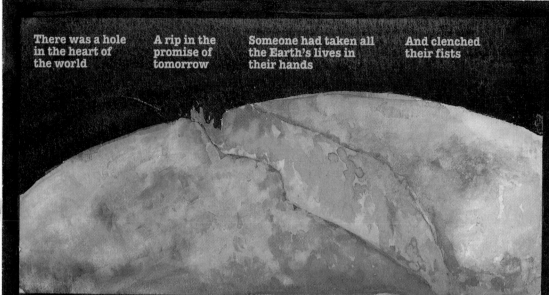

There was a hole in the heart of the world

A rip in the promise of tomorrow

Someone had taken all the Earth's lives in their hands

And clenched their fists

One man

One mad man

One madman

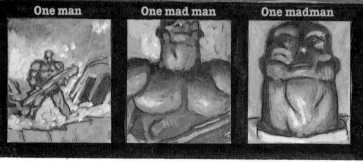

There was a hole in the heart of a hero

A sick certainty this harm could not be put right

Somehow all that was would end, and nothing could alter that

He clenched his fists

This man

This super man

This Superman

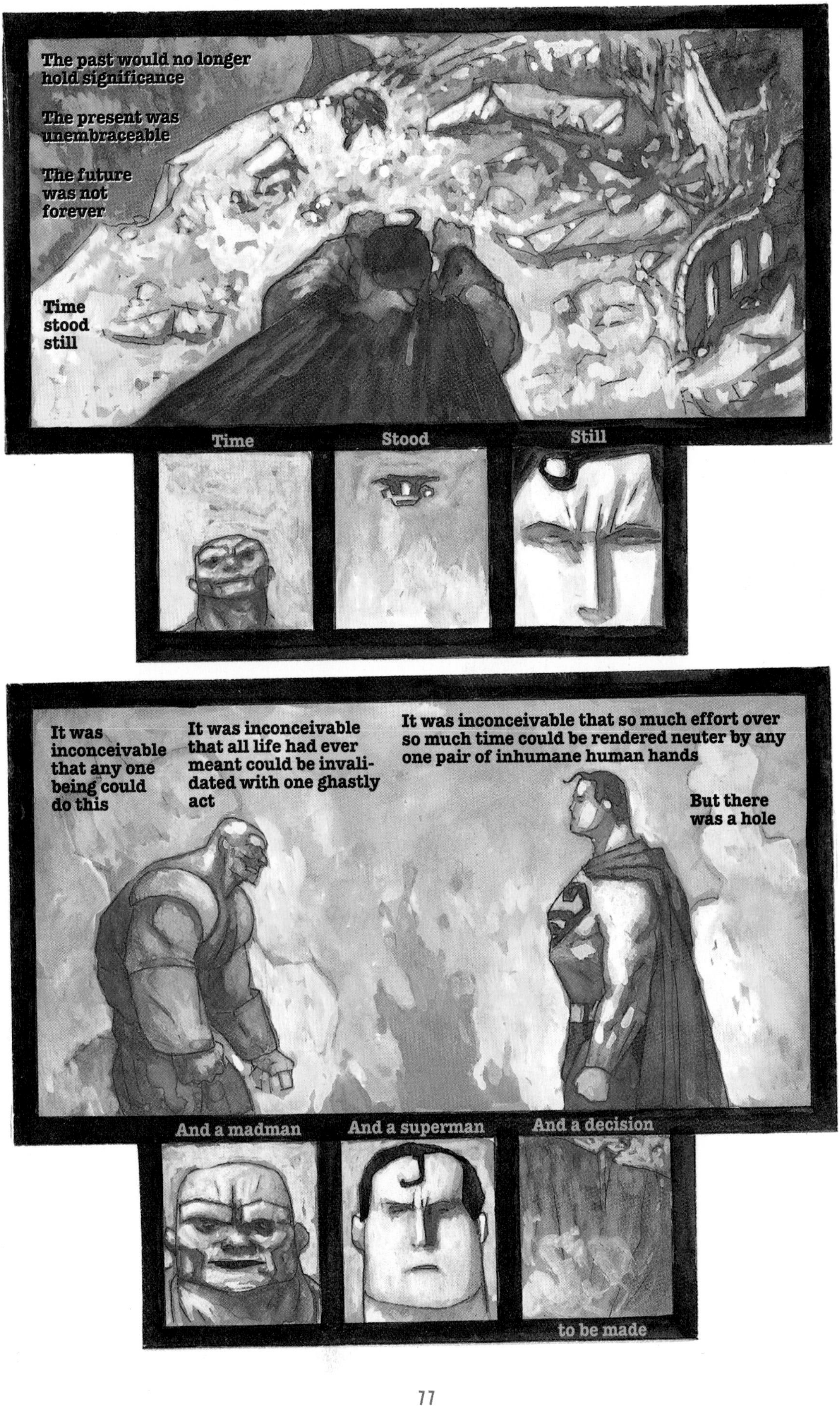

The past would no longer hold significance
The present was unembraceable
The future was not forever
Time stood still
Time
Stood
Still
It was inconceivable that any one being could do this
It was inconceivable that all life had ever meant could be invalidated with one ghastly act
It was inconceivable that so much effort over so much time could be rendered neuter by any one pair of inhumane human hands
But there was a hole
And a madman
And a superman
And a decision
to be made

At the end of the day   At the end of the world   What is justice?

The superman could hurl the madman into the abyss he had opened

Is justice the fierce pain of flesh scalded from bone by sulfuric steam?

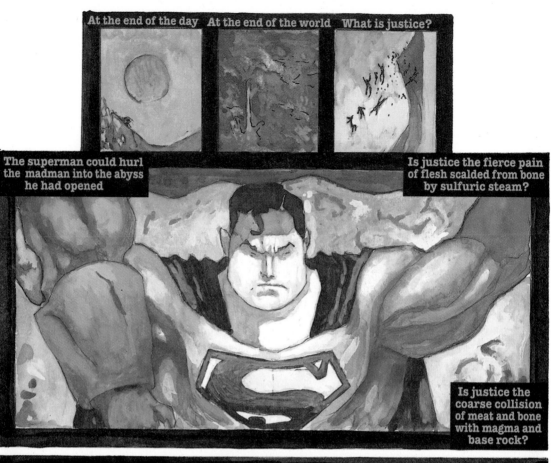

Is justice the coarse collision of meat and bone with magma and base rock?

The superman could force the madman to witness the final days of the planet he had crippled

Is justice the realization that one has brought doom to that which gave him life?

Is justice living out the life sentence he has condemned others to serve?

Or is justice nothing more than an ideal?   Which, after a point, becomes purely

Academic

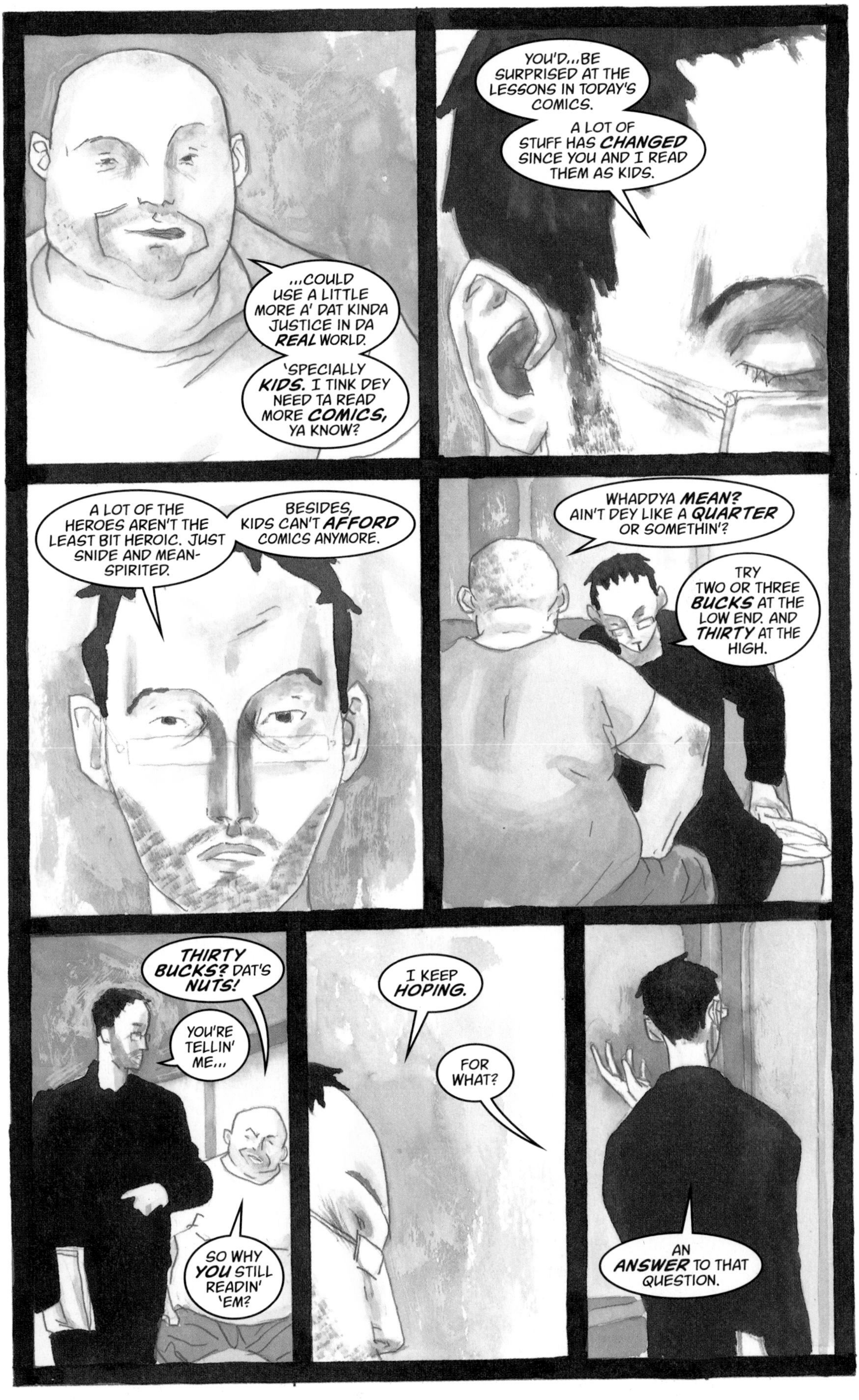
...COULD USE A LITTLE MORE A' DAT KINDA JUSTICE IN DA REAL WORLD.
'SPECIALLY KIDS. I TINK DEY NEED TA READ MORE COMICS, YA KNOW?
YOU'D...BE SURPRISED AT THE LESSONS IN TODAY'S COMICS.
A LOT OF STUFF HAS CHANGED SINCE YOU AND I READ THEM AS KIDS.
A LOT OF THE HEROES AREN'T THE LEAST BIT HEROIC. JUST SNIDE AND MEAN-SPIRITED.
BESIDES, KIDS CAN'T AFFORD COMICS ANYMORE.
WHADDYA MEAN? AIN'T DEY LIKE A QUARTER OR SOMETHIN'?
TRY TWO OR THREE BUCKS AT THE LOW END. AND THIRTY AT THE HIGH.
THIRTY BUCKS? DAT'S NUTS!
YOU'RE TELLIN' ME...
SO WHY YOU STILL READIN' 'EM?
I KEEP HOPING.
FOR WHAT?
AN ANSWER TO THAT QUESTION.

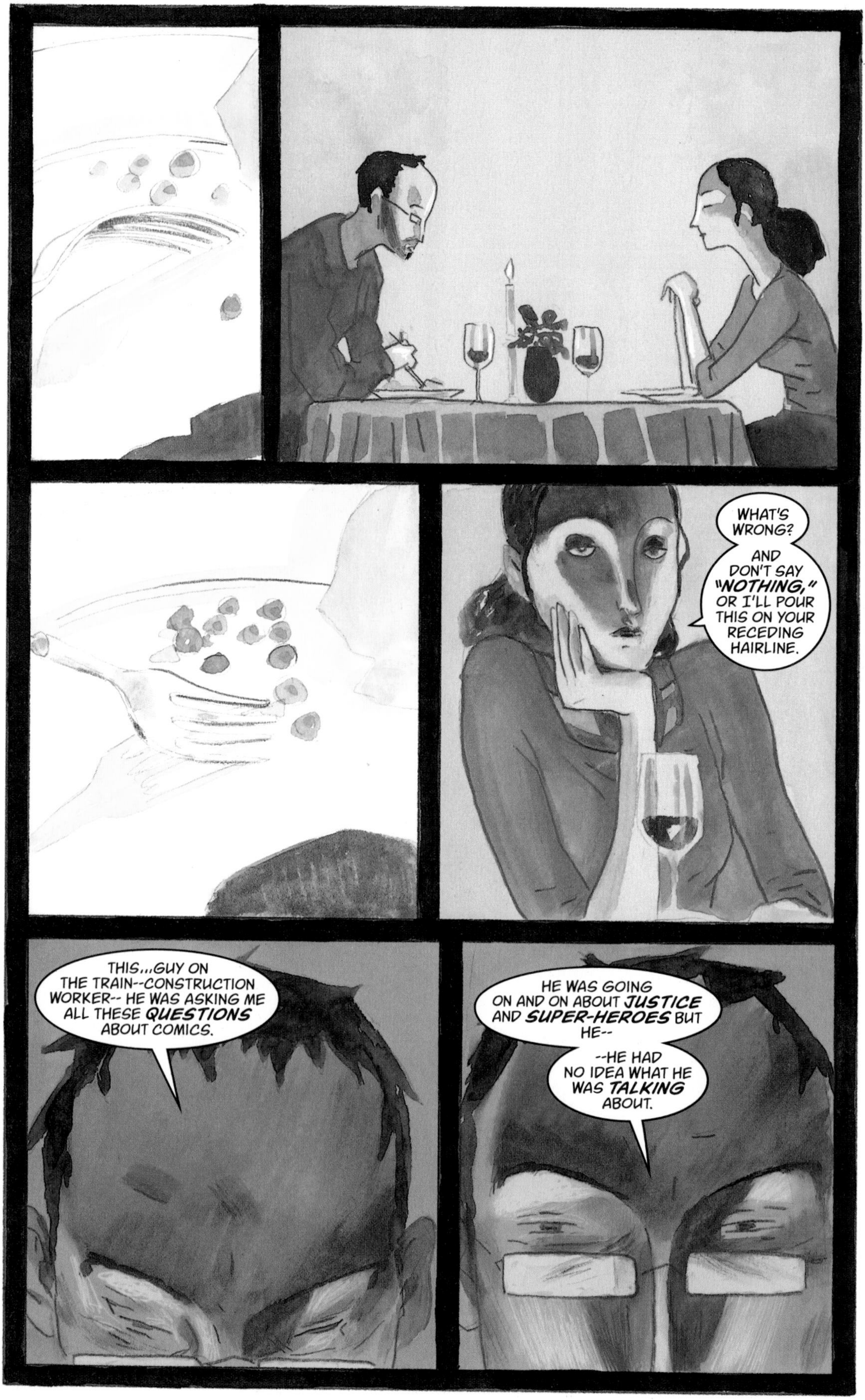
WHAT'S WRONG?
AND DON'T SAY "NOTHING," OR I'LL POUR THIS ON YOUR RECEDING HAIRLINE.
THIS...GUY ON THE TRAIN--CONSTRUCTION WORKER-- HE WAS ASKING ME ALL THESE QUESTIONS ABOUT COMICS.
HE WAS GOING ON AND ON ABOUT JUSTICE AND SUPER-HEROES BUT HE--
--HE HAD NO IDEA WHAT HE WAS TALKING ABOUT.

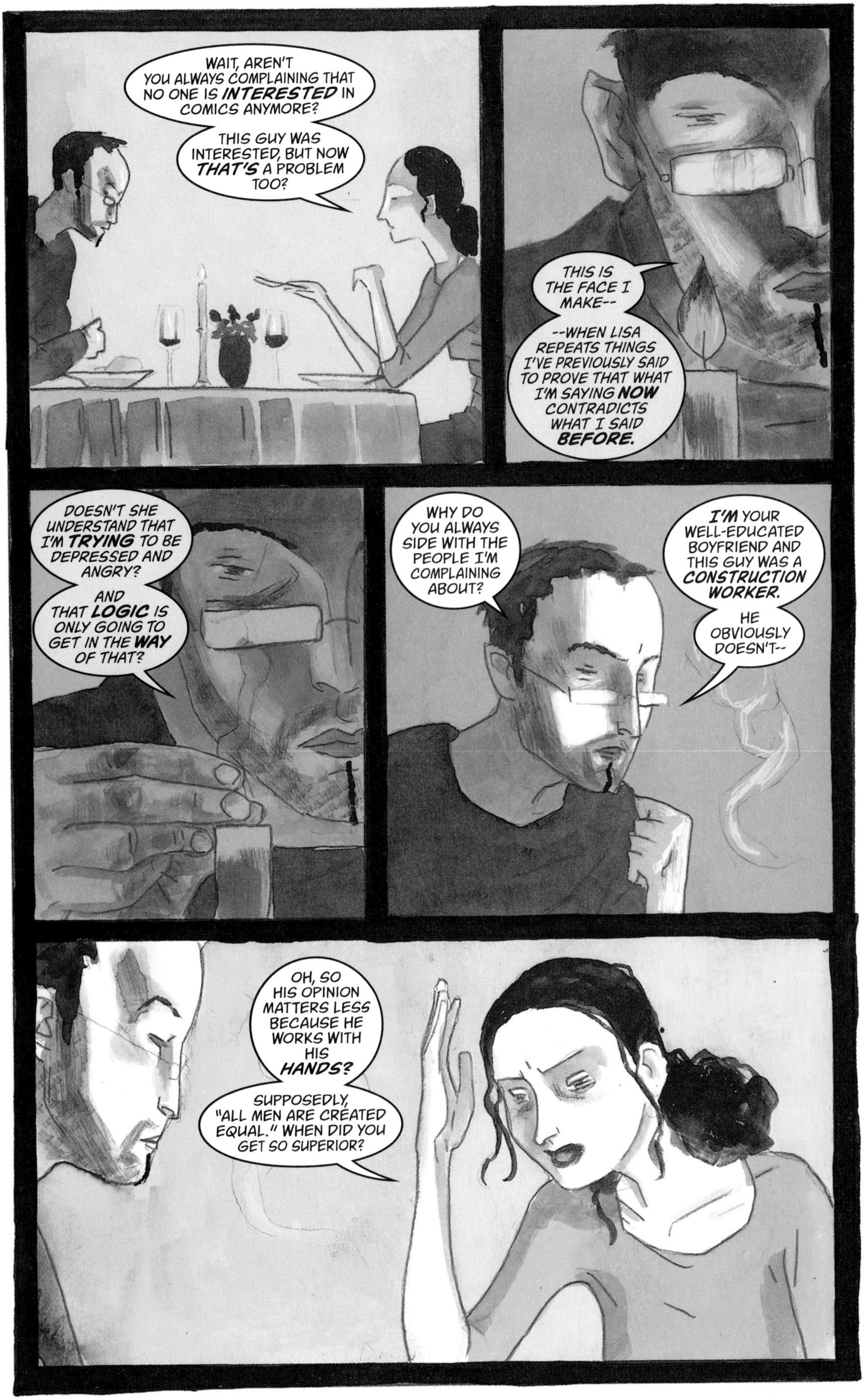
WAIT, AREN'T YOU ALWAYS COMPLAINING THAT NO ONE IS *INTERESTED* IN COMICS ANYMORE?
THIS GUY WAS INTERESTED, BUT NOW *THAT'S* A PROBLEM TOO?
THIS IS THE FACE I MAKE--
--WHEN LISA REPEATS THINGS I'VE PREVIOUSLY SAID TO PROVE THAT WHAT I'M SAYING *NOW* CONTRADICTS WHAT I SAID *BEFORE.*
DOESN'T SHE UNDERSTAND THAT I'M *TRYING* TO BE DEPRESSED AND ANGRY?
AND THAT *LOGIC* IS ONLY GOING TO GET IN THE *WAY* OF THAT?
WHY DO YOU ALWAYS SIDE WITH THE PEOPLE I'M COMPLAINING ABOUT?
I'M YOUR WELL-EDUCATED BOYFRIEND AND THIS GUY WAS A *CONSTRUCTION WORKER.*
HE OBVIOUSLY DOESN'T--
OH, SO HIS OPINION MATTERS LESS BECAUSE HE WORKS WITH HIS *HANDS?*
SUPPOSEDLY, "ALL MEN ARE CREATED EQUAL." WHEN DID YOU GET SO SUPERIOR?

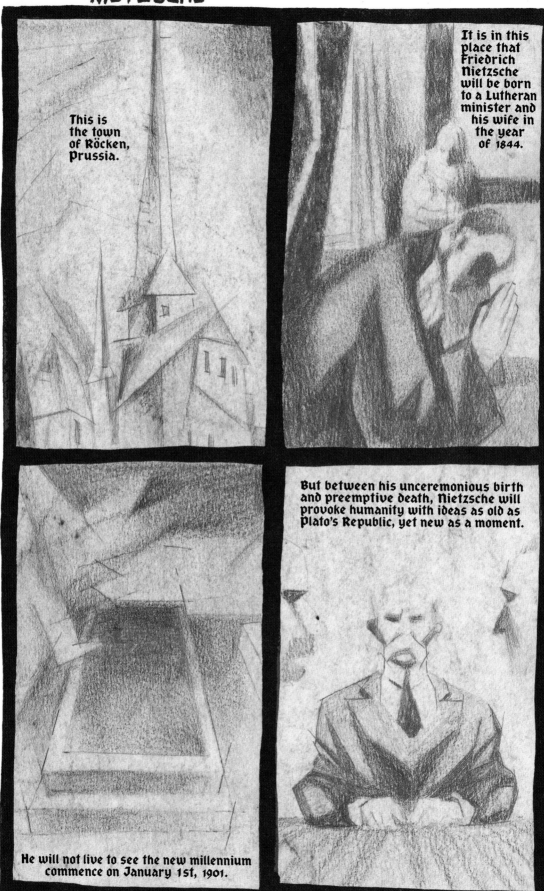

This is the town of Röcken, Prussia.

It is in this place that Friedrich Nietzsche will be born to a Lutheran minister and his wife in the year of 1844.

But between his unceremonious birth and preemptive death, Nietzsche will provoke humanity with ideas as old as Plato's Republic, yet new as a moment.

He will not live to see the new millennium commence on January 1st, 1901.

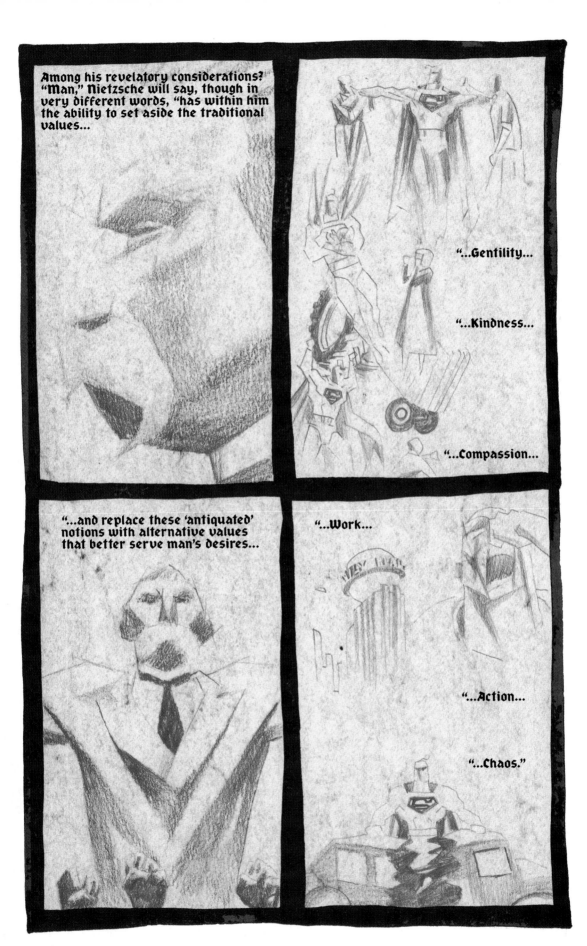

Among his revelatory considerations? "Man," Nietzsche will say, though in very different words, "has within him the ability to set aside the traditional values...

"...Gentility...

"...Kindness...

"...Compassion...

"...and replace these 'antiquated' notions with alternative values that better serve man's desires...

"...Work...

"...Action...

"...Chaos."

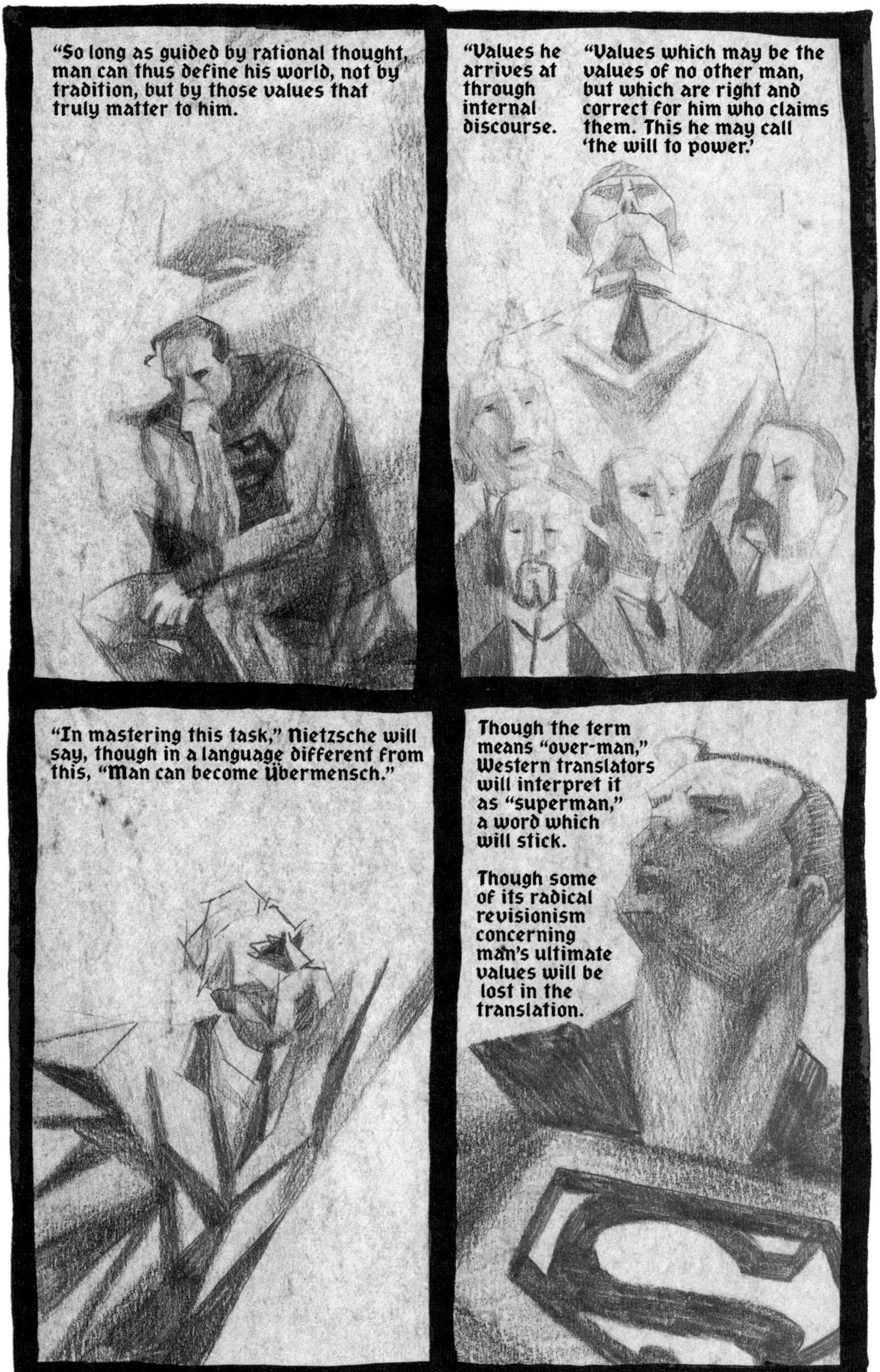
"So long as guided by rational thought, man can thus define his world, not by tradition, but by those values that truly matter to him.
"Values he arrives at through internal discourse.
"Values which may be the values of no other man, but which are right and correct for him who claims them. This he may call 'the will to power.'
"In mastering this task," Nietzsche will say, though in a language different from this, "Man can become Übermensch."
Though the term means "over-man," Western translators will interpret it as "superman," a word which will stick.
Though some of its radical revisionism concerning man's ultimate values will be lost in the translation.

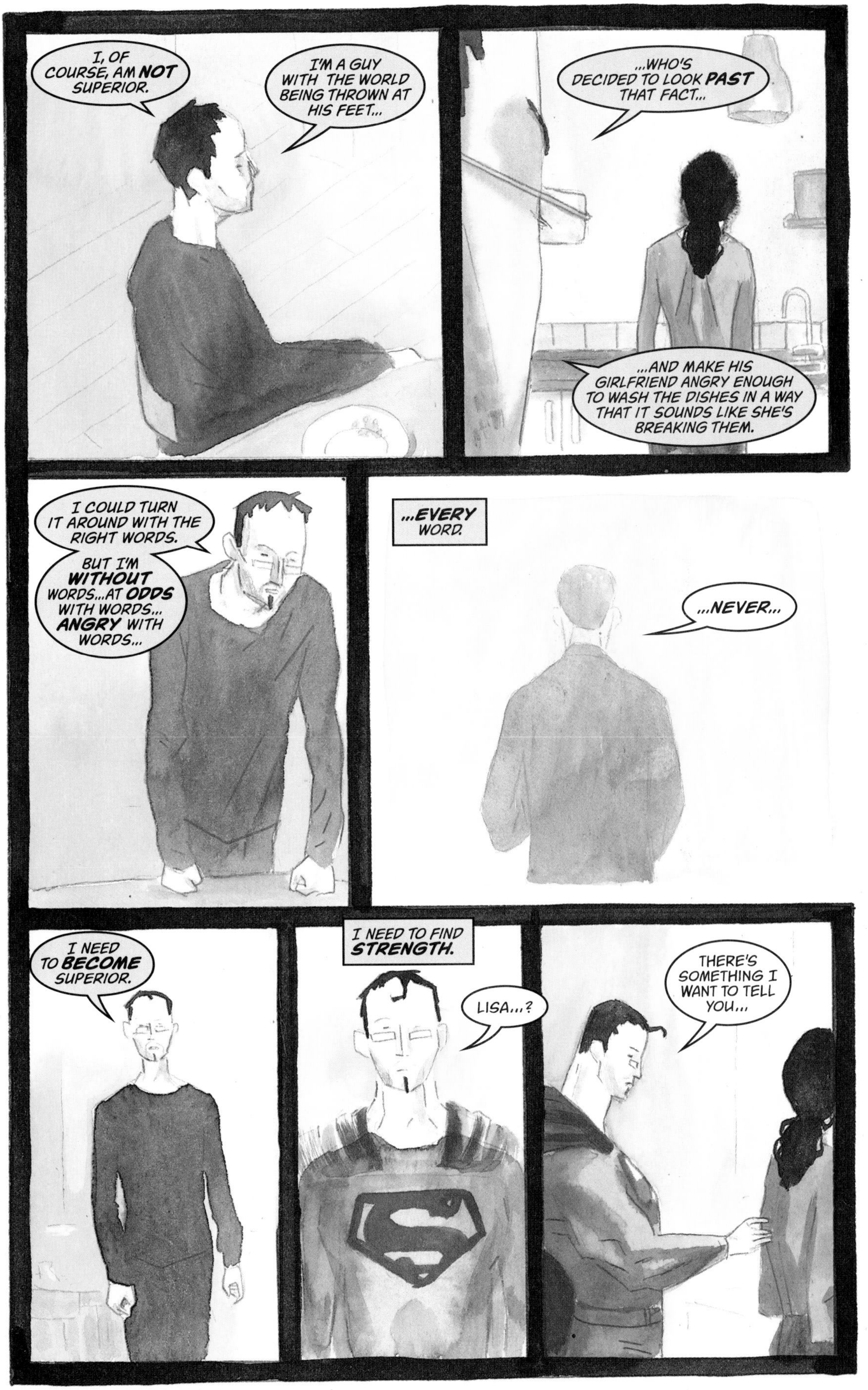
I, OF COURSE, AM NOT SUPERIOR.
I'M A GUY WITH THE WORLD BEING THROWN AT HIS FEET...
...WHO'S DECIDED TO LOOK PAST THAT FACT...
...AND MAKE HIS GIRLFRIEND ANGRY ENOUGH TO WASH THE DISHES IN A WAY THAT IT SOUNDS LIKE SHE'S BREAKING THEM.
I COULD TURN IT AROUND WITH THE RIGHT WORDS.
BUT I'M WITHOUT WORDS...AT ODDS WITH WORDS... ANGRY WITH WORDS...
...EVERY WORD.
...NEVER...
I NEED TO BECOME SUPERIOR.
I NEED TO FIND STRENGTH.
LISA...?
THERE'S SOMETHING I WANT TO TELL YOU...

COURAGE

What is it with you, Nelson Corby?

Twilight was supposed to find you dining at "Nemo's" with your assistant, Nora.

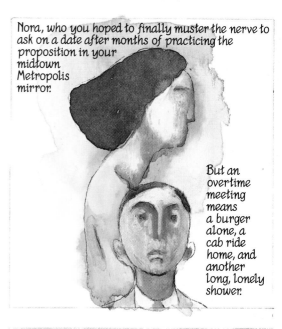

Nora, who you hoped to finally muster the nerve to ask on a date after months of practicing the proposition in your midtown Metropolis mirror.

But an overtime meeting means a burger alone, a cab ride home, and another long, lonely shower.

It also means the chance for you to make a difference in someone's life.

And all it requires... is courage.

If the girl is to live, someone has to challenge the rushing bus.

Someone must be willing to risk his own life to earn a chance at saving hers.

Who will that someone be?

Not you, Nelson. You've long suspected, but learned today-- conclusively--

--that most hearts hold so much courage... but only so much, and then no more.

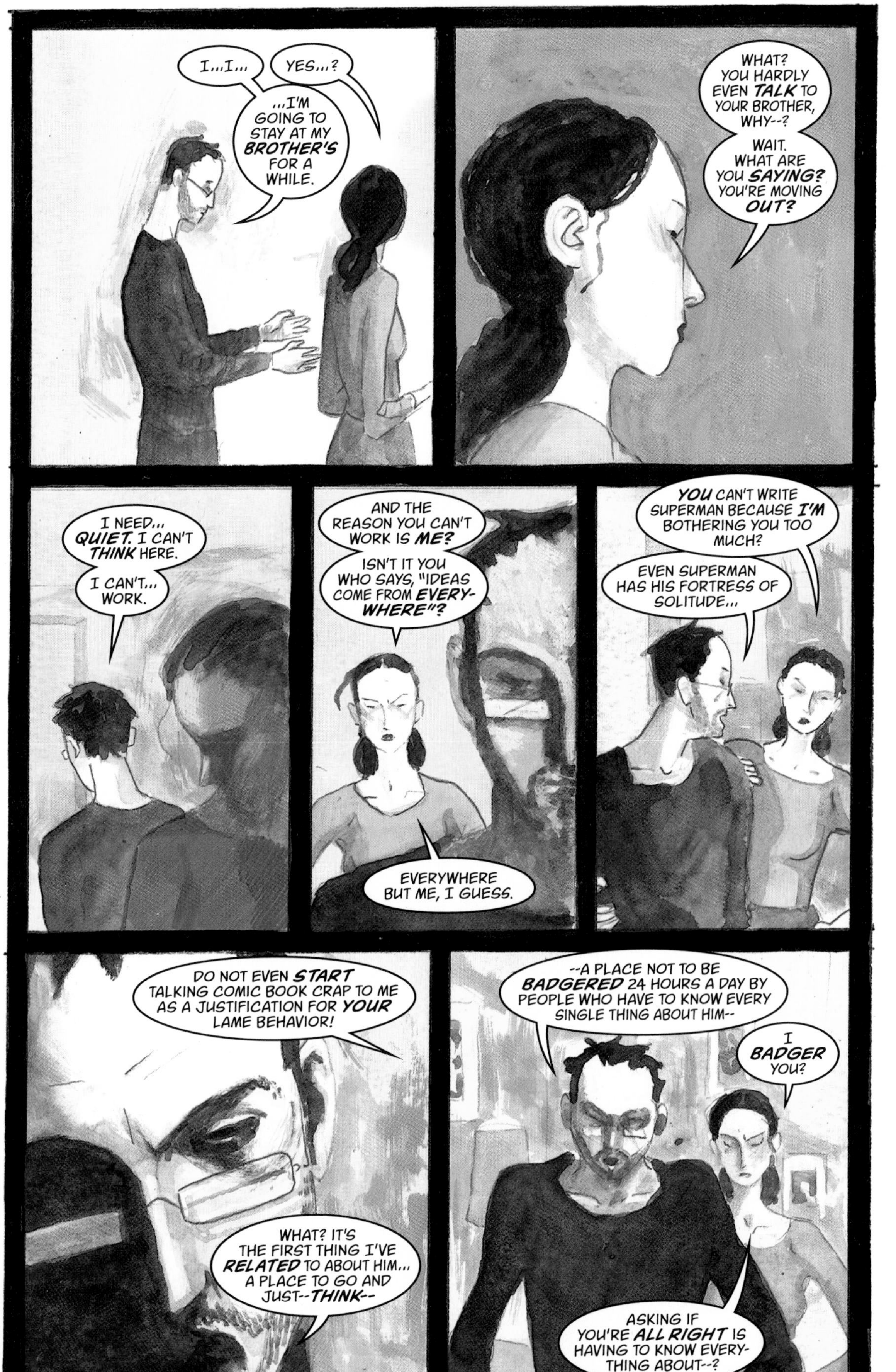
I...I...
YES...?
...I'M GOING TO STAY AT MY BROTHER'S FOR A WHILE.
WHAT? YOU HARDLY EVEN TALK TO YOUR BROTHER, WHY--?
WAIT. WHAT ARE YOU SAYING? YOU'RE MOVING OUT?
I NEED... QUIET. I CAN'T THINK HERE.
I CAN'T... WORK.
AND THE REASON YOU CAN'T WORK IS ME?
ISN'T IT YOU WHO SAYS, "IDEAS COME FROM EVERY-WHERE"?
EVERYWHERE BUT ME, I GUESS.
YOU CAN'T WRITE SUPERMAN BECAUSE I'M BOTHERING YOU TOO MUCH?
EVEN SUPERMAN HAS HIS FORTRESS OF SOLITUDE...
DO NOT EVEN START TALKING COMIC BOOK CRAP TO ME AS A JUSTIFICATION FOR YOUR LAME BEHAVIOR!
WHAT? IT'S THE FIRST THING I'VE RELATED TO ABOUT HIM... A PLACE TO GO AND JUST--THINK--
--A PLACE NOT TO BE BADGERED 24 HOURS A DAY BY PEOPLE WHO HAVE TO KNOW EVERY SINGLE THING ABOUT HIM--
I BADGER YOU?
ASKING IF YOU'RE ALL RIGHT IS HAVING TO KNOW EVERY-THING ABOUT--?

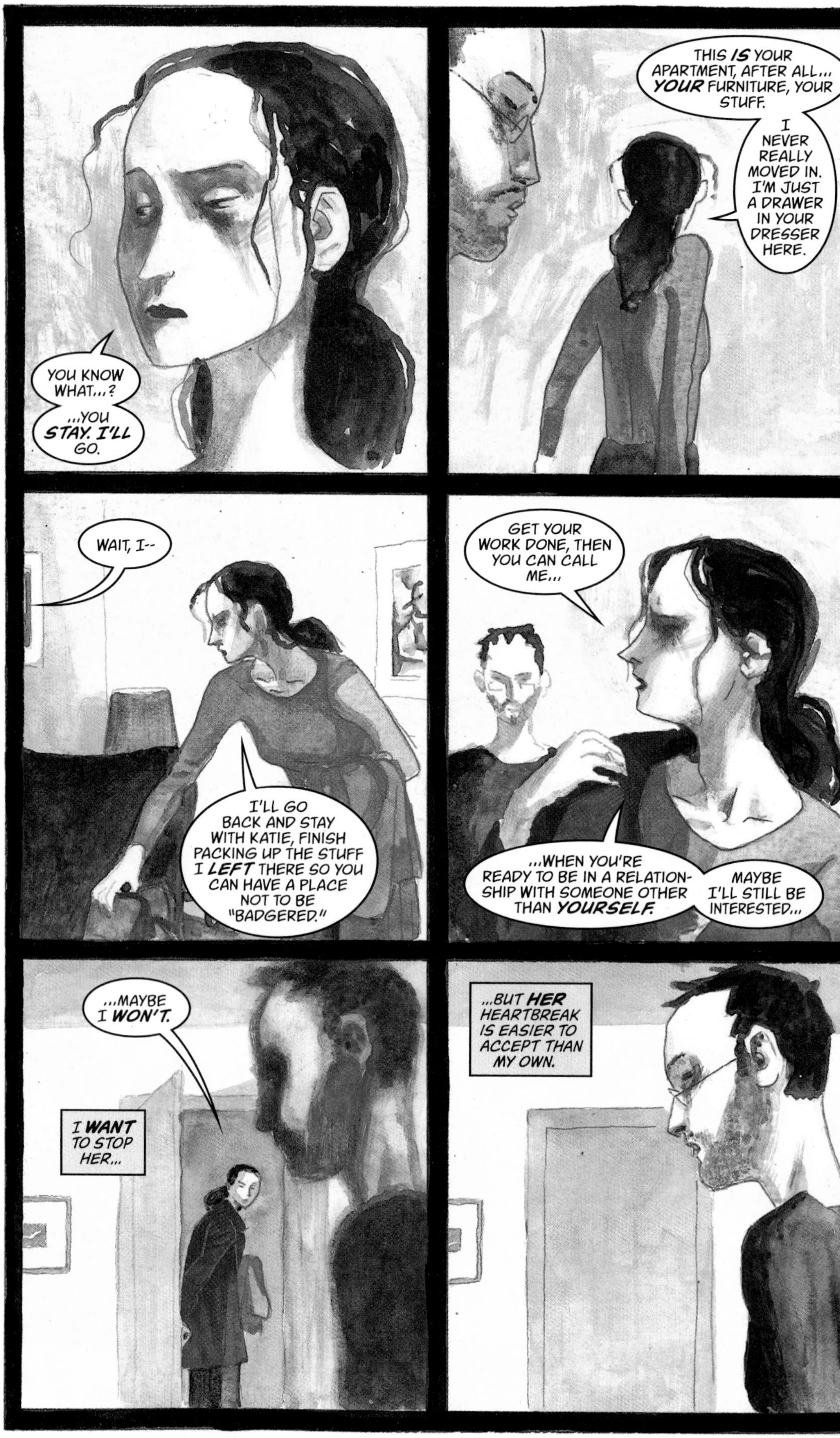
YOU KNOW WHAT...?
...YOU STAY. I'LL GO.
THIS IS YOUR APARTMENT, AFTER ALL... YOUR FURNITURE, YOUR STUFF.
I NEVER REALLY MOVED IN. I'M JUST A DRAWER IN YOUR DRESSER HERE.
WAIT, I--
I'LL GO BACK AND STAY WITH KATIE, FINISH PACKING UP THE STUFF I LEFT THERE SO YOU CAN HAVE A PLACE NOT TO BE "BADGERED."
GET YOUR WORK DONE, THEN YOU CAN CALL ME...
...WHEN YOU'RE READY TO BE IN A RELATIONSHIP WITH SOMEONE OTHER THAN YOURSELF.
MAYBE I'LL STILL BE INTERESTED...
...MAYBE I WON'T.
I WANT TO STOP HER...
...BUT HER HEARTBREAK IS EASIER TO ACCEPT THAN MY OWN.

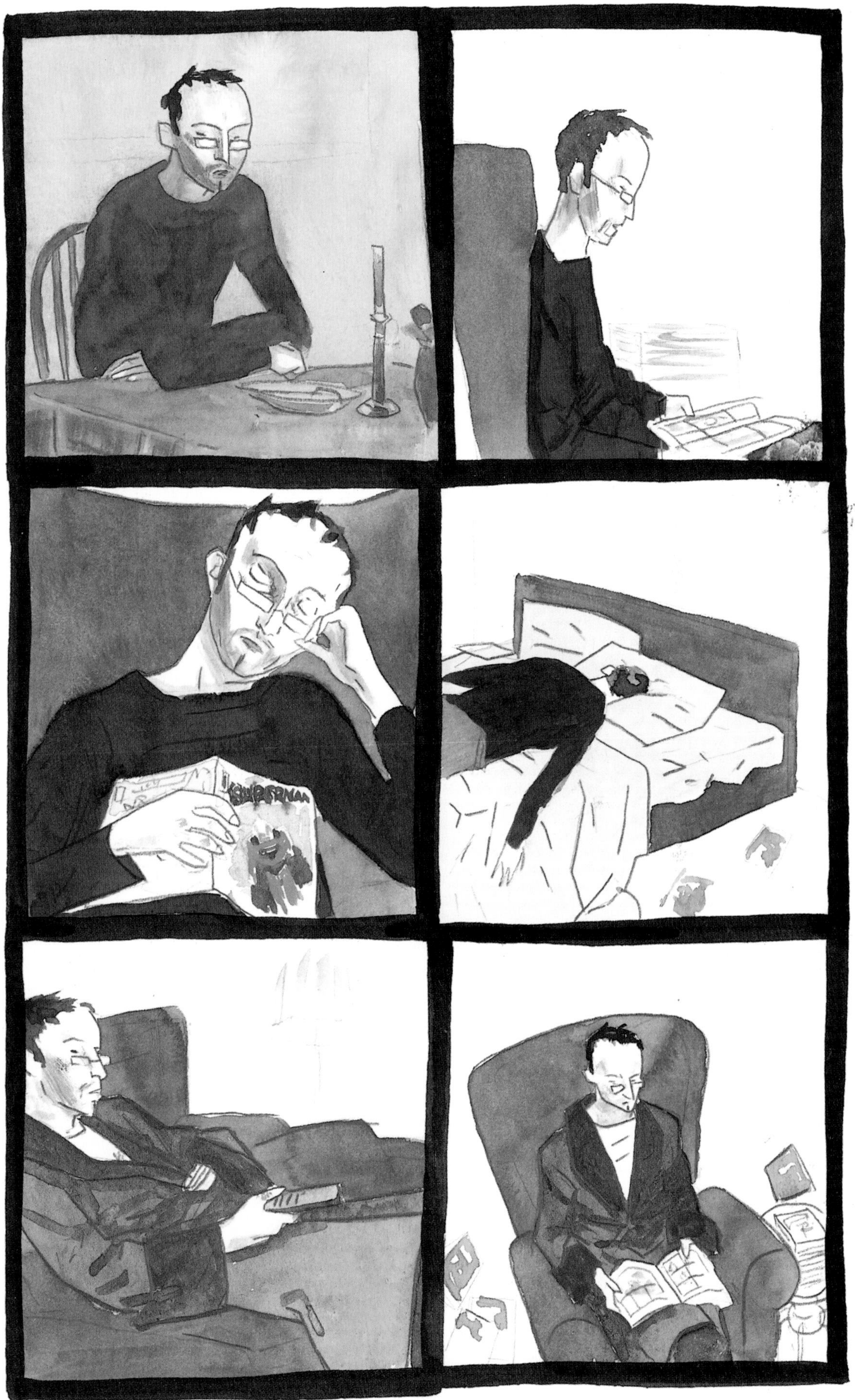
SUPERMAN

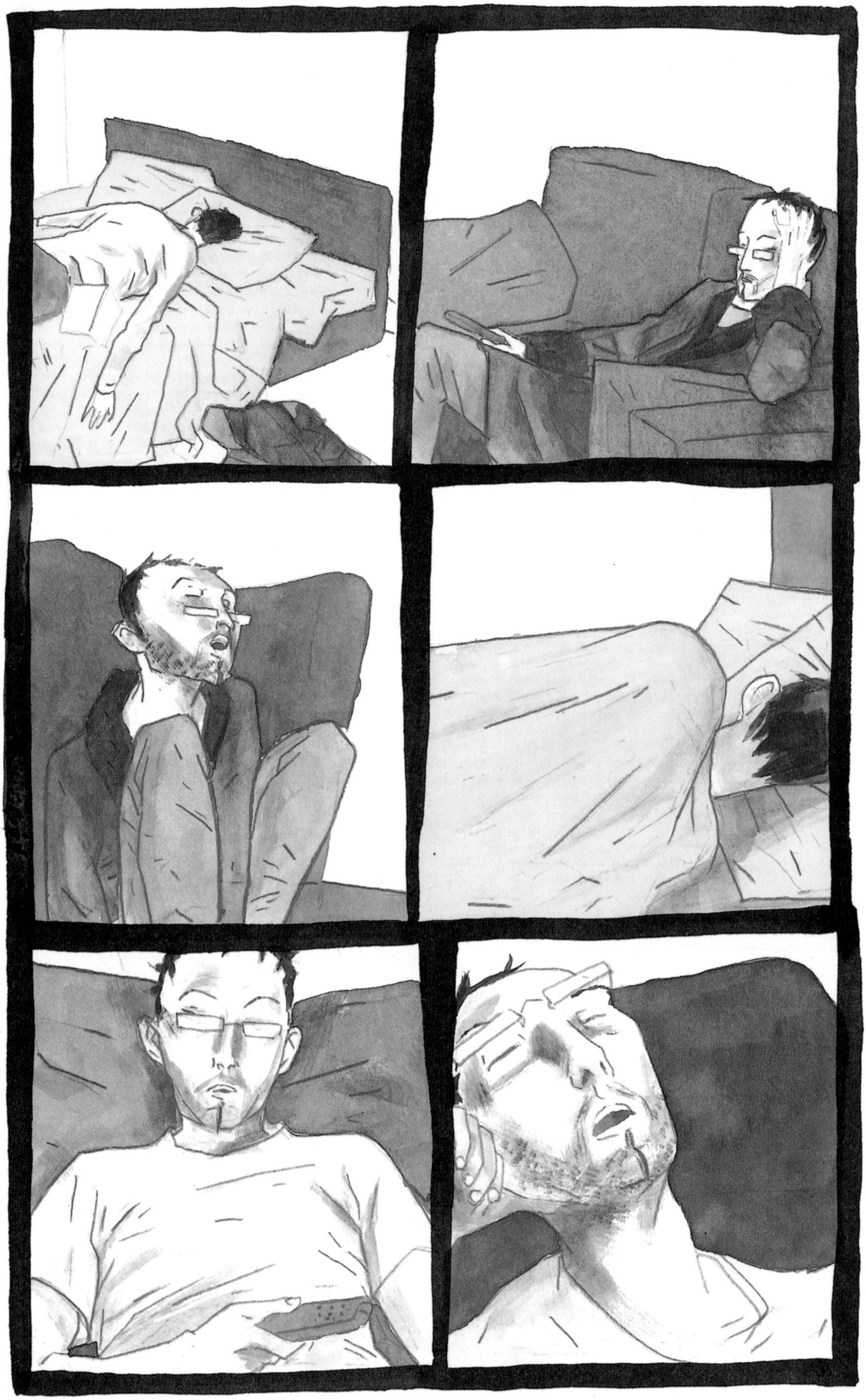

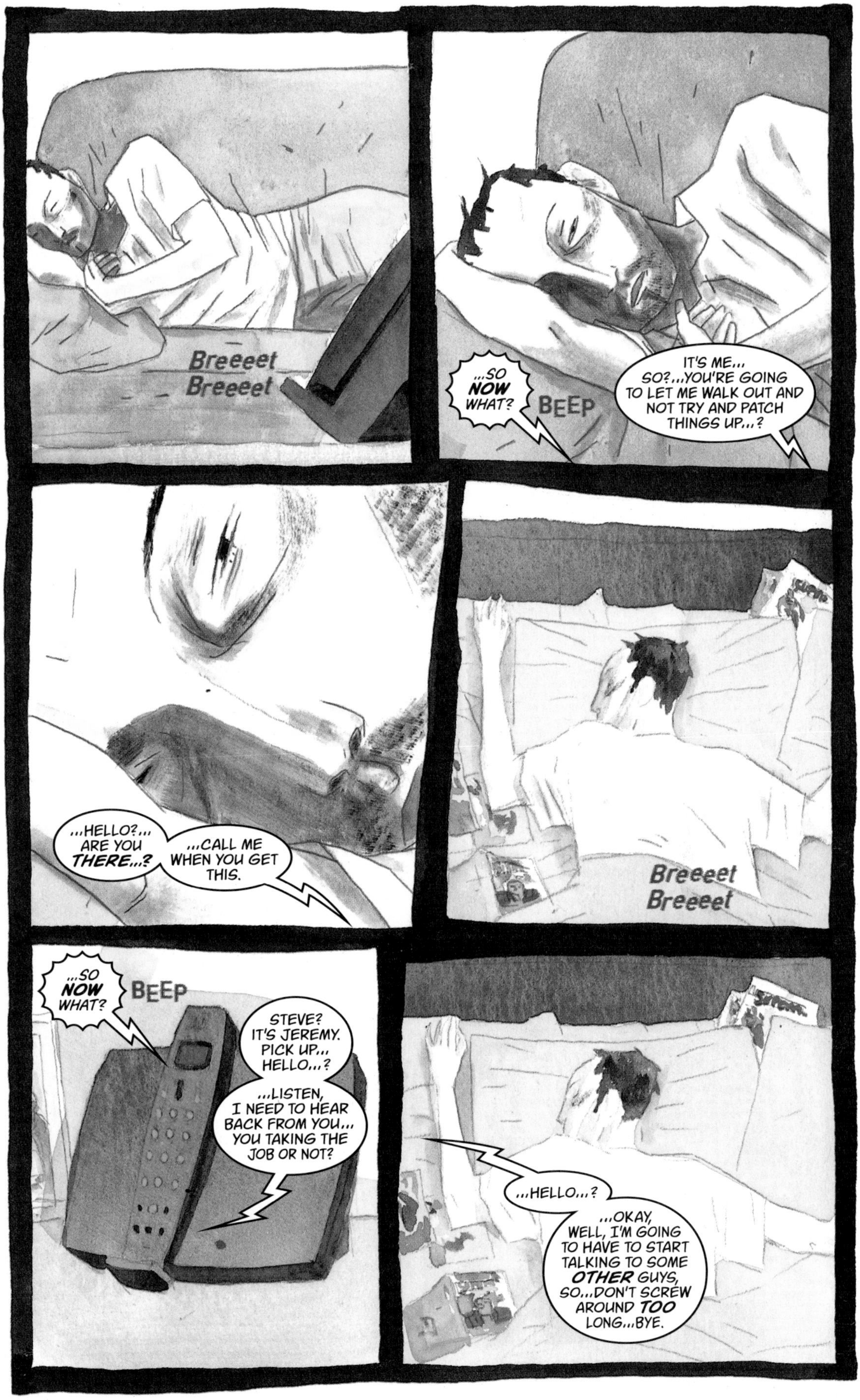

Breeeet
Breeeet
...SO NOW WHAT?
BEEP
IT'S ME... SO?...YOU'RE GOING TO LET ME WALK OUT AND NOT TRY AND PATCH THINGS UP...?
...HELLO?... ARE YOU THERE...?
...CALL ME WHEN YOU GET THIS.
Breeeet
Breeeet
...SO NOW WHAT?
BEEP
STEVE? IT'S JEREMY. PICK UP... HELLO...?
...LISTEN, I NEED TO HEAR BACK FROM YOU... YOU TAKING THE JOB OR NOT?
...HELLO...?
...OKAY, WELL, I'M GOING TO HAVE TO START TALKING TO SOME OTHER GUYS, SO...DON'T SCREW AROUND TOO LONG...BYE.

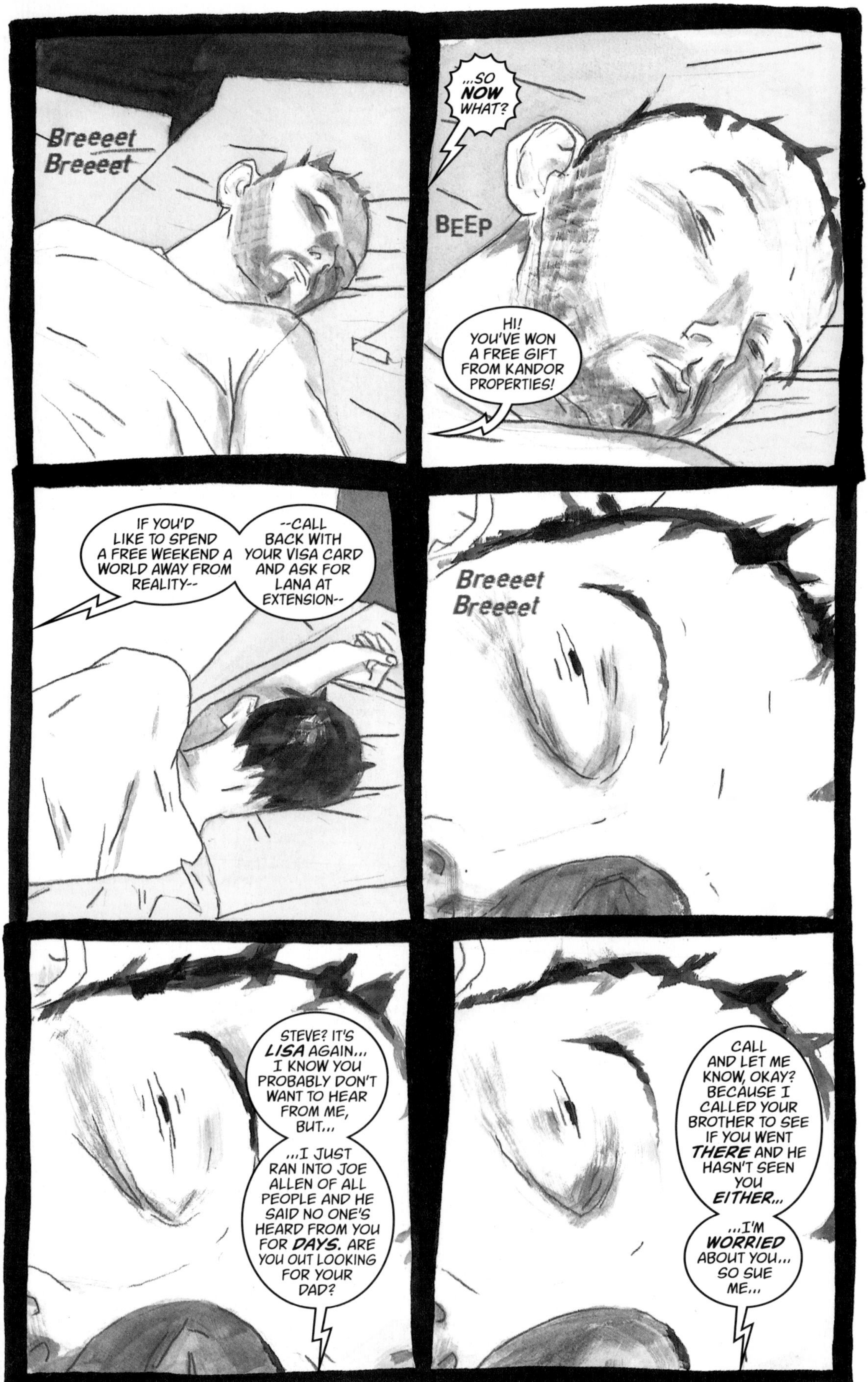

Breeeet
Breeeet
...SO NOW WHAT?
BEEP
HI! YOU'VE WON A FREE GIFT FROM KANDOR PROPERTIES!
IF YOU'D LIKE TO SPEND A FREE WEEKEND A WORLD AWAY FROM REALITY--
--CALL BACK WITH YOUR VISA CARD AND ASK FOR LANA AT EXTENSION--
Breeeet
Breeeet
STEVE? IT'S LISA AGAIN... I KNOW YOU PROBABLY DON'T WANT TO HEAR FROM ME, BUT...
...I JUST RAN INTO JOE ALLEN OF ALL PEOPLE AND HE SAID NO ONE'S HEARD FROM YOU FOR DAYS. ARE YOU OUT LOOKING FOR YOUR DAD?
CALL AND LET ME KNOW, OKAY? BECAUSE I CALLED YOUR BROTHER TO SEE IF YOU WENT THERE AND HE HASN'T SEEN YOU EITHER...
...I'M WORRIED ABOUT YOU... SO SUE ME...

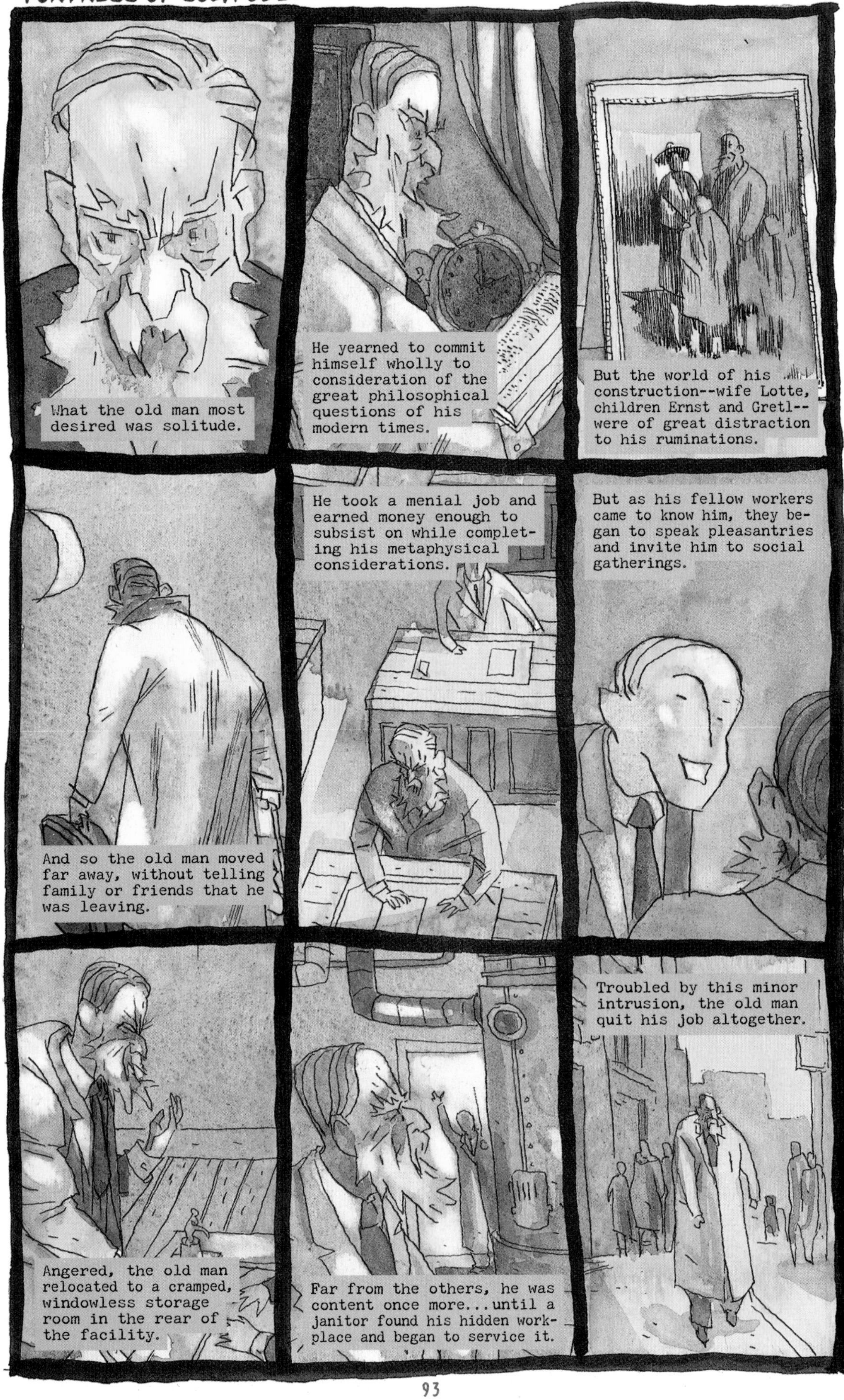
What the old man most desired was solitude.
He yearned to commit himself wholly to consideration of the great philosophical questions of his modern times.
But the world of his construction--wife Lotte, children Ernst and Gretl--were of great distraction to his ruminations.
And so the old man moved far away, without telling family or friends that he was leaving.
He took a menial job and earned money enough to subsist on while complet-ing his metaphysical considerations.
But as his fellow workers came to know him, they be-gan to speak pleasantries and invite him to social gatherings.
Angered, the old man relocated to a cramped, windowless storage room in the rear of the facility.
Far from the others, he was content once more...until a janitor found his hidden work-place and began to service it.
Troubled by this minor intrusion, the old man quit his job altogether.

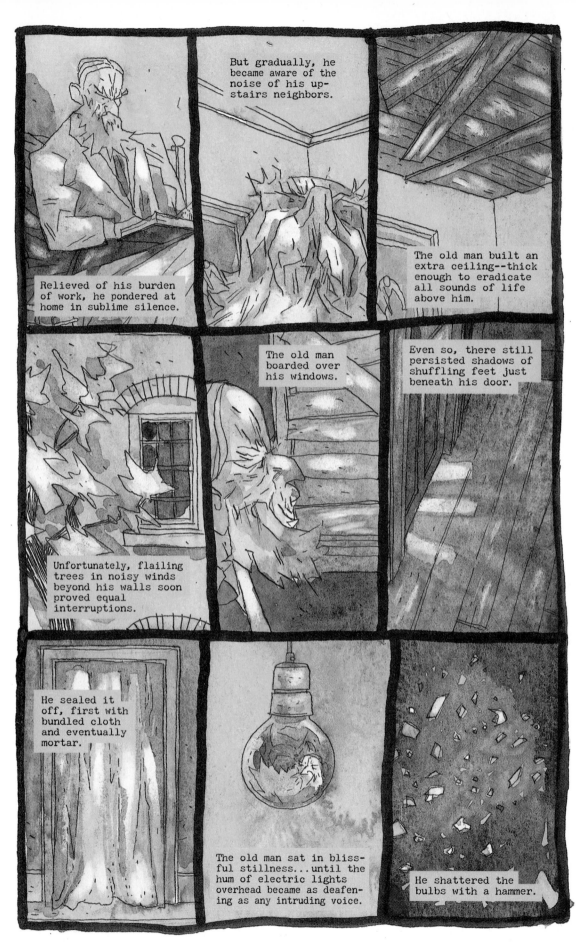

Relieved of his burden of work, he pondered at home in sublime silence.

But gradually, he became aware of the noise of his upstairs neighbors.

The old man built an extra ceiling--thick enough to eradicate all sounds of life above him.

Unfortunately, flailing trees in noisy winds beyond his walls soon proved equal interruptions.

The old man boarded over his windows.

Even so, there still persisted shadows of shuffling feet just beneath his door.

He sealed it off, first with bundled cloth and eventually mortar.

The old man sat in blissful stillness...until the hum of electric lights overhead became as deafening as any intruding voice.

He shattered the bulbs with a hammer.

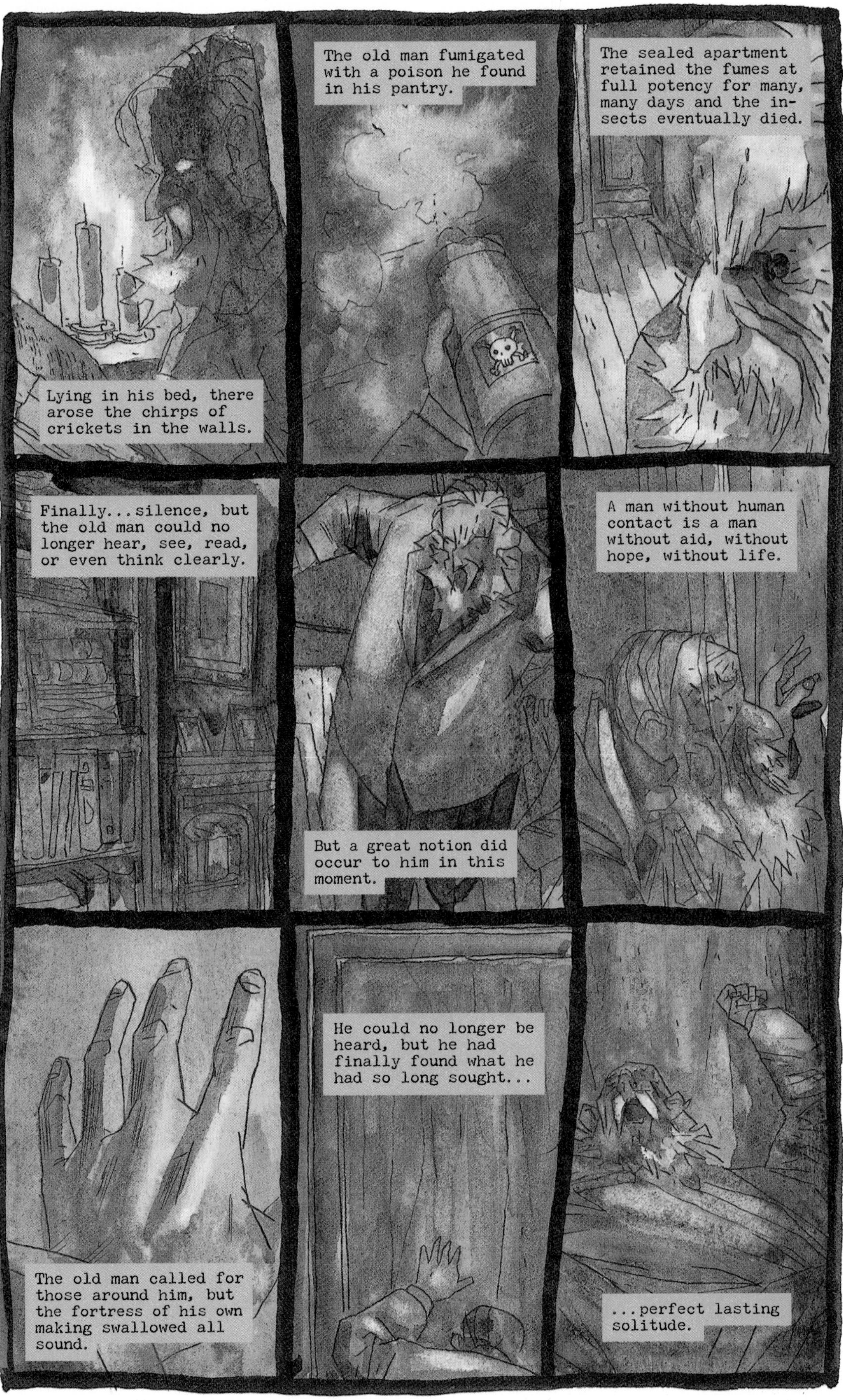
Lying in his bed, there arose the chirps of crickets in the walls.
The old man fumigated with a poison he found in his pantry.
The sealed apartment retained the fumes at full potency for many, many days and the insects eventually died.
Finally...silence, but the old man could no longer hear, see, read, or even think clearly.
But a great notion did occur to him in this moment.
A man without human contact is a man without aid, without hope, without life.
The old man called for those around him, but the fortress of his own making swallowed all sound.
He could no longer be heard, but he had finally found what he had so long sought...
...perfect lasting solitude.

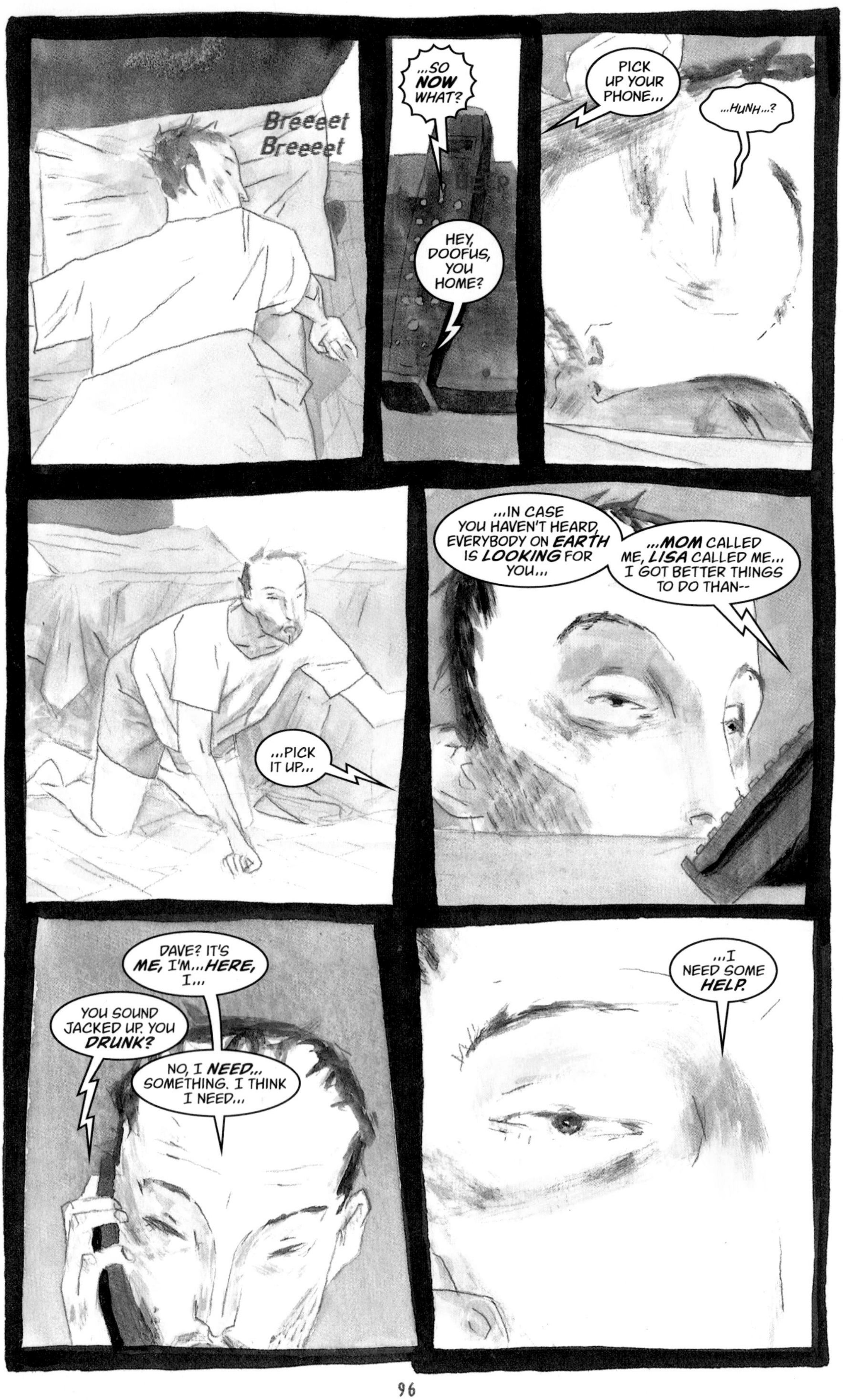
Breeeet
Breeeet
...SO NOW WHAT?
HEY, DOOFUS, YOU HOME?
PICK UP YOUR PHONE...
...HUNH...?
...PICK IT UP...
...IN CASE YOU HAVEN'T HEARD, EVERYBODY ON EARTH IS LOOKING FOR YOU...
...MOM CALLED ME, LISA CALLED ME... I GOT BETTER THINGS TO DO THAN--
DAVE? IT'S ME, I'M...HERE, I...
YOU SOUND JACKED UP. YOU DRUNK?
NO, I NEED... SOMETHING. I THINK I NEED...
...I NEED SOME HELP.

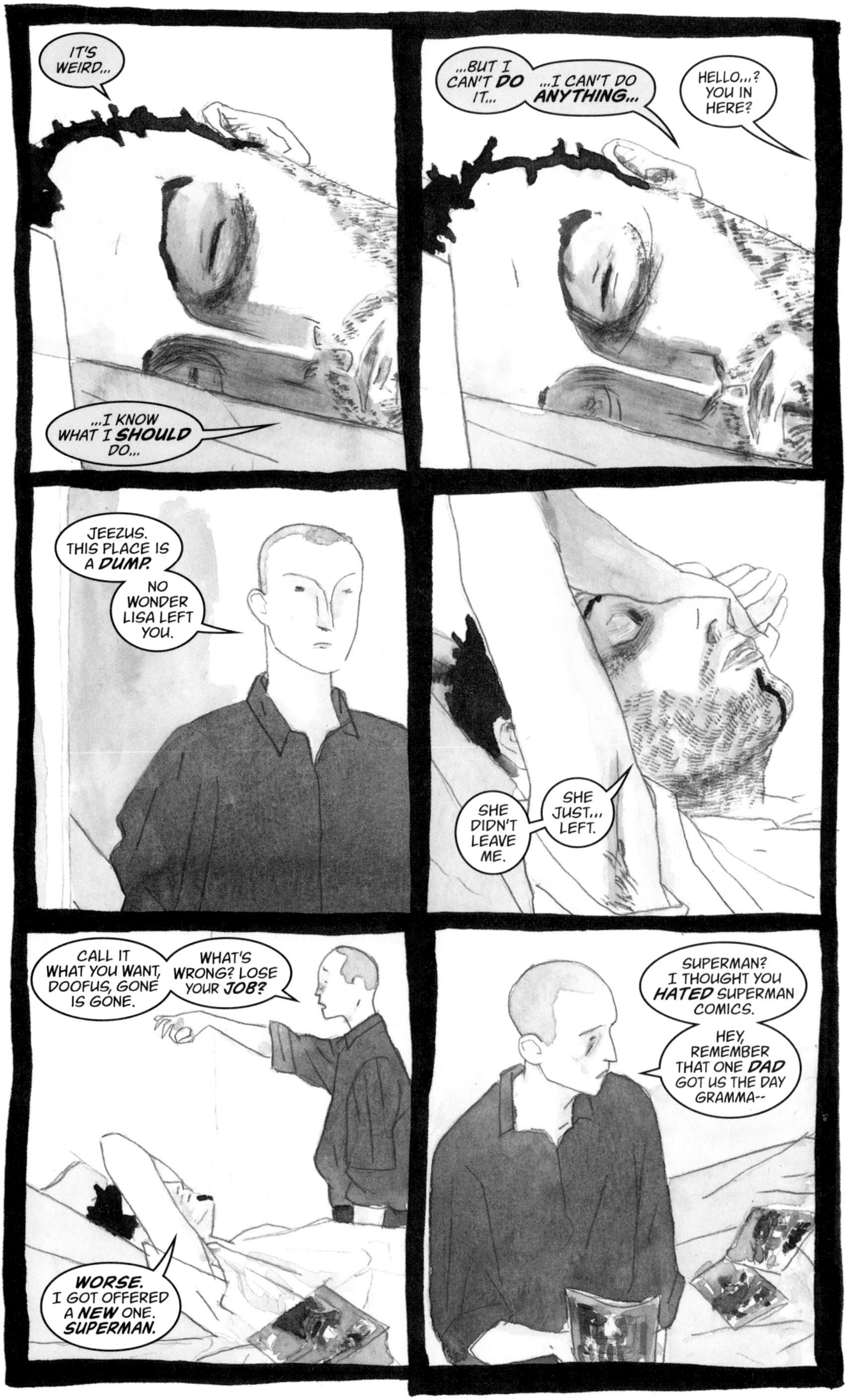
IT'S WEIRD...
...I KNOW WHAT I SHOULD DO...
...BUT I CAN'T DO IT...
...I CAN'T DO ANYTHING...
HELLO...? YOU IN HERE?
JEEZUS. THIS PLACE IS A DUMP.
NO WONDER LISA LEFT YOU.
SHE DIDN'T LEAVE ME.
SHE JUST... LEFT.
CALL IT WHAT YOU WANT, DOOFUS, GONE IS GONE.
WHAT'S WRONG? LOSE YOUR JOB?
WORSE. I GOT OFFERED A NEW ONE. SUPERMAN.
SUPERMAN? I THOUGHT YOU HATED SUPERMAN COMICS.
HEY, REMEMBER THAT ONE DAD GOT US THE DAY GRAMMA--

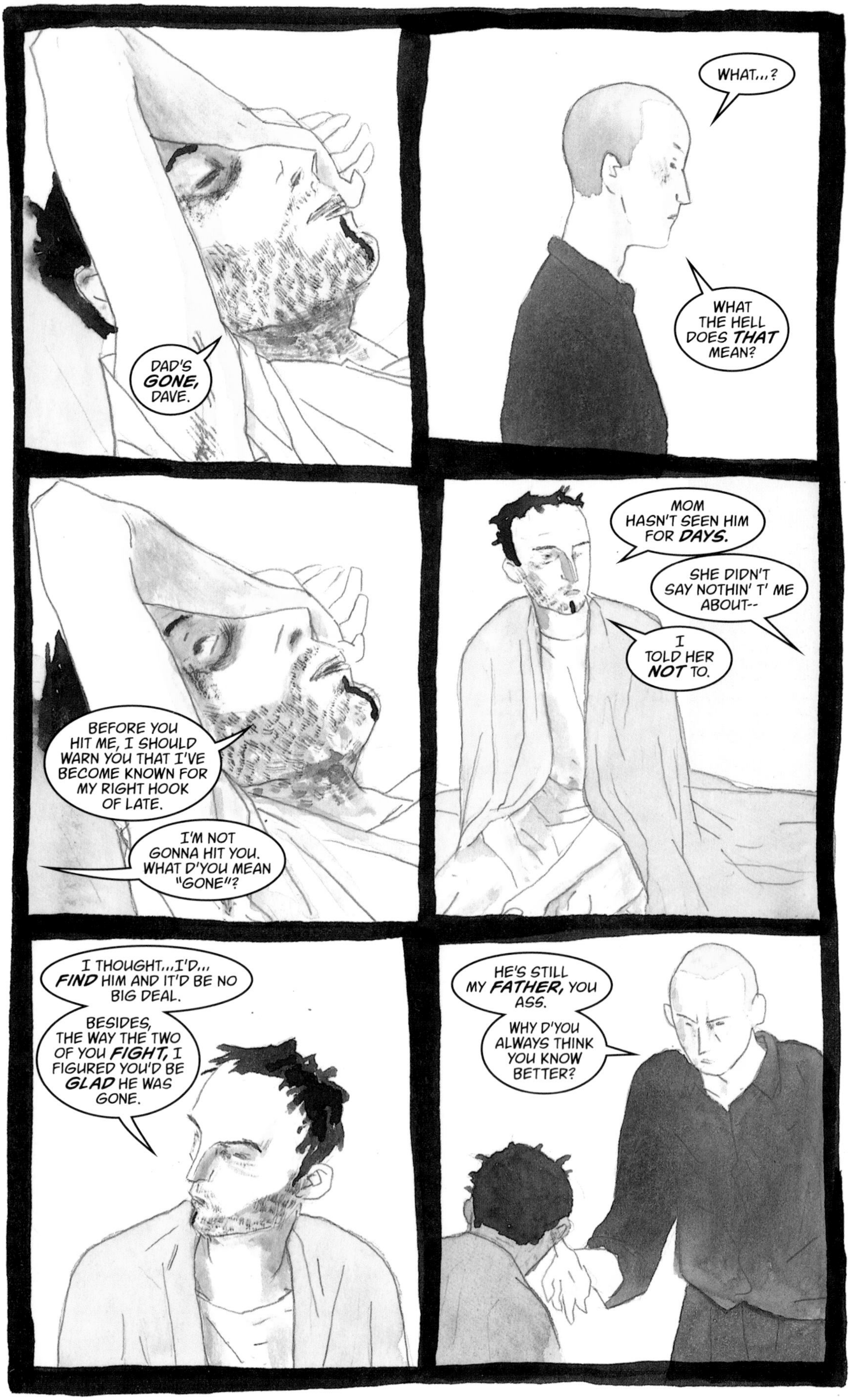
DAD'S GONE, DAVE.
WHAT...?
WHAT THE HELL DOES THAT MEAN?
BEFORE YOU HIT ME, I SHOULD WARN YOU THAT I'VE BECOME KNOWN FOR MY RIGHT HOOK OF LATE.
I'M NOT GONNA HIT YOU. WHAT D'YOU MEAN "GONE"?
MOM HASN'T SEEN HIM FOR DAYS.
SHE DIDN'T SAY NOTHIN' T' ME ABOUT--
I TOLD HER NOT TO.
I THOUGHT...I'D... FIND HIM AND IT'D BE NO BIG DEAL.
BESIDES, THE WAY THE TWO OF YOU FIGHT, I FIGURED YOU'D BE GLAD HE WAS GONE.
HE'S STILL MY FATHER, YOU ASS.
WHY D'YOU ALWAYS THINK YOU KNOW BETTER?

ALTERNATE REALITY

No matter how fast you walk, there are things you see that make you stop—

—and think twice about your life...

...incidents begging the question...

..."Are you adding to the world or taking away from it?"

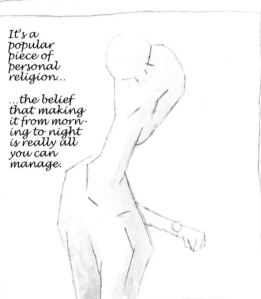

It's a popular piece of personal religion...

...the belief that making it from morning to night is really all you can manage.

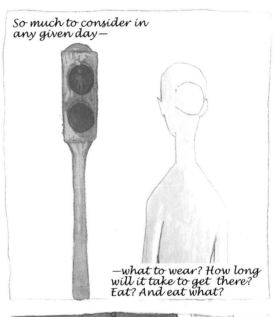

So much to consider in any given day—

—what to wear? How long will it take to get there? Eat? And eat what?

Pebbly problems piling up more precisely than the stones at Giza.

Have you paid your bills? Is today someone's birthday? Where are your keys?

And how can you possibly balance the two existing worlds...

...work and home?

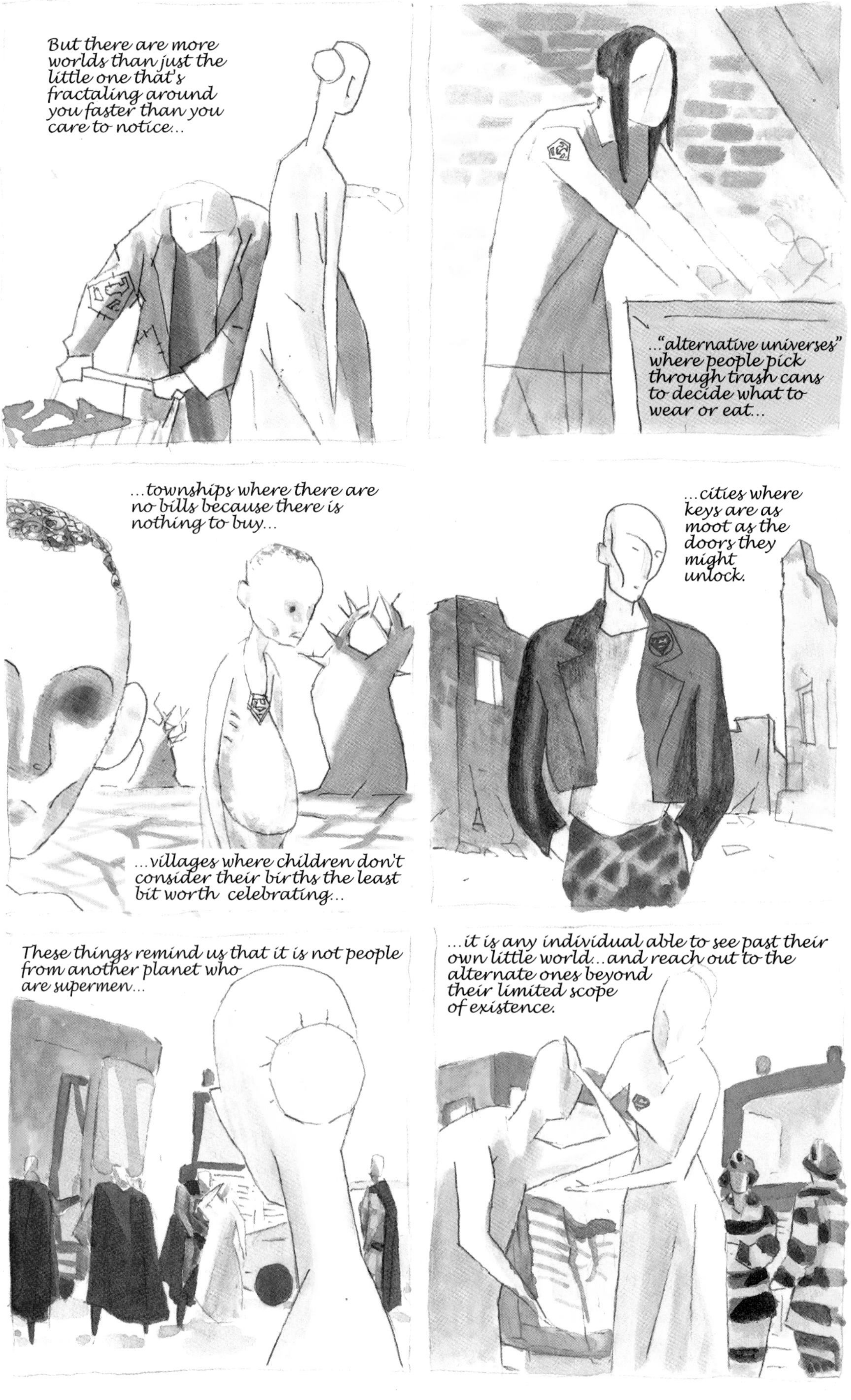
But there are more worlds than just the little one that's fractaling around you faster than you care to notice...
..."alternative universes" where people pick through trash cans to decide what to wear or eat...
...townships where there are no bills because there is nothing to buy...
...villages where children don't consider their births the least bit worth celebrating...
...cities where keys are as moot as the doors they might unlock.
These things remind us that it is not people from another planet who are supermen...
...it is any individual able to see past their own little world...and reach out to the alternate ones beyond their limited scope of existence.

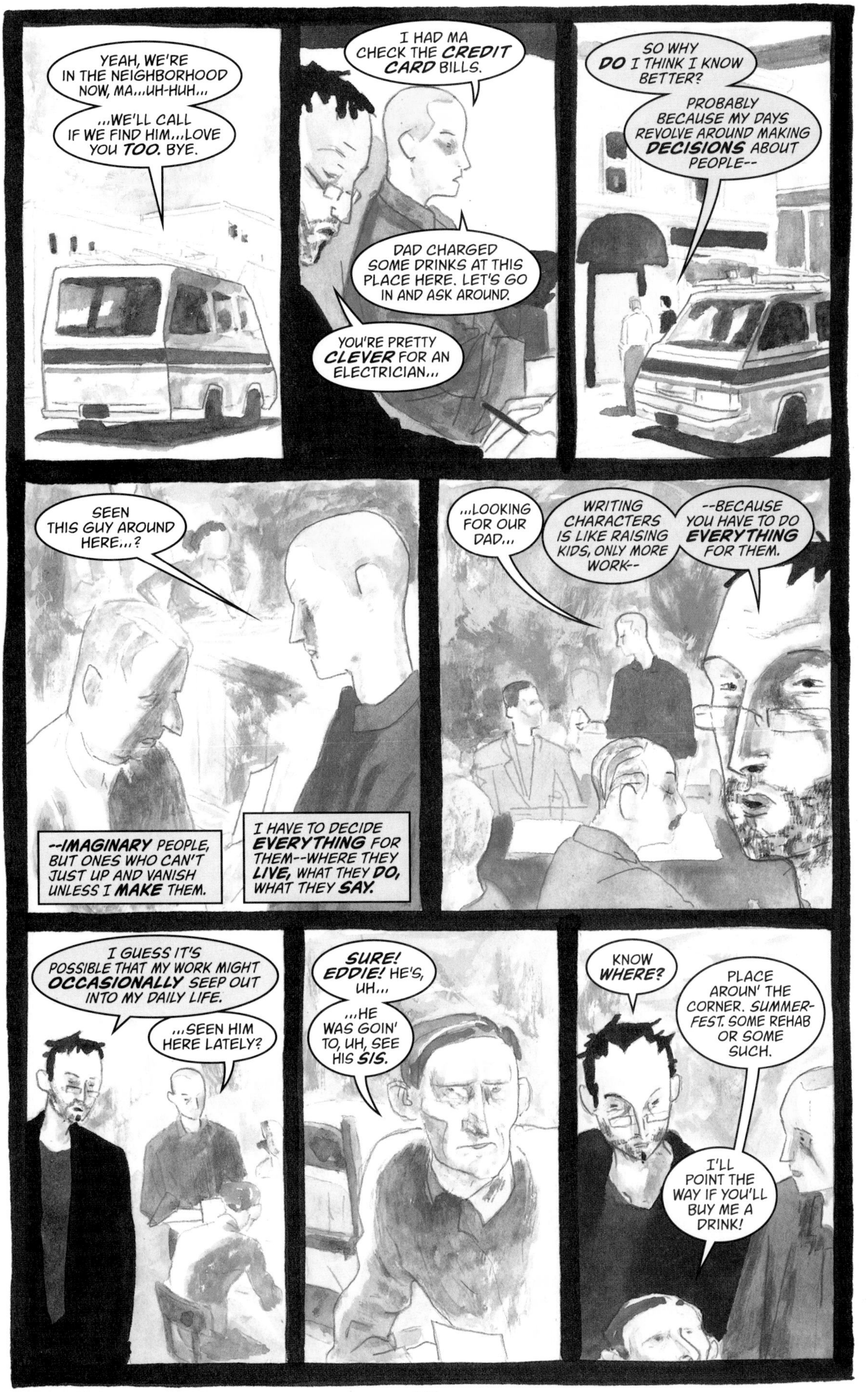
YEAH, WE'RE IN THE NEIGHBORHOOD NOW, MA...UH-HUH...
...WE'LL CALL IF WE FIND HIM...LOVE YOU TOO. BYE.
I HAD MA CHECK THE CREDIT CARD BILLS.
DAD CHARGED SOME DRINKS AT THIS PLACE HERE. LET'S GO IN AND ASK AROUND.
YOU'RE PRETTY CLEVER FOR AN ELECTRICIAN...
SO WHY DO I THINK I KNOW BETTER?
PROBABLY BECAUSE MY DAYS REVOLVE AROUND MAKING DECISIONS ABOUT PEOPLE--
SEEN THIS GUY AROUND HERE...?
--IMAGINARY PEOPLE, BUT ONES WHO CAN'T JUST UP AND VANISH UNLESS I MAKE THEM.
I HAVE TO DECIDE EVERYTHING FOR THEM--WHERE THEY LIVE, WHAT THEY DO, WHAT THEY SAY.
...LOOKING FOR OUR DAD...
WRITING CHARACTERS IS LIKE RAISING KIDS, ONLY MORE WORK--
--BECAUSE YOU HAVE TO DO EVERYTHING FOR THEM.
I GUESS IT'S POSSIBLE THAT MY WORK MIGHT OCCASIONALLY SEEP OUT INTO MY DAILY LIFE.
...SEEN HIM HERE LATELY?
SURE! EDDIE! HE'S, UH...
...HE WAS GOIN' TO, UH, SEE HIS SIS.
KNOW WHERE?
PLACE AROUN' THE CORNER. SUMMER-FEST. SOME REHAB OR SOME SUCH.
I'LL POINT THE WAY IF YOU'LL BUY ME A DRINK!

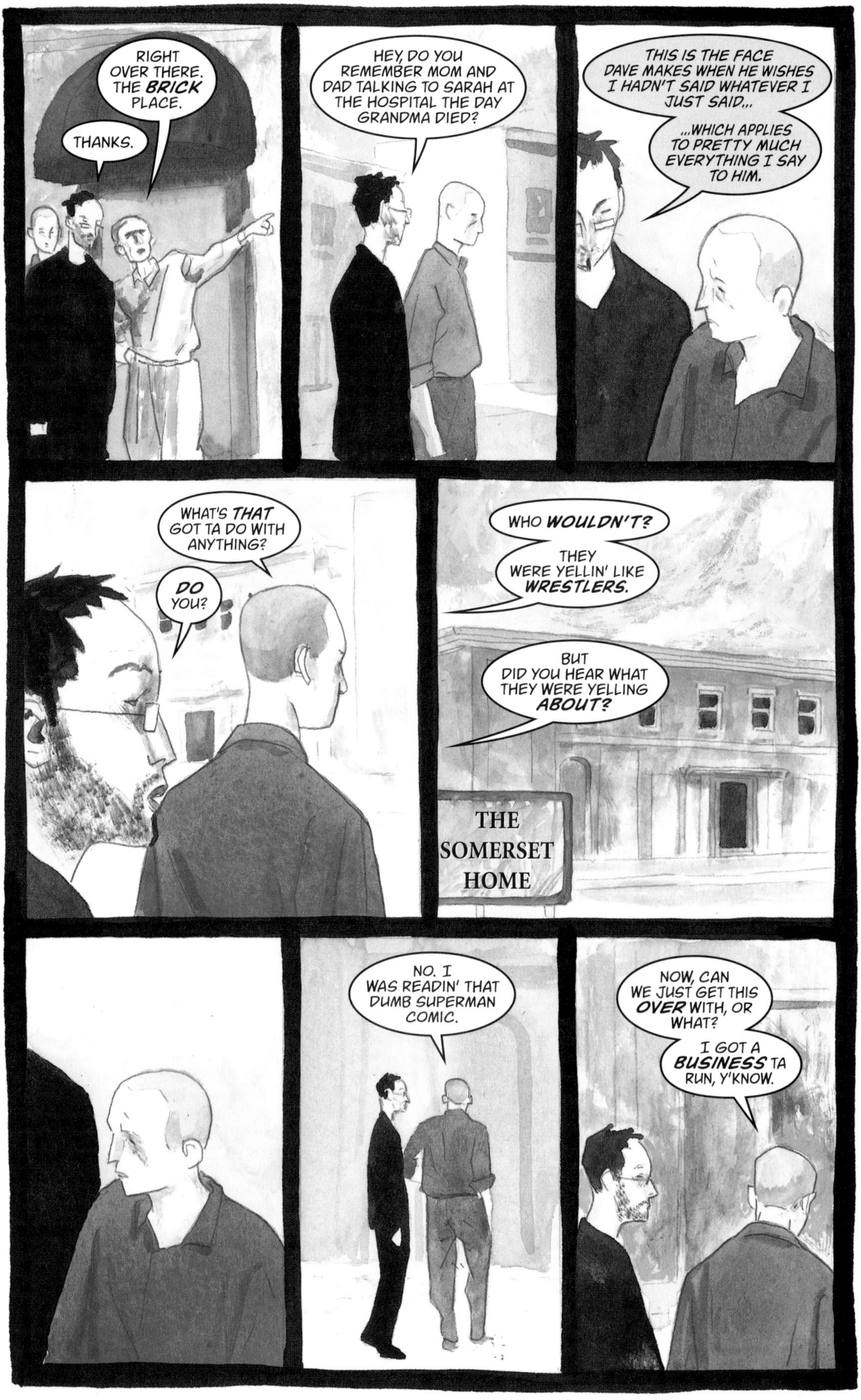
RIGHT OVER THERE. THE BRICK PLACE.
THANKS.
HEY, DO YOU REMEMBER MOM AND DAD TALKING TO SARAH AT THE HOSPITAL THE DAY GRANDMA DIED?
THIS IS THE FACE DAVE MAKES WHEN HE WISHES I HADN'T SAID WHATEVER I JUST SAID...
...WHICH APPLIES TO PRETTY MUCH EVERYTHING I SAY TO HIM.
WHAT'S THAT GOT TA DO WITH ANYTHING?
DO YOU?
WHO WOULDN'T?
THEY WERE YELLIN' LIKE WRESTLERS.
BUT DID YOU HEAR WHAT THEY WERE YELLING ABOUT?
THE SOMERSET HOME
NO. I WAS READIN' THAT DUMB SUPERMAN COMIC.
NOW, CAN WE JUST GET THIS OVER WITH, OR WHAT?
I GOT A BUSINESS TA RUN, Y'KNOW.

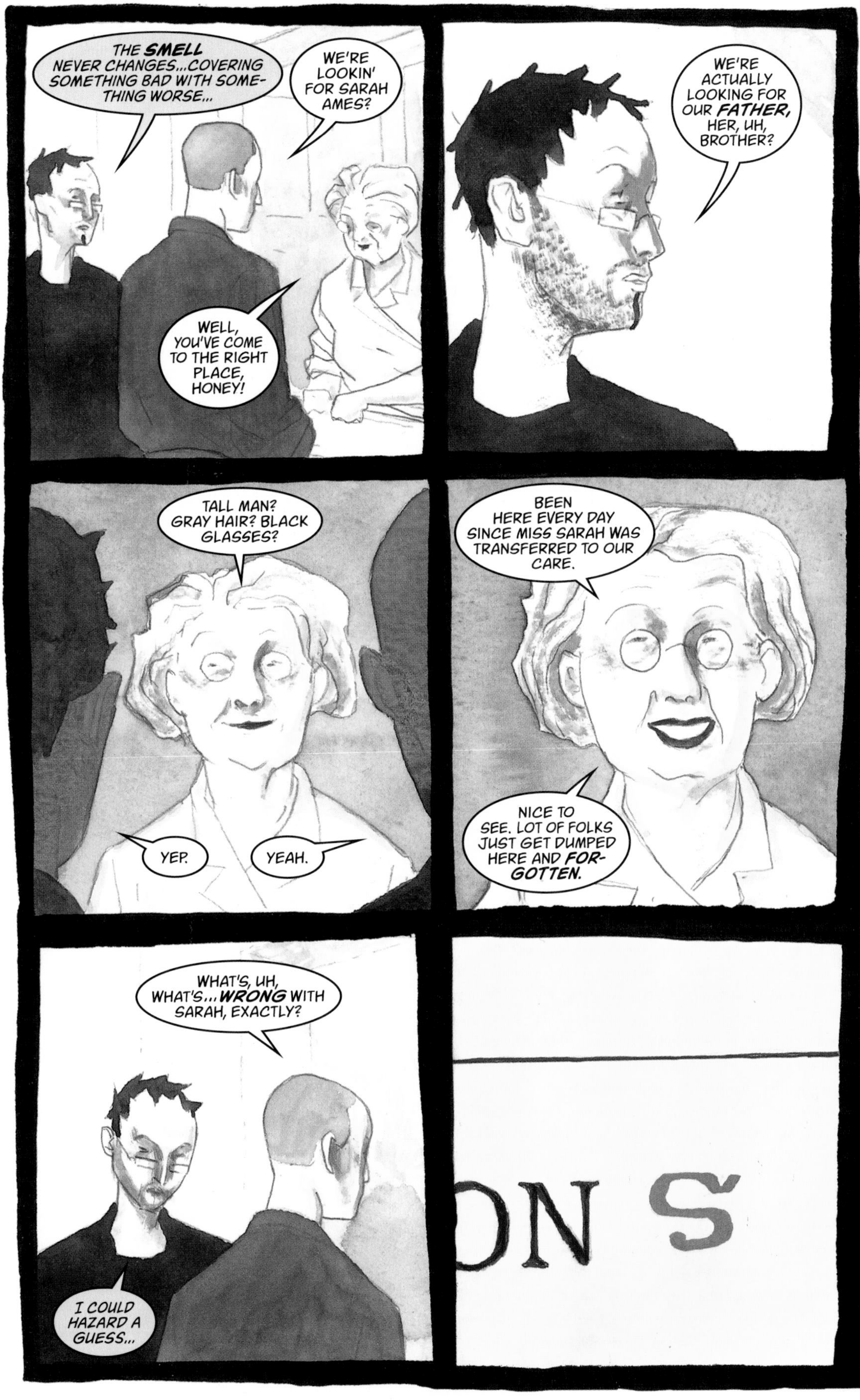
THE SMELL NEVER CHANGES...COVERING SOMETHING BAD WITH SOME-THING WORSE...
WE'RE LOOKIN' FOR SARAH AMES?
WELL, YOU'VE COME TO THE RIGHT PLACE, HONEY!
WE'RE ACTUALLY LOOKING FOR OUR FATHER, HER, UH, BROTHER?
TALL MAN? GRAY HAIR? BLACK GLASSES?
YEP.
YEAH.
BEEN HERE EVERY DAY SINCE MISS SARAH WAS TRANSFERRED TO OUR CARE.
NICE TO SEE. LOT OF FOLKS JUST GET DUMPED HERE AND FOR-GOTTEN.
WHAT'S, UH, WHAT'S...WRONG WITH SARAH, EXACTLY?
I COULD HAZARD A GUESS...
ON S

"s"

Huntington's

SERPENT SWIRL OF
THE ALPHABET SET.

MORE SO THAN ANY
OTHER ROMAN
LETTER...

...THE "S" WIELDS
SURPRISING
POWERS.

CONSIDER THE "S."

S

LIKE THE ABILITY
TO PLURAL.

words
WORDS
WORDSWORD
WordsWordsWo
words
WORD   Words
Words
Words
Words   Words
Words   Words

IT CAN MAKE A "WORD"
INTO "WORDS."

Victim

victims

victimsvictimsvictim
victim

victimsvictimsv

TURN AN ISOLATED
TRAGEDY...

...INTO AN EPIDEMIC.

MULTIPLY A SYMBOL INTO
SYMBOLS AT THE DROP
OF A CONSONANT.

Brother

THE "S" CAN ALSO
POSSESS.

Brother's

TAKE WHAT IT
WANTS THROUGH
ASSOCIATION.

IT CAN TURN
"FATHER TIME"...

...INTO "FATHER'S TIME."

A SINGLE LETTER THAT
CAN LITERALLY STEAL
TIME.

VICTIMS

MAKING MANY OUT
OF ONE.

Huntington's

OWNING WHAT IT
TOUCHES.

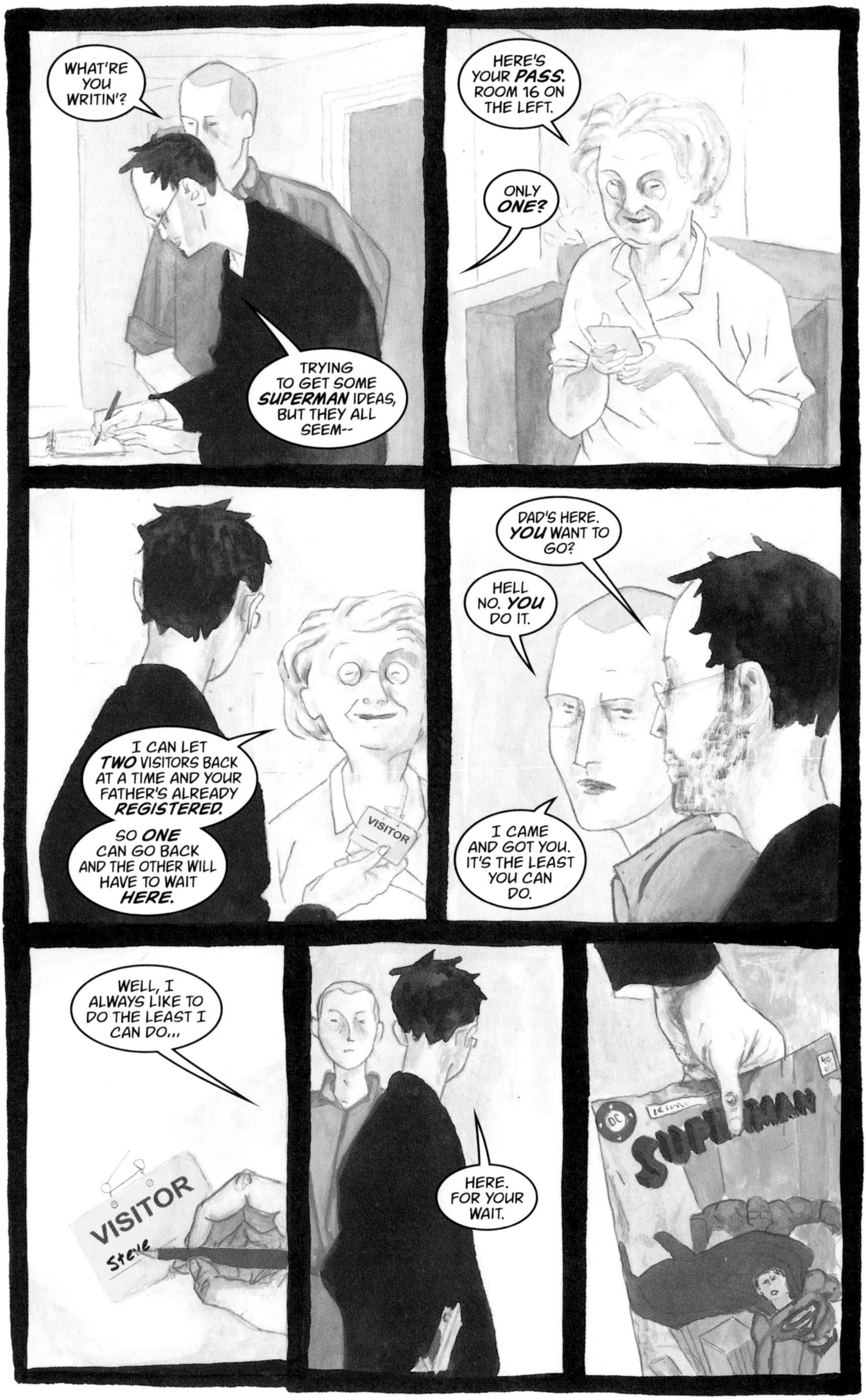
WHAT'RE YOU WRITIN'?
TRYING TO GET SOME SUPERMAN IDEAS, BUT THEY ALL SEEM--
HERE'S YOUR PASS. ROOM 16 ON THE LEFT.
ONLY ONE?
I CAN LET TWO VISITORS BACK AT A TIME AND YOUR FATHER'S ALREADY REGISTERED.
SO ONE CAN GO BACK AND THE OTHER WILL HAVE TO WAIT HERE.
VISITOR
DAD'S HERE. YOU WANT TO GO?
HELL NO. YOU DO IT.
I CAME AND GOT YOU. IT'S THE LEAST YOU CAN DO.
WELL, I ALWAYS LIKE TO DO THE LEAST I CAN DO...
VISITOR
Steve
HERE. FOR YOUR WAIT.
SUPERMAN

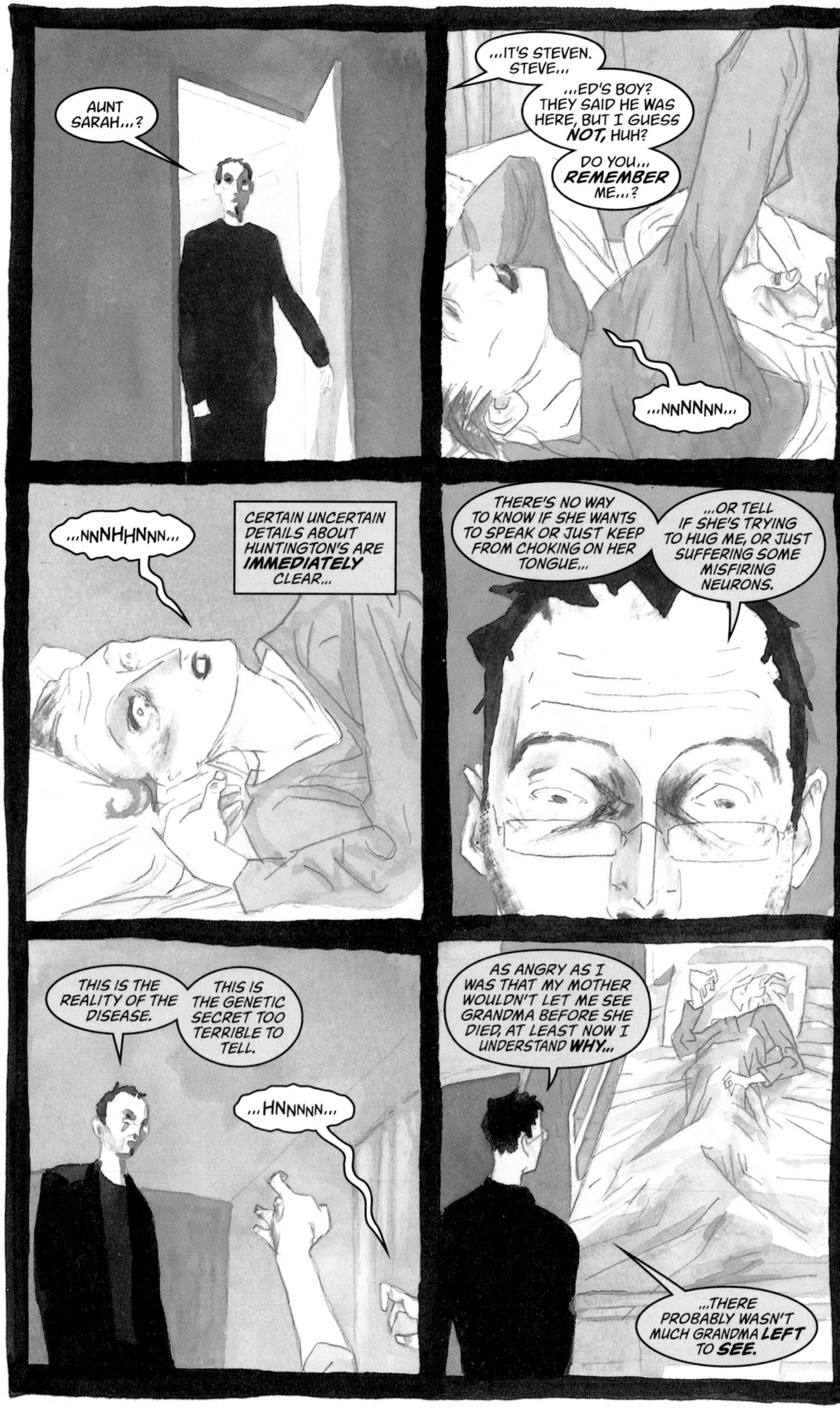
AUNT SARAH...?
...IT'S STEVEN. STEVE...
...ED'S BOY? THEY SAID HE WAS HERE, BUT I GUESS NOT, HUH?
DO YOU... REMEMBER ME...?
...NNNNNN...
...NNNHHNNN...
CERTAIN UNCERTAIN DETAILS ABOUT HUNTINGTON'S ARE IMMEDIATELY CLEAR...
THERE'S NO WAY TO KNOW IF SHE WANTS TO SPEAK OR JUST KEEP FROM CHOKING ON HER TONGUE...
...OR TELL IF SHE'S TRYING TO HUG ME, OR JUST SUFFERING SOME MISFIRING NEURONS.
THIS IS THE REALITY OF THE DISEASE.
THIS IS THE GENETIC SECRET TOO TERRIBLE TO TELL.
...HNNNNN...
AS ANGRY AS I WAS THAT MY MOTHER WOULDN'T LET ME SEE GRANDMA BEFORE SHE DIED, AT LEAST NOW I UNDERSTAND WHY...
...THERE PROBABLY WASN'T MUCH GRANDMA LEFT TO SEE.

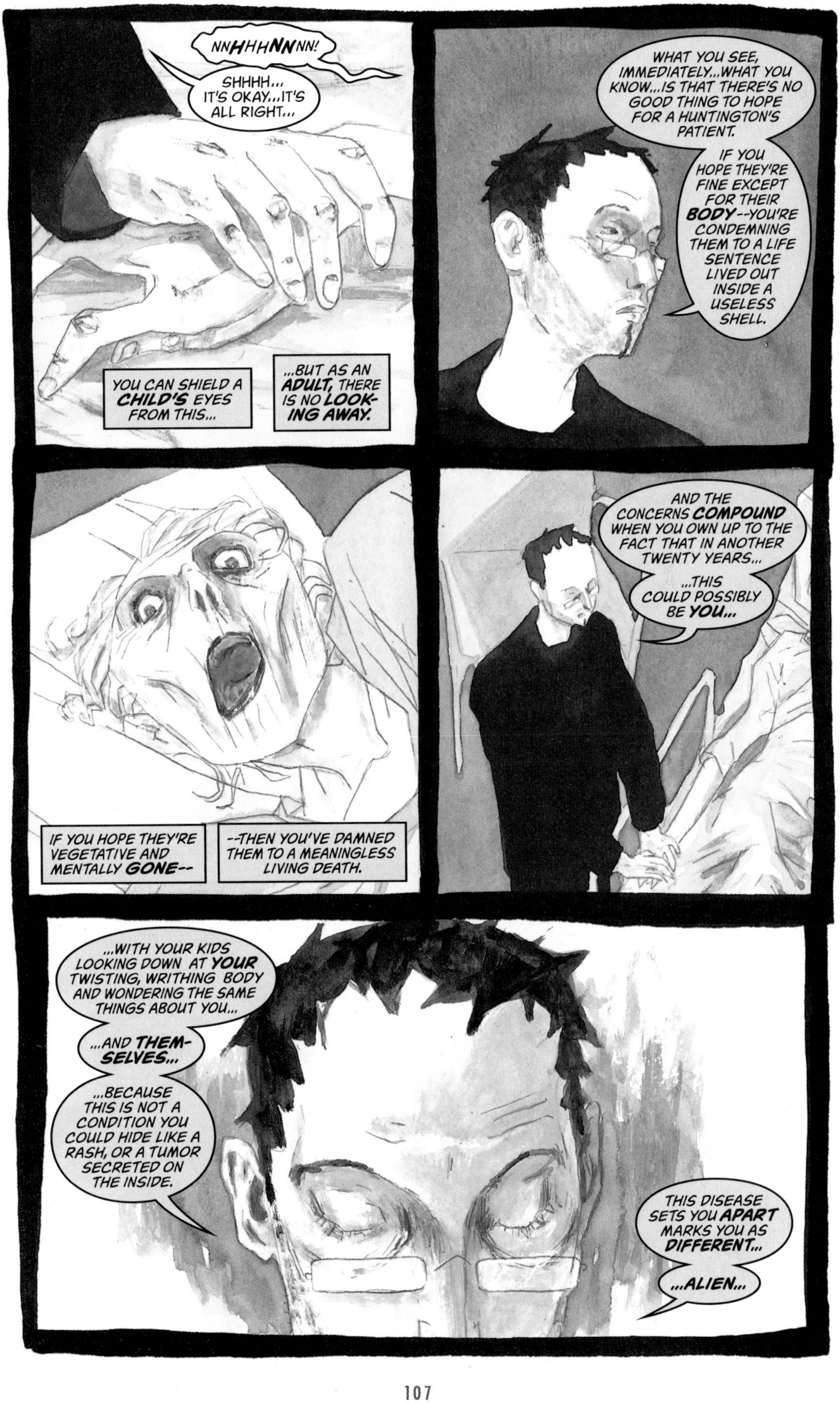
NNHHHNNNN!
SHHHH... IT'S OKAY...IT'S ALL RIGHT...
YOU CAN SHIELD A CHILD'S EYES FROM THIS...
...BUT AS AN ADULT, THERE IS NO LOOKING AWAY.
WHAT YOU SEE, IMMEDIATELY...WHAT YOU KNOW...IS THAT THERE'S NO GOOD THING TO HOPE FOR A HUNTINGTON'S PATIENT.
IF YOU HOPE THEY'RE FINE EXCEPT FOR THEIR BODY--YOU'RE CONDEMNING THEM TO A LIFE SENTENCE LIVED OUT INSIDE A USELESS SHELL.
IF YOU HOPE THEY'RE VEGETATIVE AND MENTALLY GONE--
--THEN YOU'VE DAMNED THEM TO A MEANINGLESS LIVING DEATH.
AND THE CONCERNS COMPOUND WHEN YOU OWN UP TO THE FACT THAT IN ANOTHER TWENTY YEARS...
...THIS COULD POSSIBLY BE YOU...
...WITH YOUR KIDS LOOKING DOWN AT YOUR TWISTING, WRITHING BODY AND WONDERING THE SAME THINGS ABOUT YOU...
...AND THEMSELVES...
...BECAUSE THIS IS NOT A CONDITION YOU COULD HIDE LIKE A RASH, OR A TUMOR SECRETED ON THE INSIDE.
THIS DISEASE SETS YOU APART MARKS YOU AS DIFFERENT...
...ALIEN...

THE ALIEN

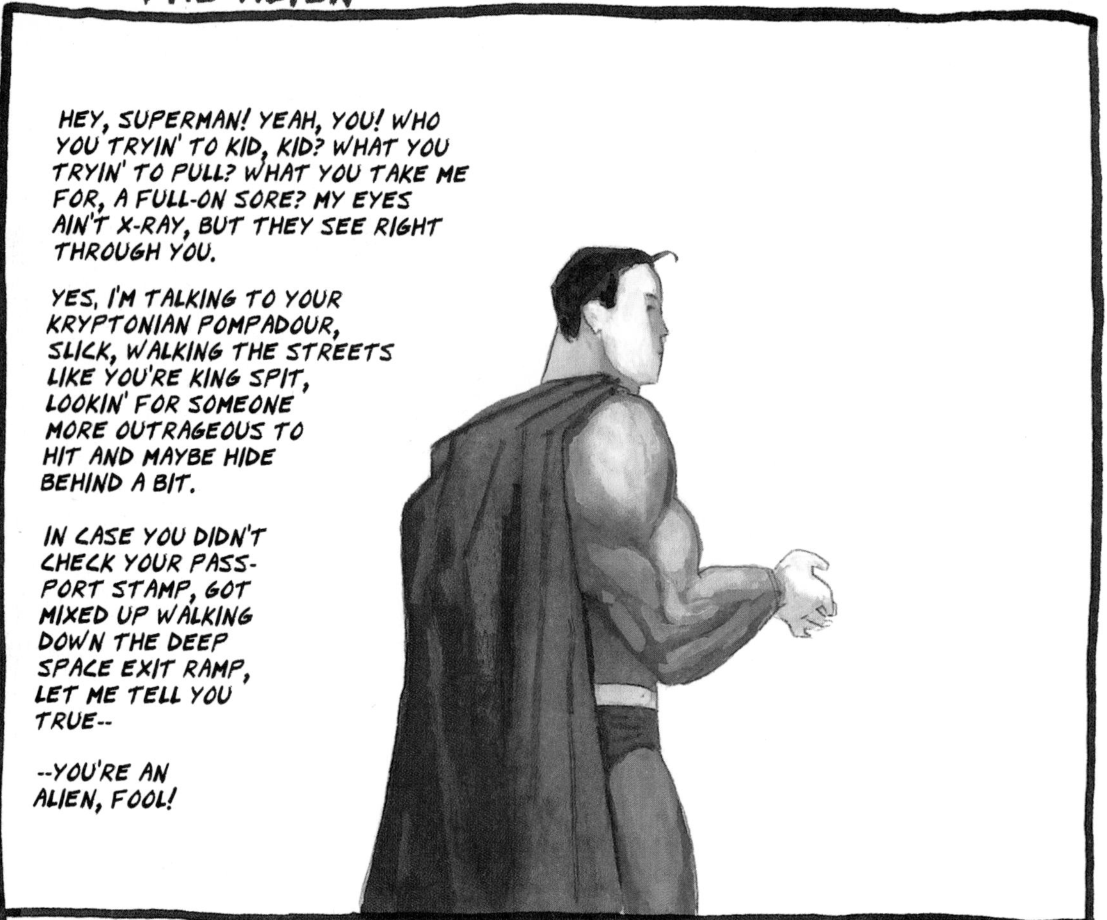
HEY, SUPERMAN! YEAH, YOU! WHO YOU TRYIN' TO KID, KID? WHAT YOU TRYIN' TO PULL? WHAT YOU TAKE ME FOR, A FULL-ON SORE? MY EYES AIN'T X-RAY, BUT THEY SEE RIGHT THROUGH YOU.
YES, I'M TALKING TO YOUR KRYPTONIAN POMPADOUR, SLICK, WALKING THE STREETS LIKE YOU'RE KING SPIT, LOOKIN' FOR SOMEONE MORE OUTRAGEOUS TO HIT AND MAYBE HIDE BEHIND A BIT.
IN CASE YOU DIDN'T CHECK YOUR PASS-PORT STAMP, GOT MIXED UP WALKING DOWN THE DEEP SPACE EXIT RAMP, LET ME TELL YOU TRUE--
--YOU'RE AN ALIEN, FOOL!

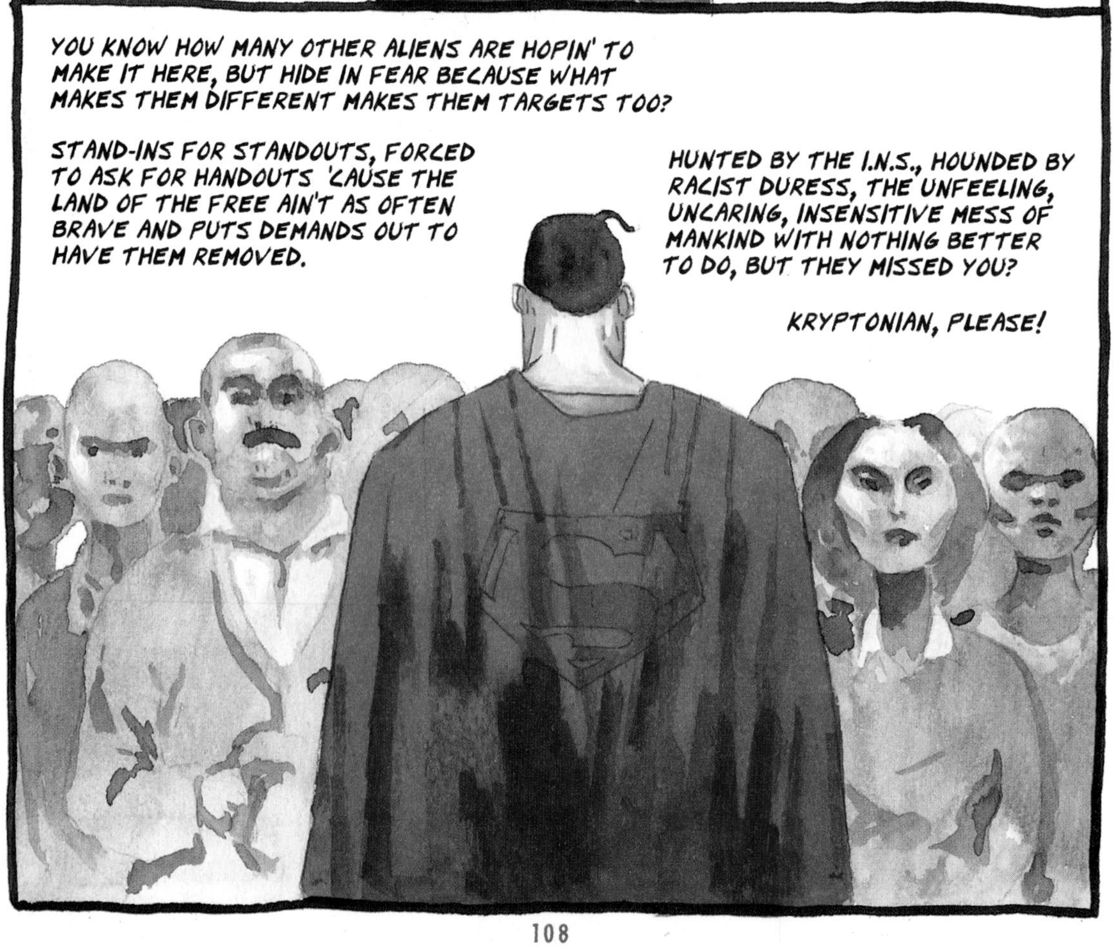
YOU KNOW HOW MANY OTHER ALIENS ARE HOPIN' TO MAKE IT HERE, BUT HIDE IN FEAR BECAUSE WHAT MAKES THEM DIFFERENT MAKES THEM TARGETS TOO?
STAND-INS FOR STANDOUTS, FORCED TO ASK FOR HANDOUTS 'CAUSE THE LAND OF THE FREE AIN'T AS OFTEN BRAVE AND PUTS DEMANDS OUT TO HAVE THEM REMOVED.
HUNTED BY THE I.N.S., HOUNDED BY RACIST DURESS, THE UNFEELING, UNCARING, INSENSITIVE MESS OF MANKIND WITH NOTHING BETTER TO DO, BUT THEY MISSED YOU?
KRYPTONIAN, PLEASE!

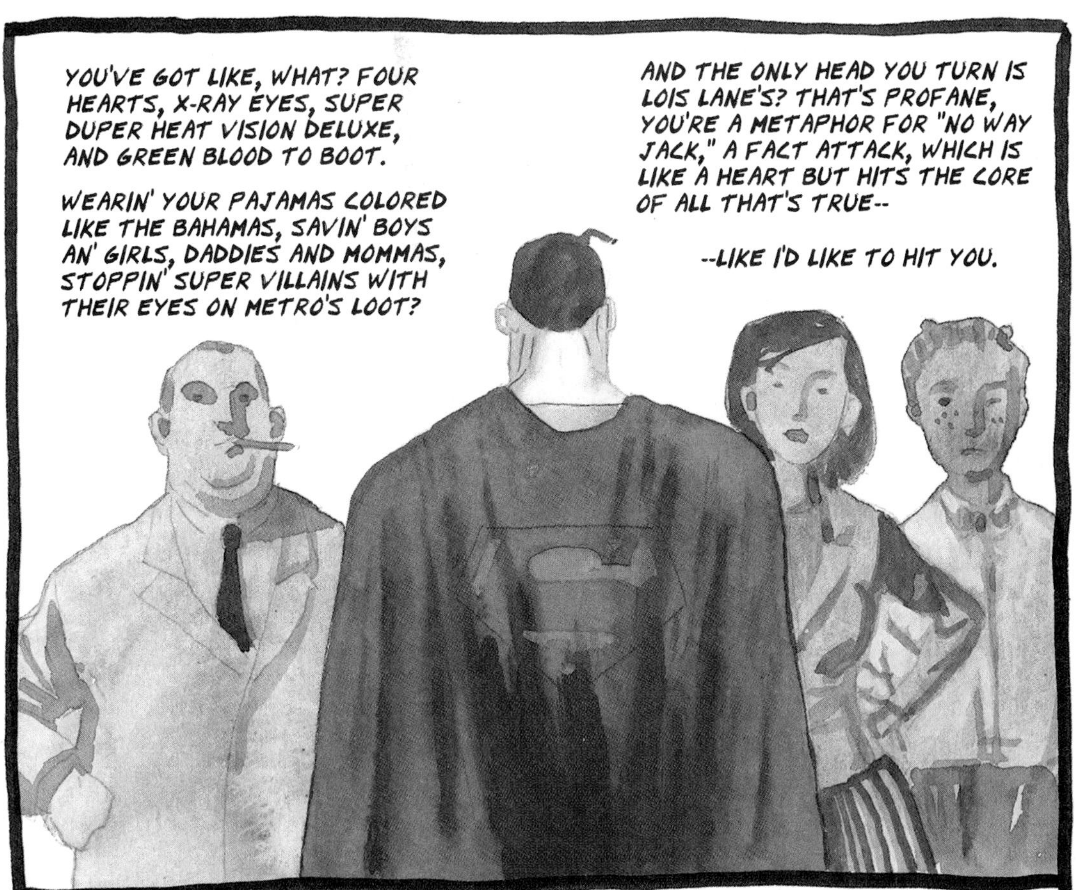
YOU'VE GOT LIKE, WHAT? FOUR HEARTS, X-RAY EYES, SUPER DUPER HEAT VISION DELUXE, AND GREEN BLOOD TO BOOT.
WEARIN' YOUR PAJAMAS COLORED LIKE THE BAHAMAS, SAVIN' BOYS AN' GIRLS, DADDIES AND MOMMAS, STOPPIN' SUPER VILLAINS WITH THEIR EYES ON METRO'S LOOT?
AND THE ONLY HEAD YOU TURN IS LOIS LANE'S? THAT'S PROFANE, YOU'RE A METAPHOR FOR "NO WAY JACK," A FACT ATTACK, WHICH IS LIKE A HEART BUT HITS THE CORE OF ALL THAT'S TRUE--
--LIKE I'D LIKE TO HIT YOU.

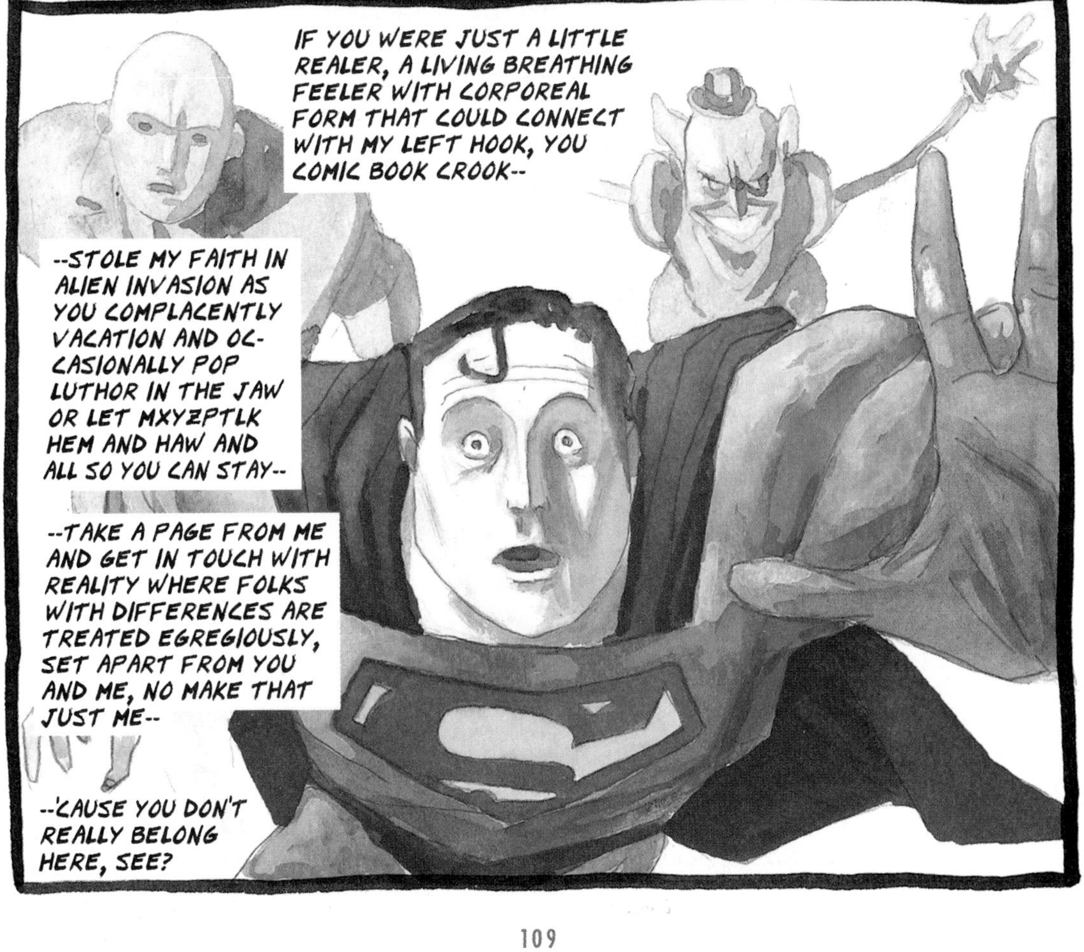
IF YOU WERE JUST A LITTLE REALER, A LIVING BREATHING FEELER WITH CORPOREAL FORM THAT COULD CONNECT WITH MY LEFT HOOK, YOU COMIC BOOK CROOK--
--STOLE MY FAITH IN ALIEN INVASION AS YOU COMPLACENTLY VACATION AND OC-CASIONALLY POP LUTHOR IN THE JAW OR LET MXYZPTLK HEM AND HAW AND ALL SO YOU CAN STAY--
--TAKE A PAGE FROM ME AND GET IN TOUCH WITH REALITY WHERE FOLKS WITH DIFFERENCES ARE TREATED EGREGIOUSLY, SET APART FROM YOU AND ME, NO MAKE THAT JUST ME--
--'CAUSE YOU DON'T REALLY BELONG HERE, SEE?

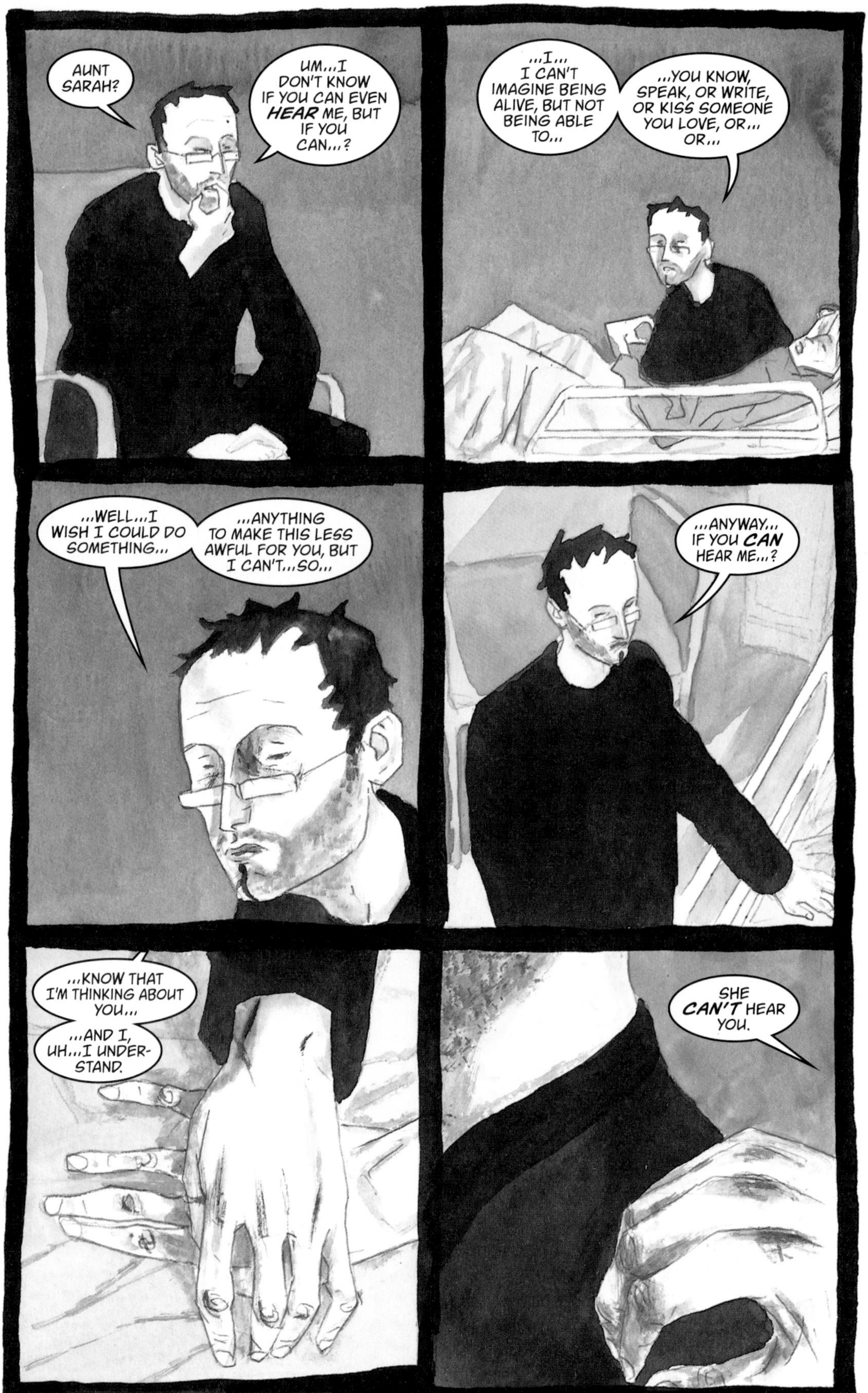
AUNT SARAH?
UM...I DON'T KNOW IF YOU CAN EVEN HEAR ME, BUT IF YOU CAN...?
...I... I CAN'T IMAGINE BEING ALIVE, BUT NOT BEING ABLE TO...
...YOU KNOW, SPEAK, OR WRITE, OR KISS SOMEONE YOU LOVE, OR... OR...
...WELL...I WISH I COULD DO SOMETHING...
...ANYTHING TO MAKE THIS LESS AWFUL FOR YOU, BUT I CAN'T...SO...
...ANYWAY... IF YOU CAN HEAR ME...?
...KNOW THAT I'M THINKING ABOUT YOU...
...AND I, UH...I UNDER-STAND.
SHE CAN'T HEAR YOU.

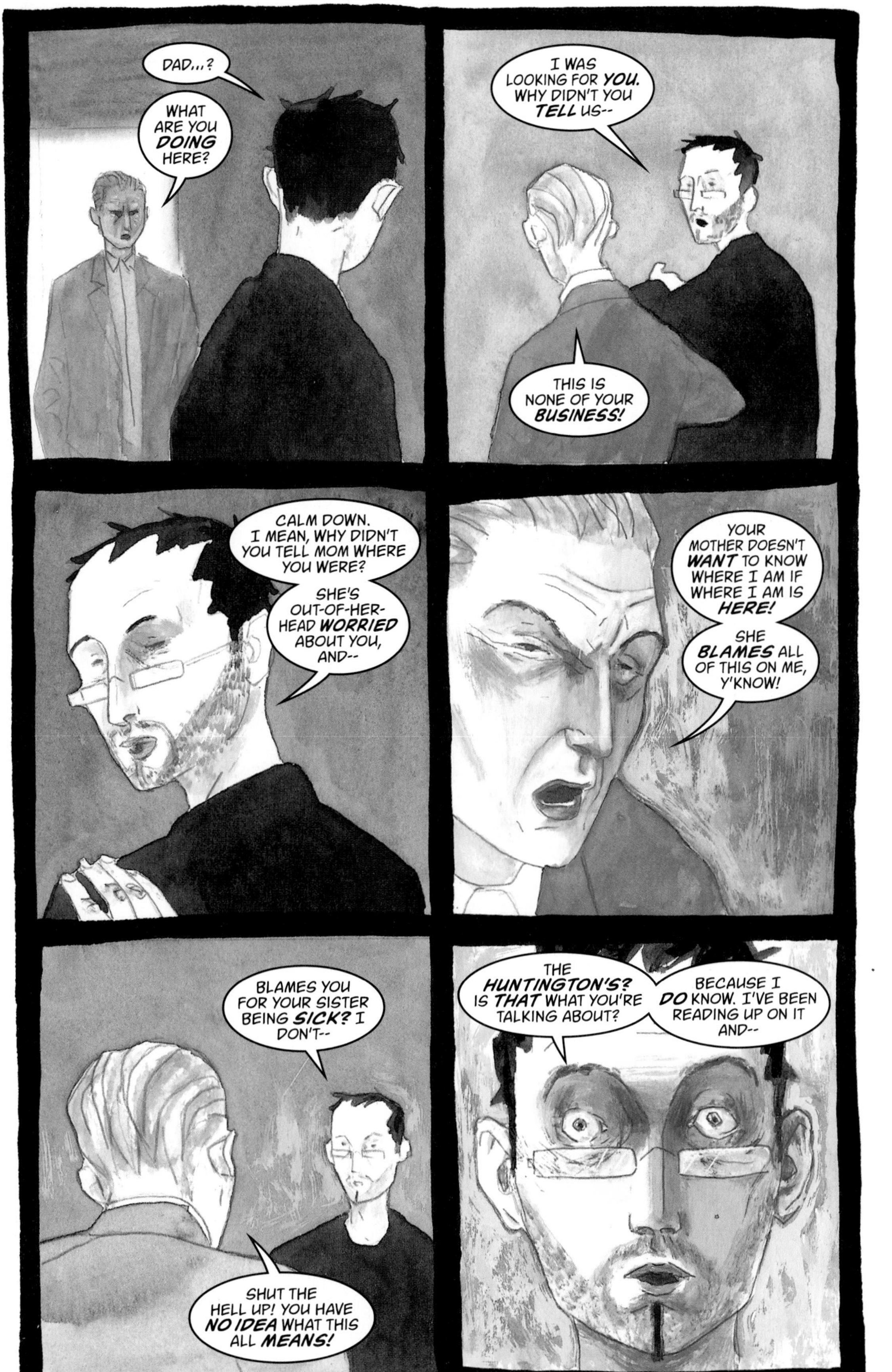
DAD...?
WHAT ARE YOU DOING HERE?
I WAS LOOKING FOR YOU. WHY DIDN'T YOU TELL US--
THIS IS NONE OF YOUR BUSINESS!
CALM DOWN. I MEAN, WHY DIDN'T YOU TELL MOM WHERE YOU WERE?
SHE'S OUT-OF-HER-HEAD WORRIED ABOUT YOU, AND--
YOUR MOTHER DOESN'T WANT TO KNOW WHERE I AM IF WHERE I AM IS HERE!
SHE BLAMES ALL OF THIS ON ME, Y'KNOW!
BLAMES YOU FOR YOUR SISTER BEING SICK? I DON'T--
SHUT THE HELL UP! YOU HAVE NO IDEA WHAT THIS ALL MEANS!
THE HUNTINGTON'S? IS THAT WHAT YOU'RE TALKING ABOUT?
BECAUSE I DO KNOW. I'VE BEEN READING UP ON IT AND--

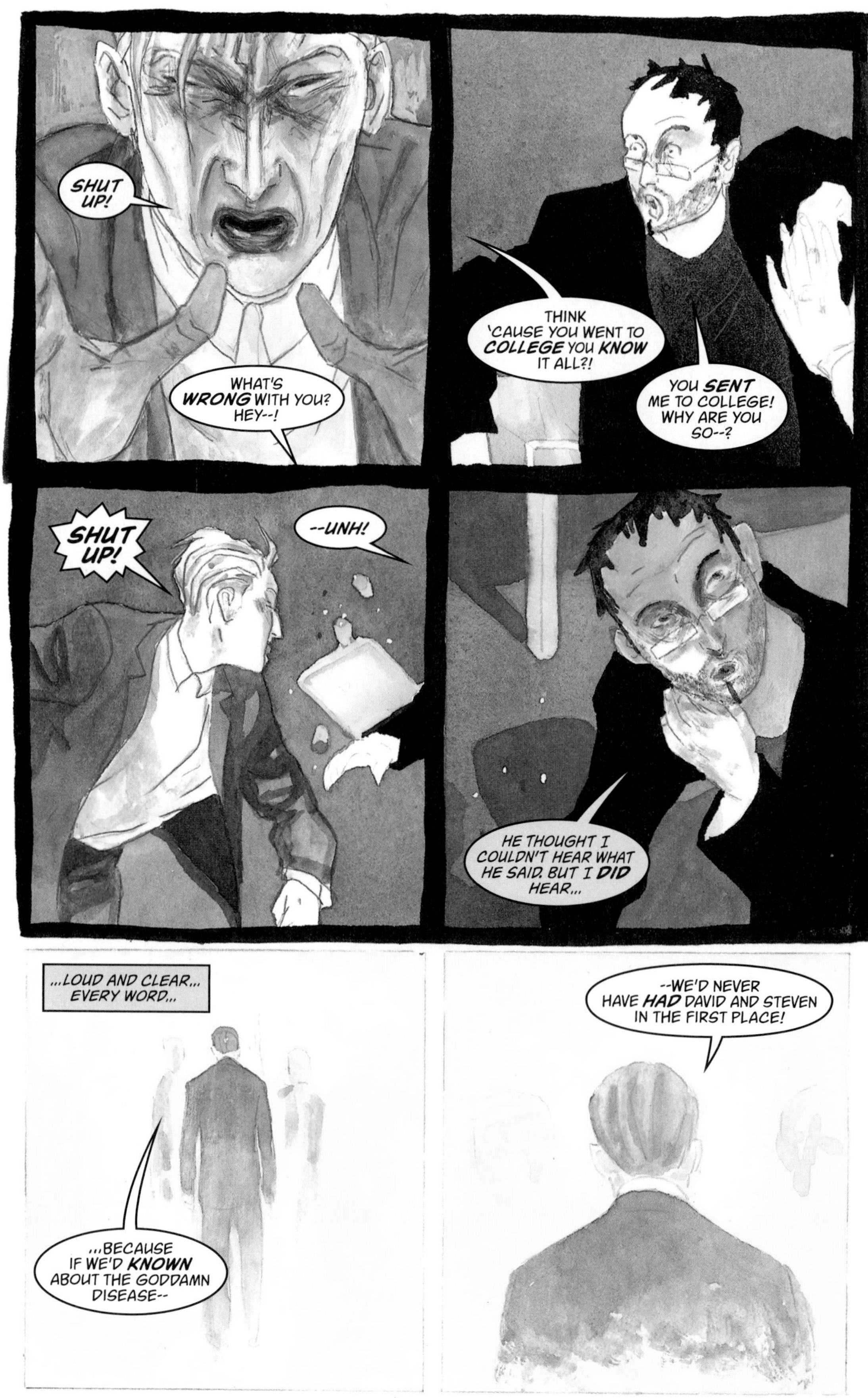
SHUT UP!
WHAT'S WRONG WITH YOU? HEY--!
THINK 'CAUSE YOU WENT TO COLLEGE YOU KNOW IT ALL?!
YOU SENT ME TO COLLEGE! WHY ARE YOU SO--?
SHUT UP!
--UNH!
HE THOUGHT I COULDN'T HEAR WHAT HE SAID. BUT I DID HEAR...
...LOUD AND CLEAR... EVERY WORD...
...BECAUSE IF WE'D KNOWN ABOUT THE GODDAMN DISEASE--
--WE'D NEVER HAVE HAD DAVID AND STEVEN IN THE FIRST PLACE!

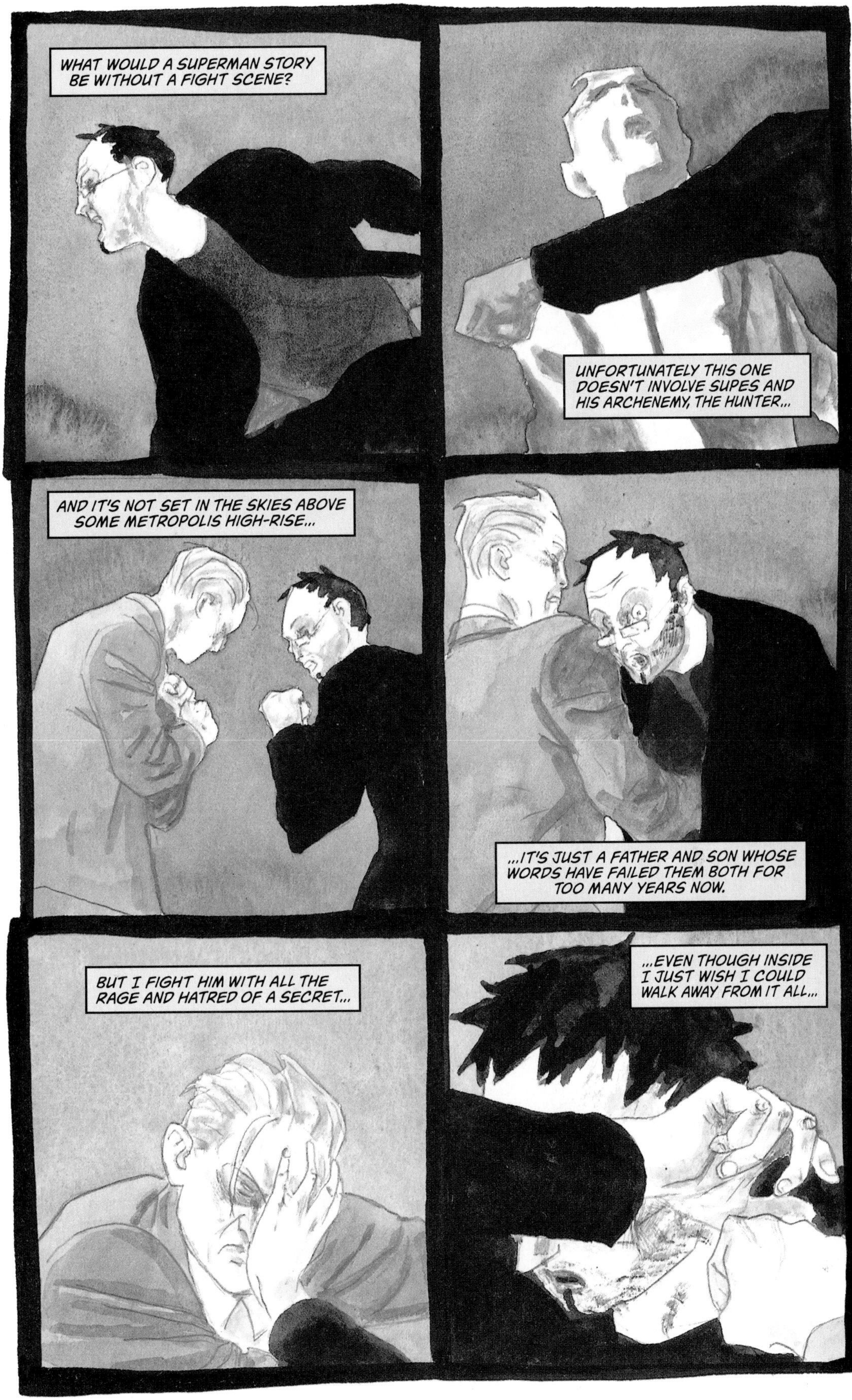
WHAT WOULD A SUPERMAN STORY BE WITHOUT A FIGHT SCENE?
UNFORTUNATELY THIS ONE DOESN'T INVOLVE SUPES AND HIS ARCHENEMY, THE HUNTER...
AND IT'S NOT SET IN THE SKIES ABOVE SOME METROPOLIS HIGH-RISE...
...IT'S JUST A FATHER AND SON WHOSE WORDS HAVE FAILED THEM BOTH FOR TOO MANY YEARS NOW.
BUT I FIGHT HIM WITH ALL THE RAGE AND HATRED OF A SECRET...
...EVEN THOUGH INSIDE I JUST WISH I COULD WALK AWAY FROM IT ALL...

ESCAPE

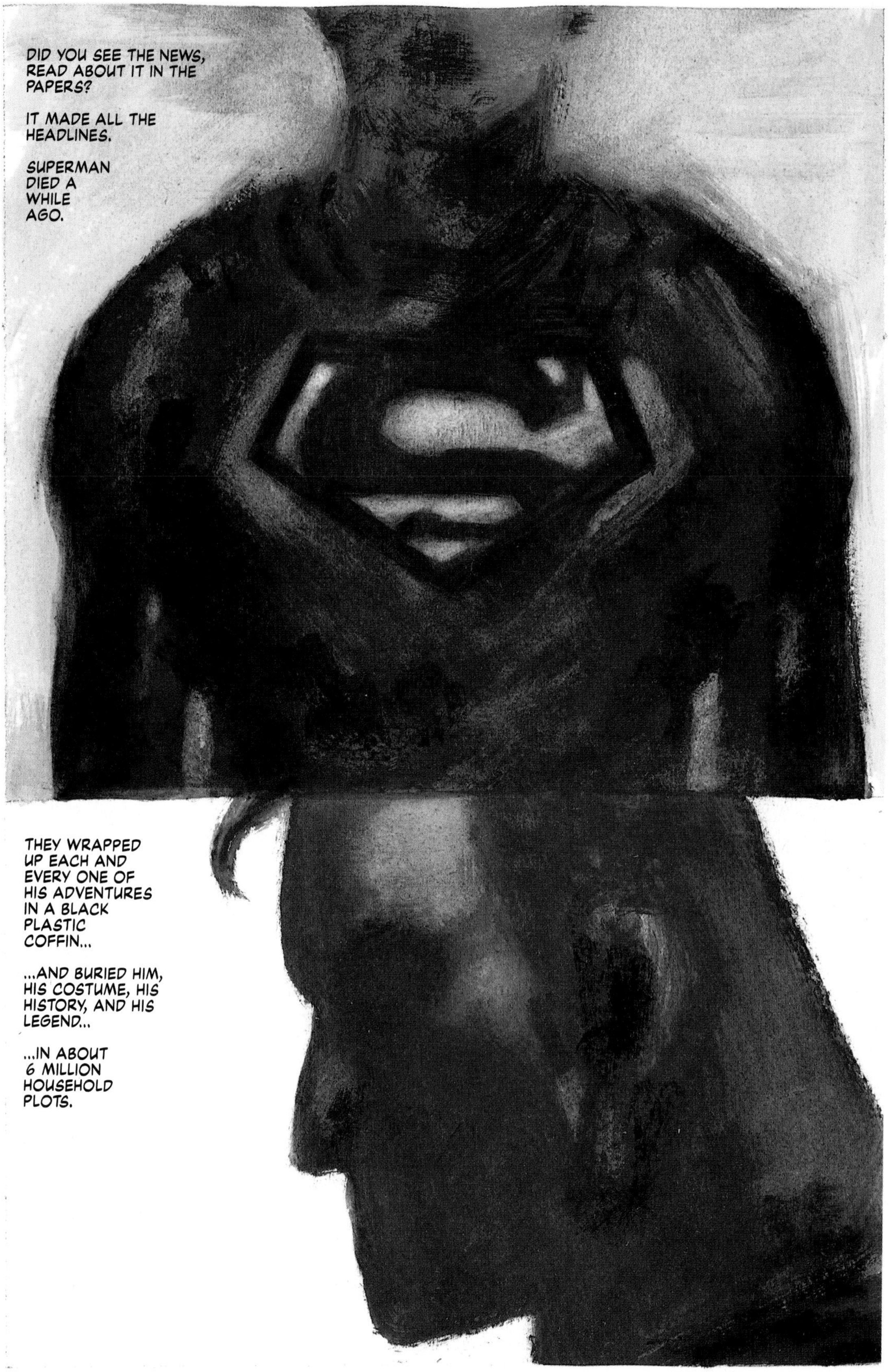
DID YOU SEE THE NEWS, READ ABOUT IT IN THE PAPERS?
IT MADE ALL THE HEADLINES.
SUPERMAN DIED A WHILE AGO.
THEY WRAPPED UP EACH AND EVERY ONE OF HIS ADVENTURES IN A BLACK PLASTIC COFFIN...
...AND BURIED HIM, HIS COSTUME, HIS HISTORY, AND HIS LEGEND...
...IN ABOUT 6 MILLION HOUSEHOLD PLOTS.

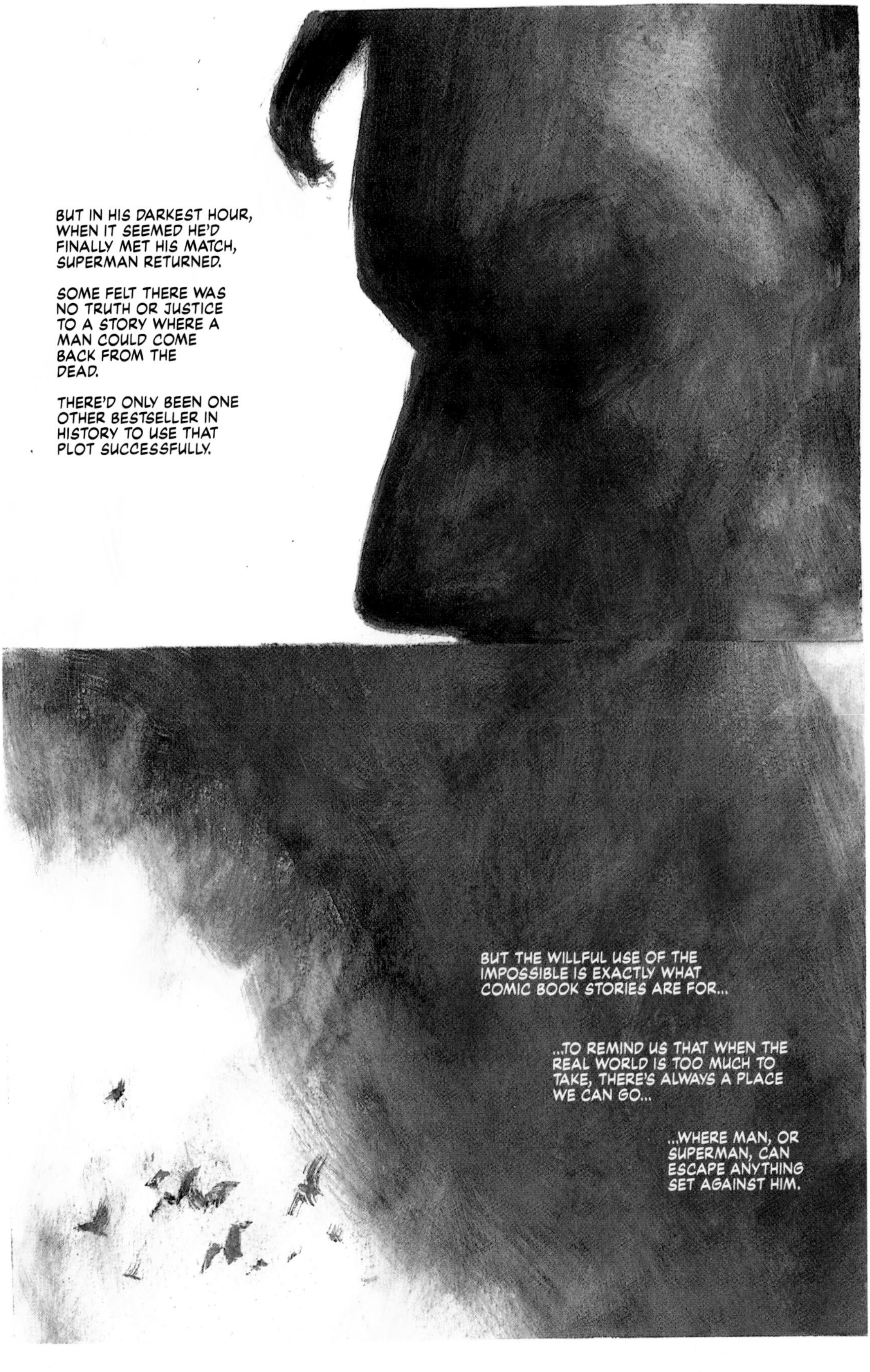
BUT IN HIS DARKEST HOUR, WHEN IT SEEMED HE'D FINALLY MET HIS MATCH, SUPERMAN RETURNED.
SOME FELT THERE WAS NO TRUTH OR JUSTICE TO A STORY WHERE A MAN COULD COME BACK FROM THE DEAD.
THERE'D ONLY BEEN ONE OTHER BESTSELLER IN HISTORY TO USE THAT PLOT SUCCESSFULLY.
BUT THE WILLFUL USE OF THE IMPOSSIBLE IS EXACTLY WHAT COMIC BOOK STORIES ARE FOR...
...TO REMIND US THAT WHEN THE REAL WORLD IS TOO MUCH TO TAKE, THERE'S ALWAYS A PLACE WE CAN GO...
...WHERE MAN, OR SUPERMAN, CAN ESCAPE ANYTHING SET AGAINST HIM.

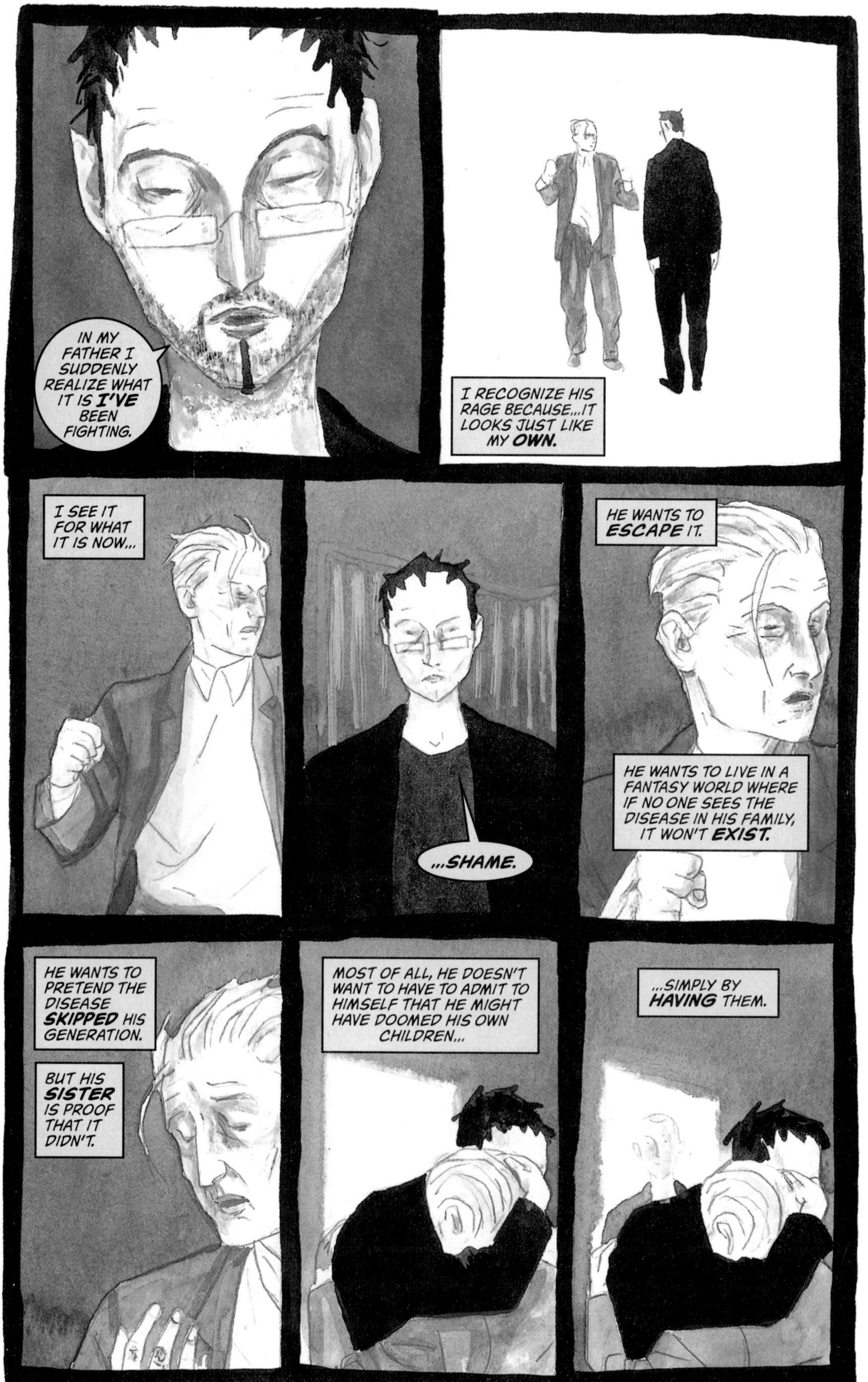
IN MY FATHER I SUDDENLY REALIZE WHAT IT IS I'VE BEEN FIGHTING.
I RECOGNIZE HIS RAGE BECAUSE...IT LOOKS JUST LIKE MY OWN.
I SEE IT FOR WHAT IT IS NOW...
...SHAME.
HE WANTS TO ESCAPE IT.
HE WANTS TO LIVE IN A FANTASY WORLD WHERE IF NO ONE SEES THE DISEASE IN HIS FAMILY, IT WON'T EXIST.
HE WANTS TO PRETEND THE DISEASE SKIPPED HIS GENERATION.
BUT HIS SISTER IS PROOF THAT IT DIDN'T.
MOST OF ALL, HE DOESN'T WANT TO HAVE TO ADMIT TO HIMSELF THAT HE MIGHT HAVE DOOMED HIS OWN CHILDREN...
...SIMPLY BY HAVING THEM.

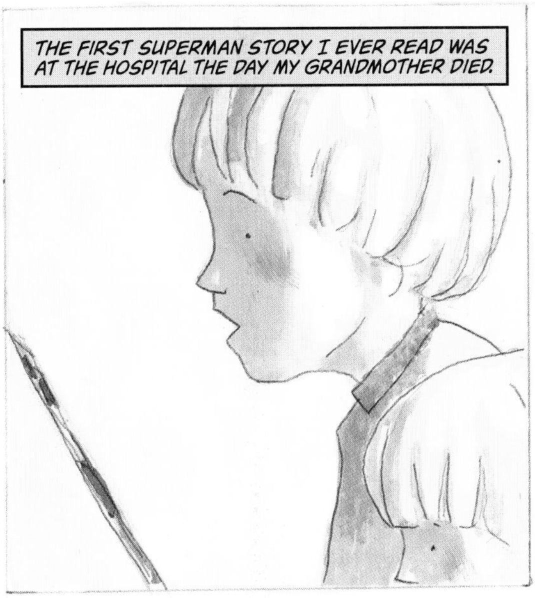
THE FIRST SUPERMAN STORY I EVER READ WAS AT THE HOSPITAL THE DAY MY GRANDMOTHER DIED.

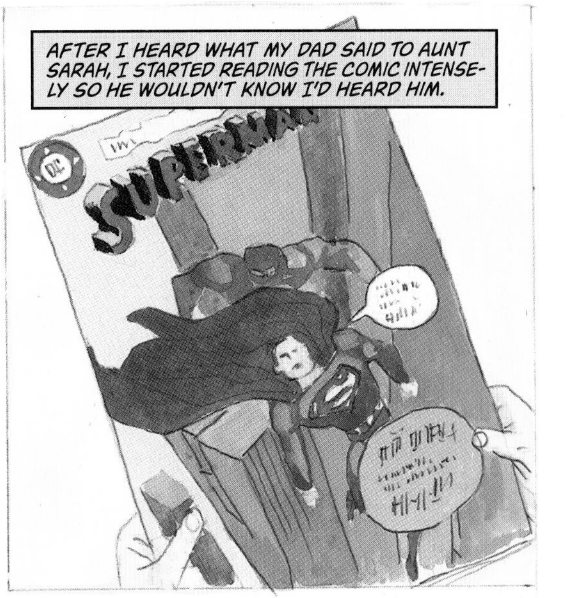
AFTER I HEARD WHAT MY DAD SAID TO AUNT SARAH, I STARTED READING THE COMIC INTENSELY SO HE WOULDN'T KNOW I'D HEARD HIM.
SUPERMAN

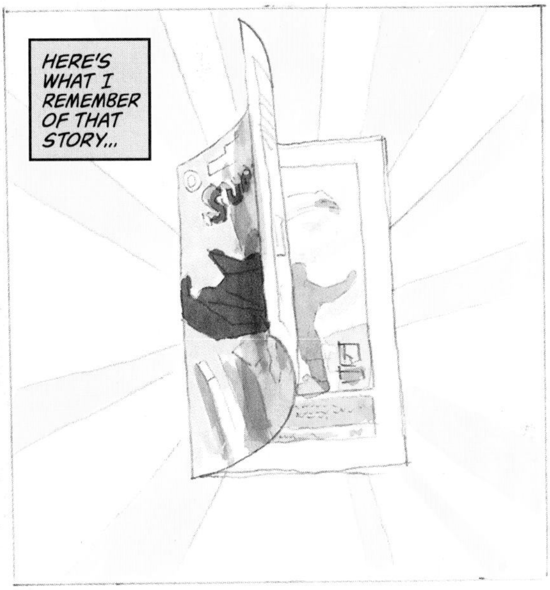
HERE'S WHAT I REMEMBER OF THAT STORY...

HERO

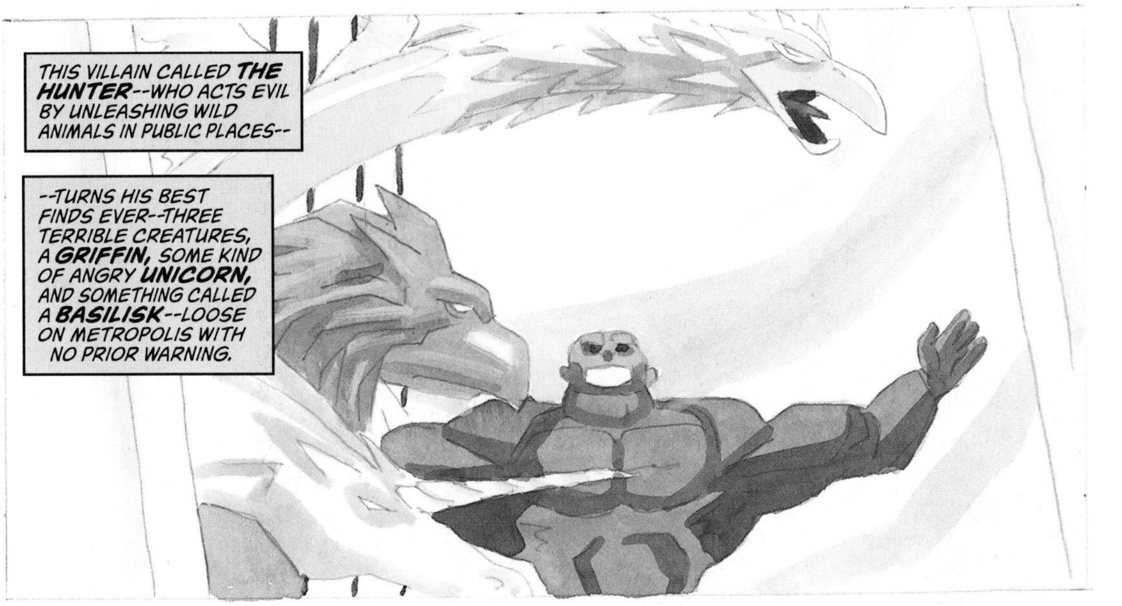
THIS VILLAIN CALLED **THE HUNTER**--WHO ACTS EVIL BY UNLEASHING WILD ANIMALS IN PUBLIC PLACES--
--TURNS HIS BEST FINDS EVER--THREE TERRIBLE CREATURES, A **GRIFFIN,** SOME KIND OF ANGRY **UNICORN,** AND SOMETHING CALLED A **BASILISK**--LOOSE ON METROPOLIS WITH NO PRIOR WARNING.

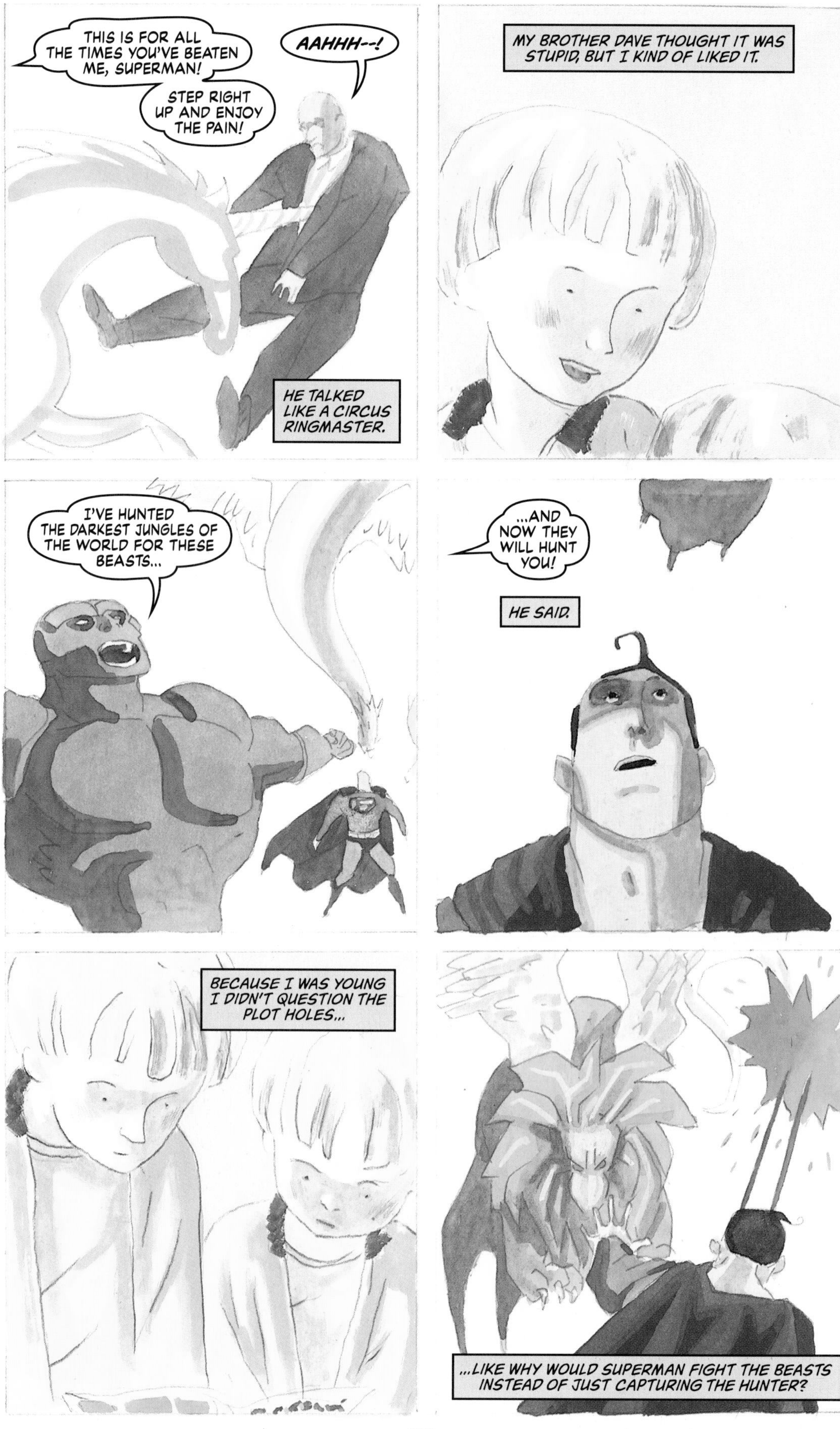
THIS IS FOR ALL THE TIMES YOU'VE BEATEN ME, SUPERMAN!
STEP RIGHT UP AND ENJOY THE PAIN!
AAHHH--!
HE TALKED LIKE A CIRCUS RINGMASTER.
MY BROTHER DAVE THOUGHT IT WAS STUPID, BUT I KIND OF LIKED IT.
I'VE HUNTED THE DARKEST JUNGLES OF THE WORLD FOR THESE BEASTS...
...AND NOW THEY WILL HUNT YOU!
HE SAID.
BECAUSE I WAS YOUNG I DIDN'T QUESTION THE PLOT HOLES...
...LIKE WHY WOULD SUPERMAN FIGHT THE BEASTS INSTEAD OF JUST CAPTURING THE HUNTER?

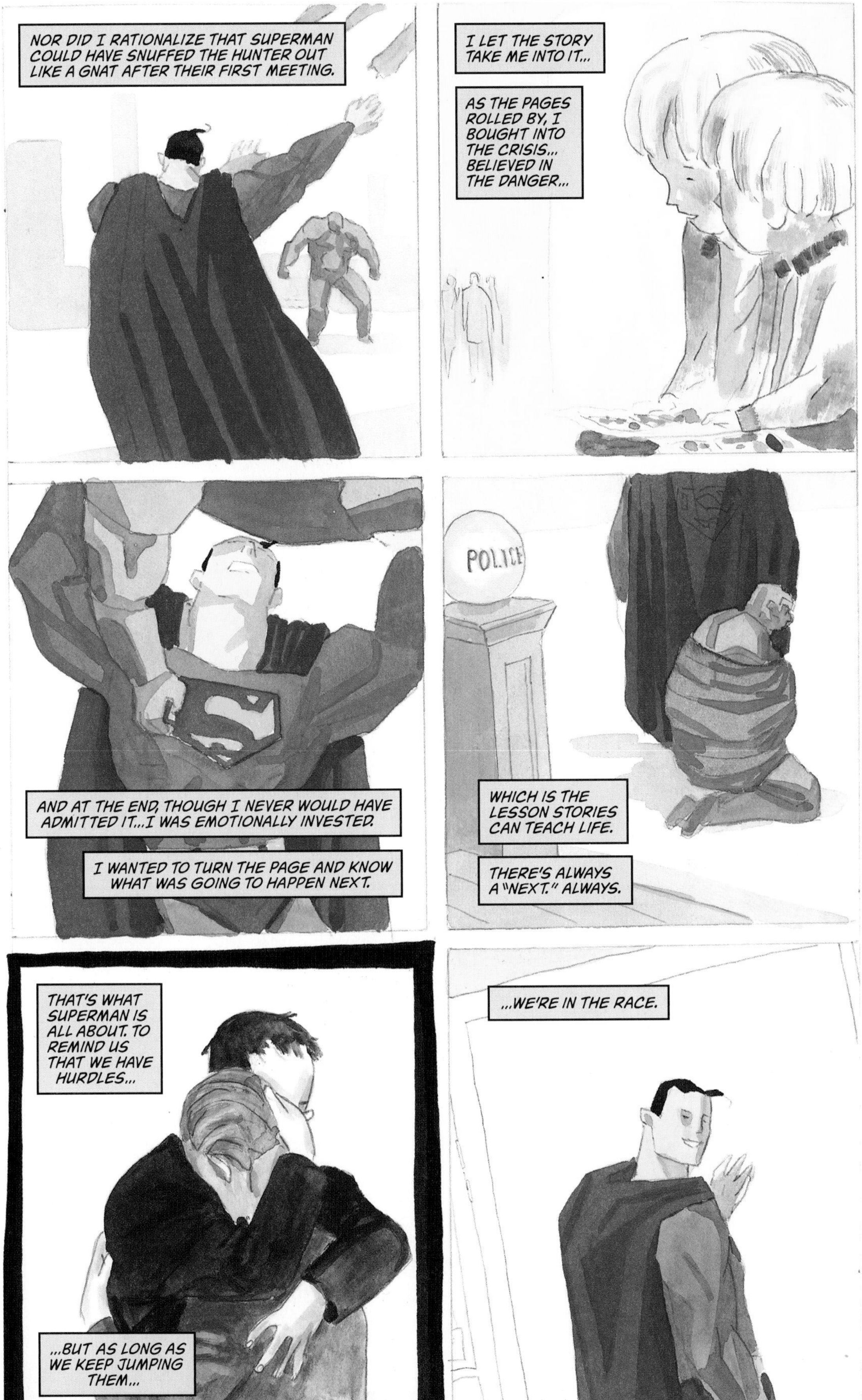
NOR DID I RATIONALIZE THAT SUPERMAN COULD HAVE SNUFFED THE HUNTER OUT LIKE A GNAT AFTER THEIR FIRST MEETING.
I LET THE STORY TAKE ME INTO IT...
AS THE PAGES ROLLED BY, I BOUGHT INTO THE CRISIS... BELIEVED IN THE DANGER...
AND AT THE END, THOUGH I NEVER WOULD HAVE ADMITTED IT...I WAS EMOTIONALLY INVESTED.
I WANTED TO TURN THE PAGE AND KNOW WHAT WAS GOING TO HAPPEN NEXT.
POLICE
WHICH IS THE LESSON STORIES CAN TEACH LIFE.
THERE'S ALWAYS A "NEXT." ALWAYS.
THAT'S WHAT SUPERMAN IS ALL ABOUT. TO REMIND US THAT WE HAVE HURDLES...
...BUT AS LONG AS WE KEEP JUMPING THEM...
...WE'RE IN THE RACE.

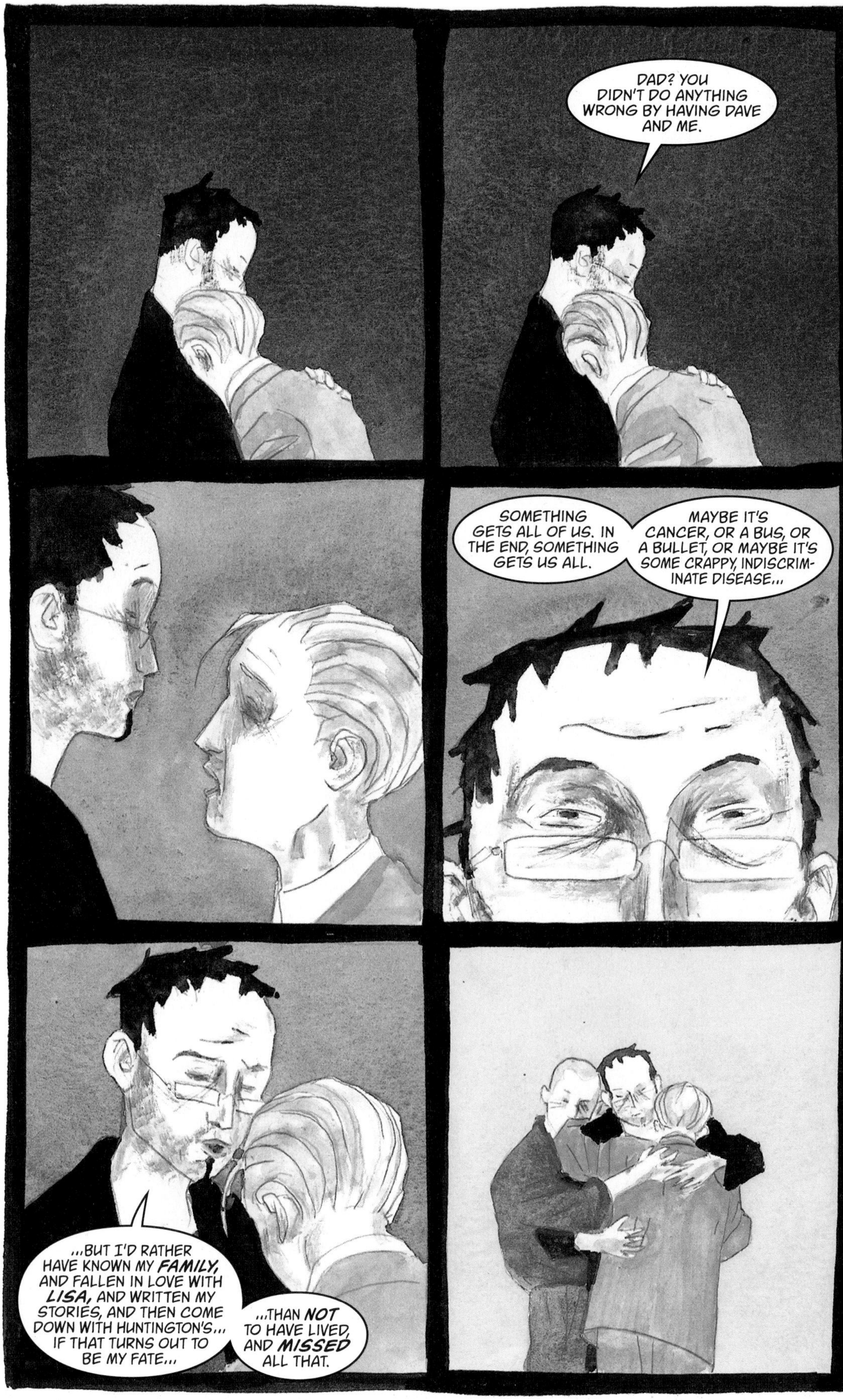
DAD? YOU DIDN'T DO ANYTHING WRONG BY HAVING DAVE AND ME.
SOMETHING GETS ALL OF US. IN THE END, SOMETHING GETS US ALL.
MAYBE IT'S CANCER, OR A BUS, OR A BULLET, OR MAYBE IT'S SOME CRAPPY, INDISCRIMINATE DISEASE...
...BUT I'D RATHER HAVE KNOWN MY FAMILY, AND FALLEN IN LOVE WITH LISA, AND WRITTEN MY STORIES, AND THEN COME DOWN WITH HUNTINGTON'S... IF THAT TURNS OUT TO BE MY FATE...
...THAN NOT TO HAVE LIVED, AND MISSED ALL THAT.

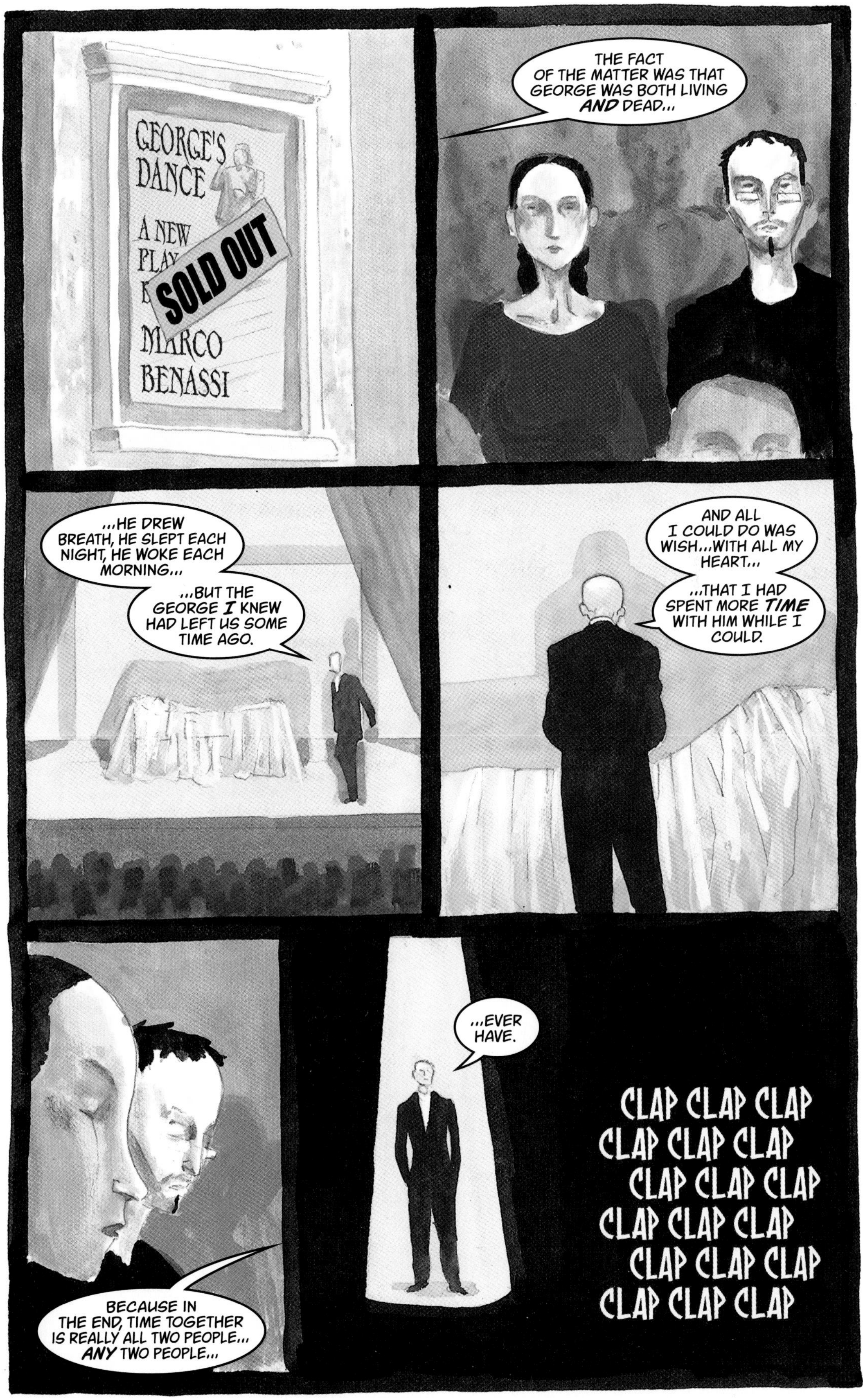
GEORGE'S DANCE
A NEW PLAY
MARCO BENASSI
SOLD OUT
THE FACT OF THE MATTER WAS THAT GEORGE WAS BOTH LIVING AND DEAD...
...HE DREW BREATH, HE SLEPT EACH NIGHT, HE WOKE EACH MORNING...
...BUT THE GEORGE I KNEW HAD LEFT US SOME TIME AGO.
AND ALL I COULD DO WAS WISH...WITH ALL MY HEART...
...THAT I HAD SPENT MORE TIME WITH HIM WHILE I COULD.
BECAUSE IN THE END, TIME TOGETHER IS REALLY ALL TWO PEOPLE... ANY TWO PEOPLE...
...EVER HAVE.
CLAP CLAP CLAP
CLAP CLAP CLAP
CLAP CLAP CLAP
CLAP CLAP CLAP
CLAP CLAP CLAP
CLAP CLAP CLAP

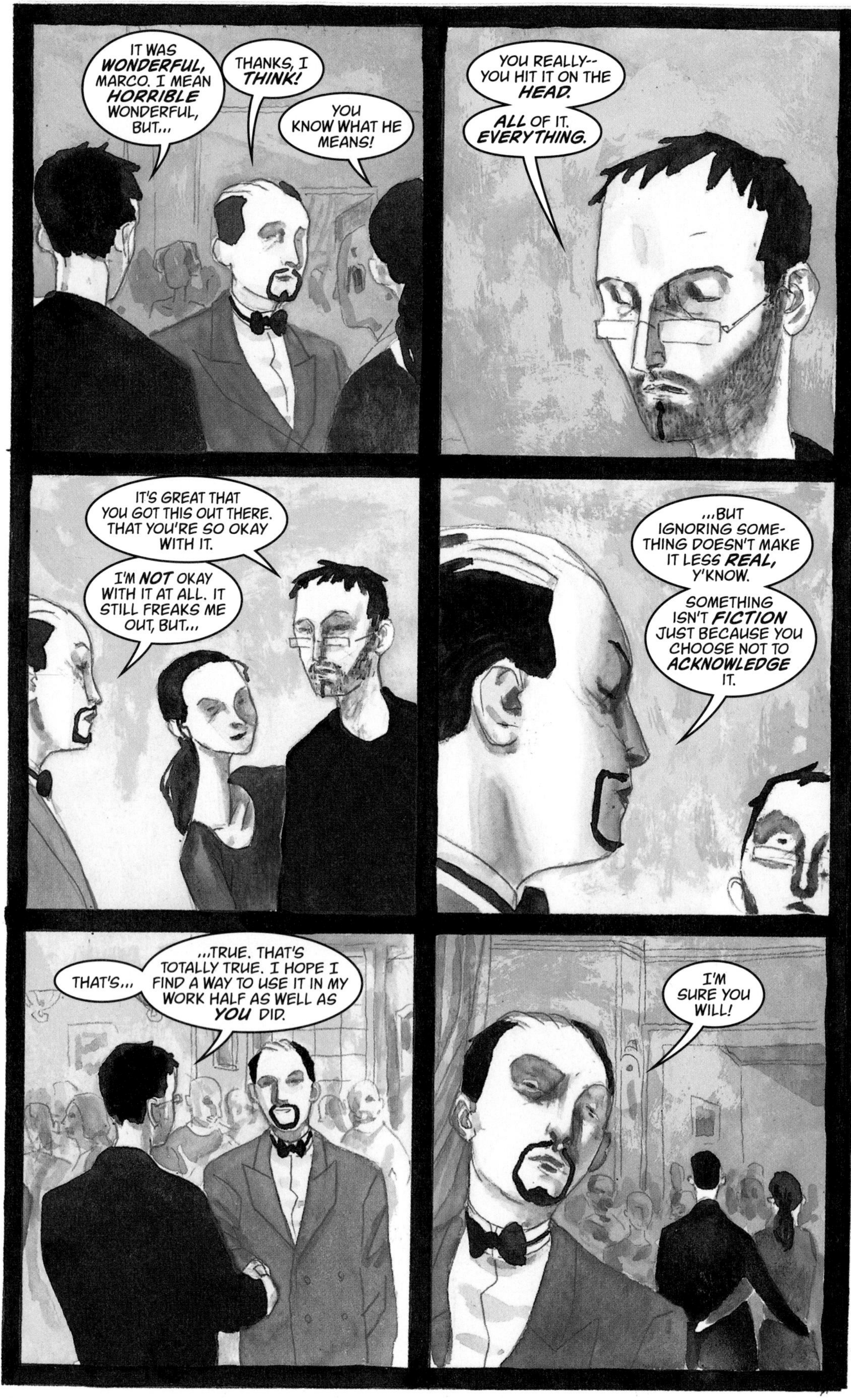
IT WAS WONDERFUL, MARCO. I MEAN HORRIBLE WONDERFUL, BUT...
THANKS, I THINK!
YOU KNOW WHAT HE MEANS!
YOU REALLY-- YOU HIT IT ON THE HEAD.
ALL OF IT. EVERYTHING.
IT'S GREAT THAT YOU GOT THIS OUT THERE. THAT YOU'RE SO OKAY WITH IT.
I'M NOT OKAY WITH IT AT ALL. IT STILL FREAKS ME OUT, BUT...
...BUT IGNORING SOME-THING DOESN'T MAKE IT LESS REAL, Y'KNOW.
SOMETHING ISN'T FICTION JUST BECAUSE YOU CHOOSE NOT TO ACKNOWLEDGE IT.
THAT'S...
...TRUE. THAT'S TOTALLY TRUE. I HOPE I FIND A WAY TO USE IT IN MY WORK HALF AS WELL AS YOU DID.
I'M SURE YOU WILL!

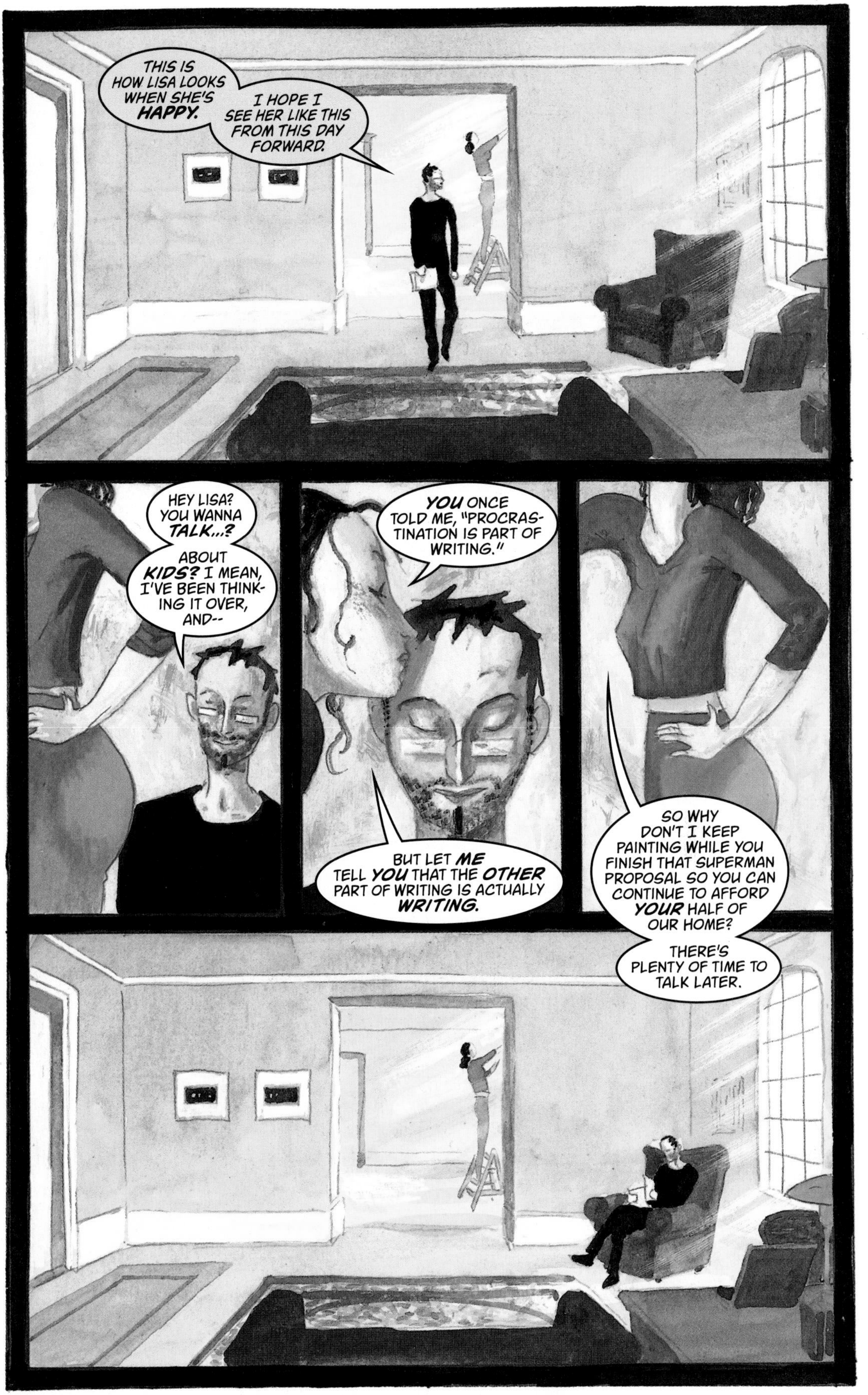
THIS IS HOW LISA LOOKS WHEN SHE'S **HAPPY.**
I HOPE I SEE HER LIKE THIS FROM THIS DAY FORWARD.
HEY LISA? YOU WANNA **TALK...?**
ABOUT **KIDS?** I MEAN, I'VE BEEN THINKING IT OVER, AND--
YOU ONCE TOLD ME, "PROCRASTINATION IS PART OF WRITING."
BUT LET **ME** TELL **YOU** THAT THE **OTHER** PART OF WRITING IS ACTUALLY **WRITING.**
SO WHY DON'T I KEEP PAINTING WHILE YOU FINISH THAT SUPERMAN PROPOSAL SO YOU CAN CONTINUE TO AFFORD **YOUR** HALF OF OUR HOME?
THERE'S PLENTY OF TIME TO TALK LATER.

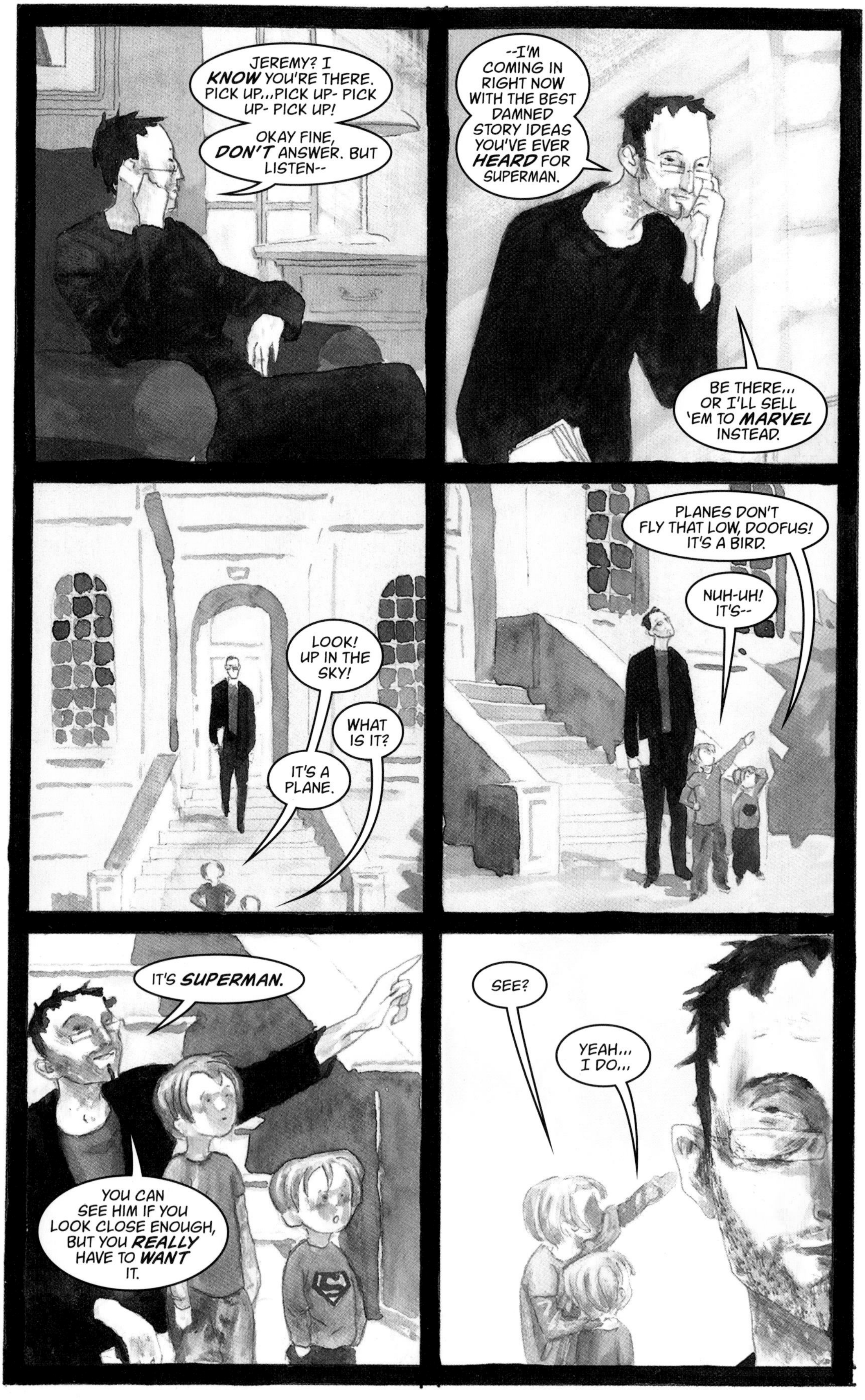
JEREMY? I **KNOW** YOU'RE THERE. PICK UP...PICK UP- PICK UP- PICK UP!
OKAY FINE, **DON'T** ANSWER. BUT LISTEN--
--I'M COMING IN RIGHT NOW WITH THE BEST DAMNED STORY IDEAS YOU'VE EVER **HEARD** FOR SUPERMAN.
BE THERE... OR I'LL SELL 'EM TO **MARVEL** INSTEAD.
LOOK! UP IN THE SKY!
WHAT IS IT?
IT'S A PLANE.
PLANES DON'T FLY THAT LOW, DOOFUS! IT'S A BIRD.
NUH-UH! IT'S--
IT'S **SUPERMAN.**
YOU CAN SEE HIM IF YOU LOOK CLOSE ENOUGH, BUT YOU **REALLY** HAVE TO **WANT** IT.
SEE?
YEAH... I DO...

Look! Up in the sky!

TON'S

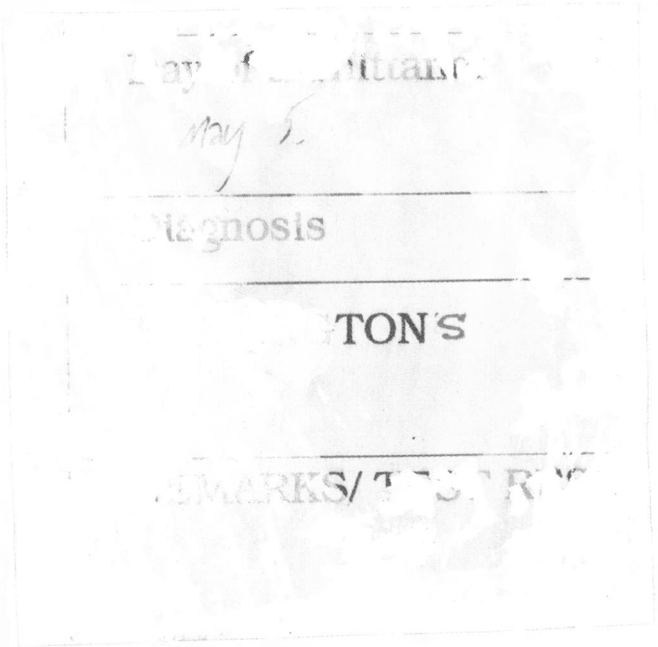

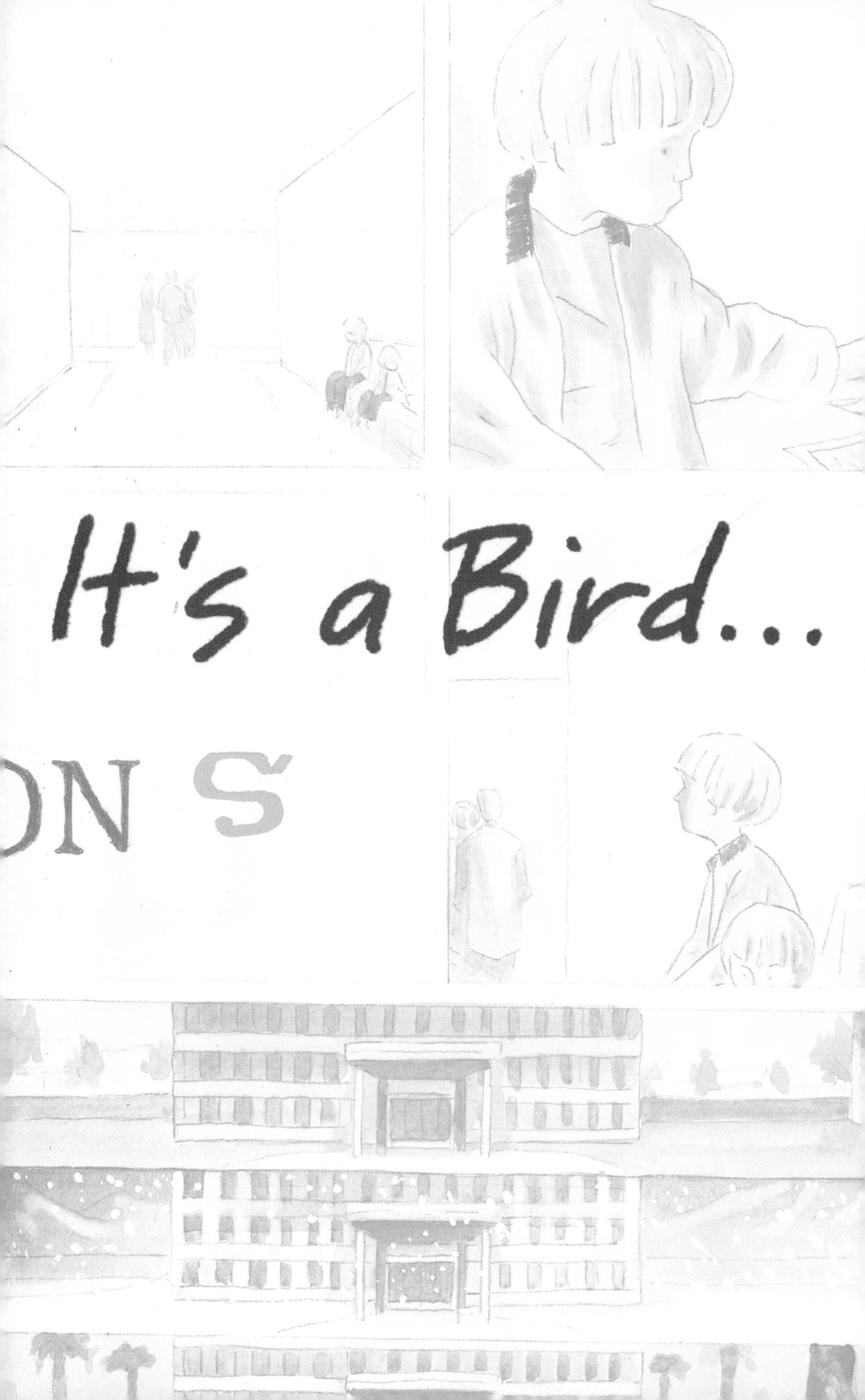
It's a Bird...
ON S

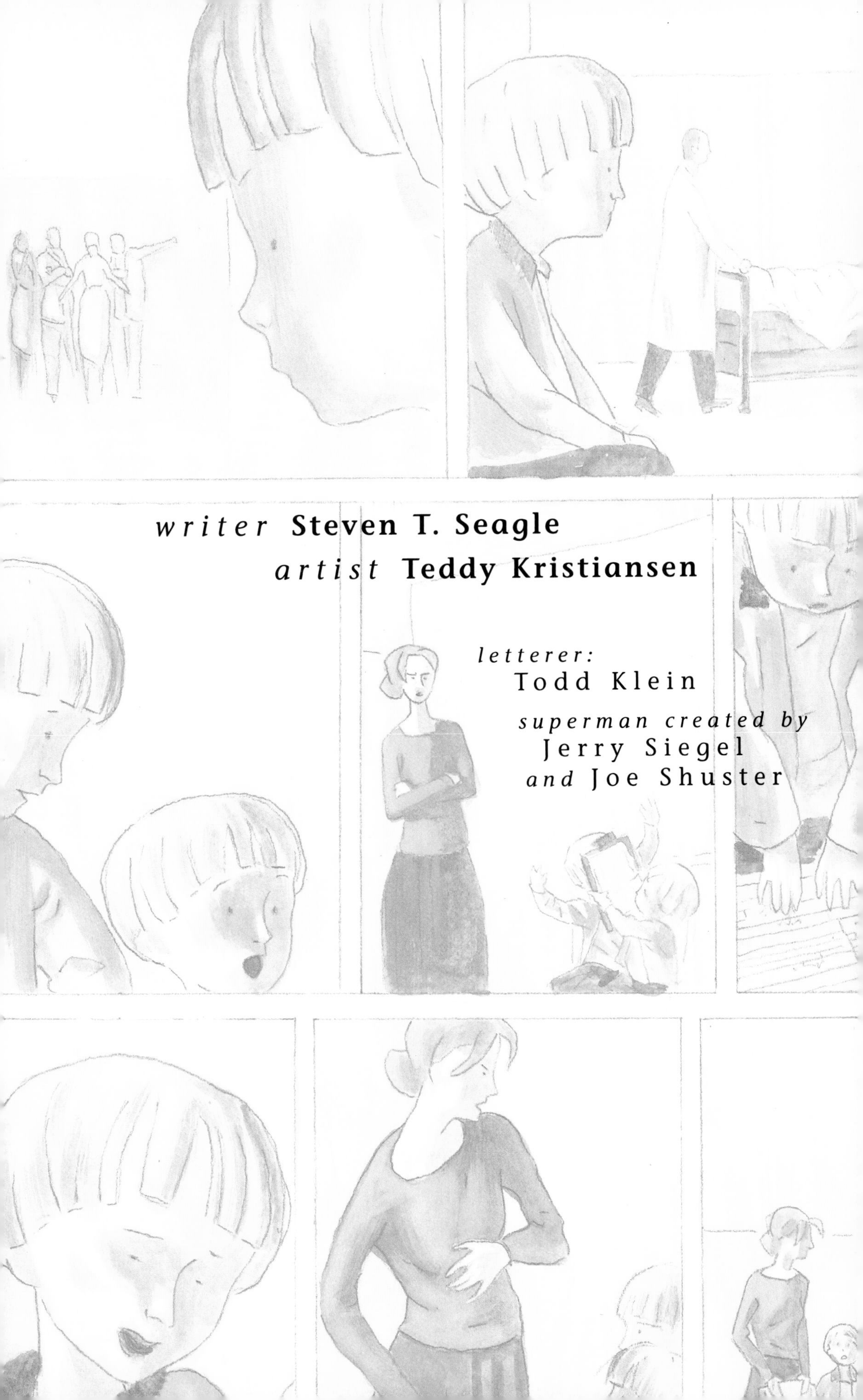
writer Steven T. Seagle
artist Teddy Kristiansen
letterer: Todd Klein
superman created by Jerry Siegel and Joe Shuster

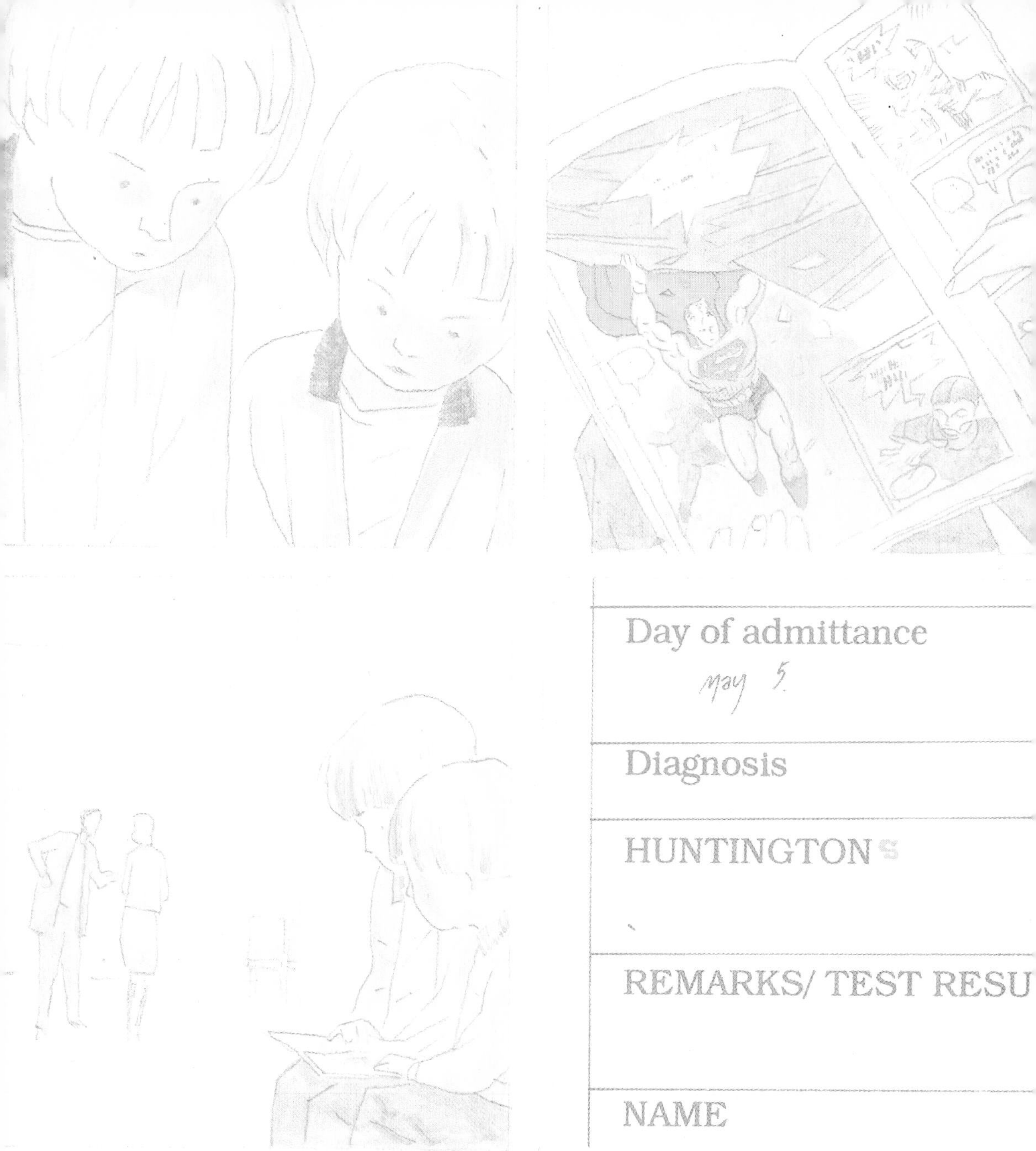
Day of admittance
may 5
Diagnosis
HUNTINGTON s
REMARKS/ TEST RESU
NAME

This book is for my Aunt Sarah who,
unfortunately, did not get to see it.
— *Steve Seagle*

To Hope, with love and thanks.
— *Teddy Kristiansen*

Teddy H. Kristiansen lives in Copenhagen, Denmark with the love of his life, Hope; his lovely daughters, Emily, Sophia, and Lulu; and his cats, Tigger and Mini. His Vertigo comics work includes HOUSE OF SECRETS: FOUNDATION and HOUSE OF SECRETS: FAÇADE (both with writer Steven T. Seagle); SANDMAN; and SANDMAN MIDNIGHT THEATRE. He has also illustrated Grendel: Four Devils, One Hell; Tarzan, and SUPERMAN: METROPOLIS. His first published work being an original Superman graphic album available only in Europe, IT'S A BIRD... marks a trip full circle of sorts for the artist. A man of many hats, Kristiansen has also worked in animation as well as commercial illustration, children's book illustration and the fine arts. His newest medium is plaster. More of his work can be found on his website, www.teddyk.dk. Next on his horizon is an issue of SOLO for DC Comics, a work which he is very proud of. He acknowledges some of the years it took him to paint this story in twenty-one distinctly different styles, but only some.

Steven T. Seagle lives in Pasadena, California with the love of his life, Liesel, and the cat of his life, Gaudi. His Vertigo comics work includes HOUSE OF SECRETS: FOUNDATION and HOUSE OF SECRETS: FAÇADE (both with artist Teddy Kristiansen); the multi-Eisner nominated SANDMAN MYSTERY THEATRE; and VERTICAL. He has also written such mainstays as Uncanny X-Men and SUPERMAN. His other writing venues include feature film, television, and, with his partners at Man of Action Studios LLC, animation and video games. His newest venture, SpeakTheaterArts.com, is writing and producing live theater in Los Angeles. He acknowledges some similarities between himself and the character "Steve" in this book, but only some.

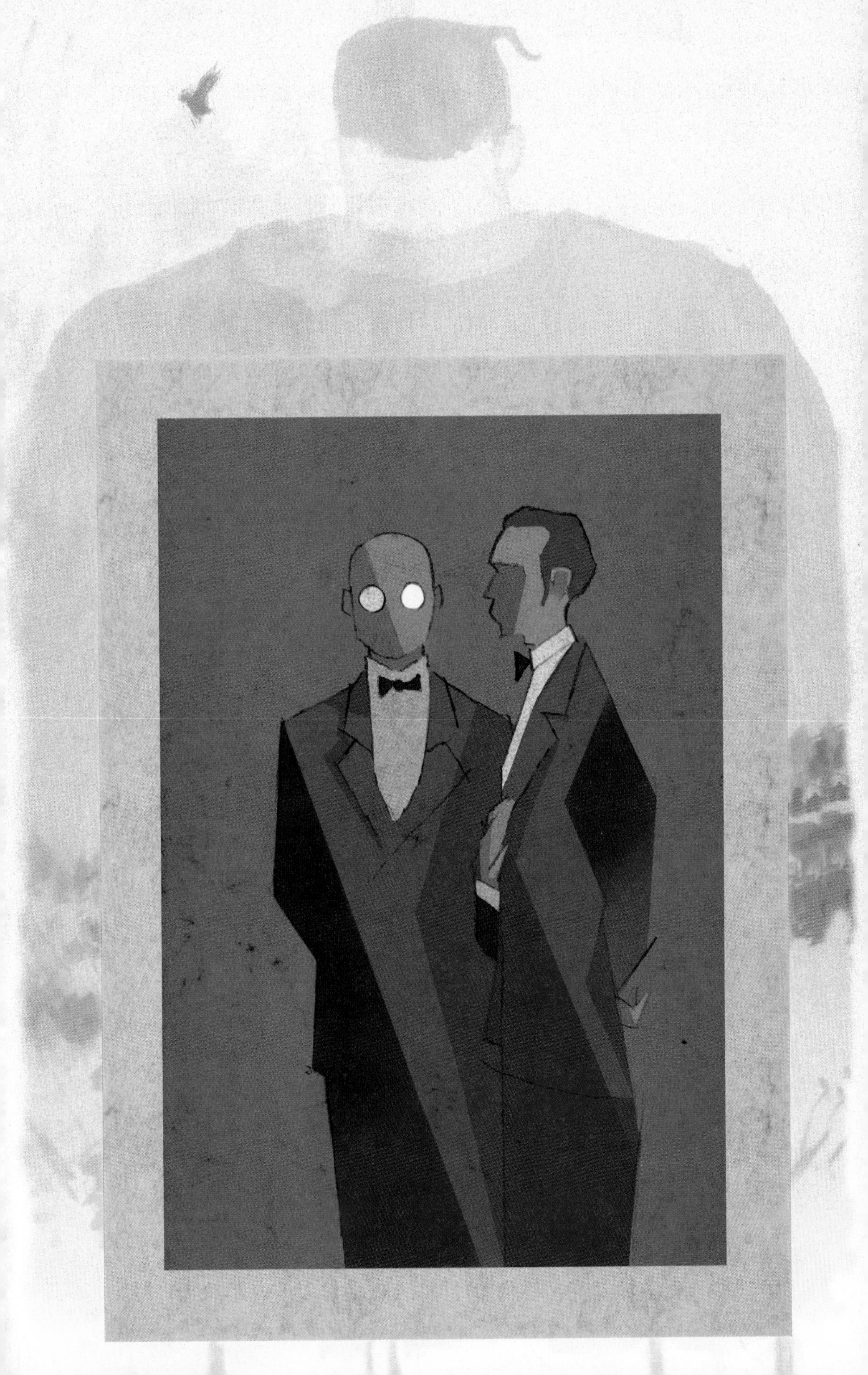

Look for these other VERTIGO books:

All Vertigo titles are Suggested for Mature Readers

100 BULLETS
Brian Azzarello/Eduardo Risso
With one special briefcase, Agent Graves gives you the chance to kill without retribution. But what is the real price for this chance — and who is setting it?
Vol 1: FIRST SHOT, LAST CALL
Vol 2: SPLIT SECOND CHANCE
Vol 3: HANG UP ON THE HANG LOW
Vol 4: A FOREGONE TOMORROW
Vol 5: THE COUNTERFIFTH DETECTIVE
Vol 6: SIX FEET UNDER THE GUN

ANIMAL MAN
Grant Morrison/Chas Truog/
Doug Hazlewood/various
A minor super-hero's consciousness is raised higher and higher until he becomes aware of his own fictitious nature in this revolutionary and existential series.
Vol 1: ANIMAL MAN
Vol 2: ORIGIN OF THE SPECIES
Vol 3: DEUS EX MACHINA

THE BOOKS OF MAGIC
Neil Gaiman/various
A quartet of fallen mystics introduce the world of magic to young Tim Hunter, who is destined to become the world's most powerful magician.

THE BOOKS OF MAGIC
John Ney Rieber/Peter
Gross/various
The continuing trials and adventures of Tim Hunter, whose magical talents bring extra trouble and confusion to his adolescence.
Vol 1: BINDINGS
Vol 2: SUMMONINGS
Vol 3: RECKONINGS
Vol 4: TRANSFORMATIONS
Vol 5: GIRL IN THE BOX
Vol 6: THE BURNING GIRL
Vol 7: DEATH AFTER DEATH

DEATH: AT DEATH'S DOOR
Jill Thompson
Part fanciful manga retelling of the acclaimed THE SANDMAN: SEASON OF MISTS and part original story of the party from Hell.

DEATH: THE HIGH COST OF LIVING
Neil Gaiman/Chris Bachalo/
Mark Buckingham
One day every century, Death assumes mortal form to learn more about the lives she must take.

DEATH: THE TIME OF YOUR LIFE
Neil Gaiman/Chris Bachalo/
Mark Buckingham/Mark Pennington
A young lesbian mother strikes a deal with Death for the life of her son in a story about fame, relationships, and rock and roll.

FABLES
Bill Willingham/Lan Medina/
Mark Buckingham/Steve
Leialoha
The immortal characters of popular fairy tales have been driven from their homelands, and now live hidden among us, trying to cope with life in 21st-century Manhattan.
Vol 1: LEGENDS IN EXILE
Vol 2: ANIMAL FARM

HELLBLAZER
Jamie Delano/Garth
Ennis/Warren Ellis/ Brian
Azzarello/Steve Dillon/
Marcelo Frusin/various
Where horror, dark magic, and bad luck meet, John Constantine is never far away.
Vol 1: ORIGINAL SINS
Vol 2: DANGEROUS HABITS
Vol 3: FEAR AND LOATHING
Vol 4: TAINTED LOVE
Vol 5: DAMNATION'S FLAME
Vol 6: RAKE AT THE GATES OF HELL
Vol 7: HAUNTED
Vol 8: HARD TIME
Vol 9: GOOD INTENTIONS
Vol 10: FREEZES OVER

THE INVISIBLES
Grant Morrison/various
The saga of a terrifying conspiracy and the resistance movement combating it — a secret underground of ultra-cool guerrilla cells trained in ontological and physical anarchy.
Vol 1: SAY YOU WANT A REVOLUTION
Vol 2: APOCALIPSTICK
Vol 3: ENTROPY IN THE U.K.
Vol 4: BLOODY HELL IN AMERICA
Vol 5: COUNTING TO NONE
Vol 6: KISSING MR. QUIMPER
Vol 7: THE INVISIBLE KINGDOM

LUCIFER
Mike Carey/Peter Gross/
Scott Hampton/Chris Weston/
Dean Ormston/various
Walking out of Hell (and out of the pages of THE SANDMAN), an ambitious Lucifer Morningstar creates a new cosmos modeled after his own image.
Vol 1: DEVIL IN THE GATEWAY
Vol 2: CHILDREN AND MONSTERS
Vol 3: A DALLIANCE WITH THE DAMNED
Vol 4: THE DIVINE COMEDY
Vol 5: INFERNO

PREACHER
Garth Ennis/Steve Dillon/various
A modern American epic of life, death, God, love, and redemption — filled with sex, booze, and blood.
Vol 1: GONE TO TEXAS
Vol 2: UNTIL THE END OF THE WORLD
Vol 3: PROUD AMERICANS
Vol 4: ANCIENT HISTORY
Vol 5: DIXIE FRIED
Vol 6: WAR IN THE SUN
Vol 7: SALVATION
Vol 8: ALL HELL'S A-COMING
Vol 9: ALAMO

THE SANDMAN
Neil Gaiman/various
One of the most acclaimed and celebrated comics titles ever published.
Vol 1: PRELUDES & NOCTURNES
Vol 2: THE DOLL'S HOUSE
Vol 3: DREAM COUNTRY
Vol 4: SEASON OF MISTS
Vol 5: A GAME OF YOU
Vol 6: FABLES & REFLECTIONS
Vol 7: BRIEF LIVES
Vol 8: WORLDS' END

Vol 9: THE KINDLY ONES
Vol 10: THE WAKE
Vol 11: ENDLESS NIGHTS

SWAMP THING: DARK GENESIS
Len Wein/Berni Wrightson
A gothic nightmare is brought to life with this horrifying yet poignant story of a man transformed into a monster.

SWAMP THING
Alan Moore/Stephen Bissette/
John Totleben/Rick Veitch/various
The writer and the series that revolutionized comics — a masterpiece of lyrical fantasy.
Vol 1: SAGA OF THE SWAMP THING
Vol 2: LOVE & DEATH
Vol 3: THE CURSE
Vol 4: A MURDER OF CROWS
Vol 5: EARTH TO EARTH
Vol 6: REUNION

TRANSMETROPOLITAN
Warren Ellis/Darick
Robertson/various
An exuberant trip into a frenetic future, where outlaw journalist Spider Jerusalem battles hypocrisy, corruption, and sobriety.
Vol 1: BACK ON THE STREET
Vol 2: LUST FOR LIFE
Vol 3: YEAR OF THE BASTARD
Vol 4: THE NEW SCUM
Vol 5: LONELY CITY
Vol 6: GOUGE AWAY
Vol 7: SPIDER'S THRASH
Vol 8: DIRGE
Vol 9: THE CURE

Y: THE LAST MAN
Brian K. Vaughan/Pia Guerra/
José Marzán, Jr.
An unexplained plague kills every male mammal on Earth — all except Yorick Brown and his pet monkey. Will he survive this new, emasculated world to discover what killed his fellow men?
Vol 1: UNMANNED
Vol 2: CYCLES

BARNUM!
Howard Chaykin/David
Tischman/Niko Henrichon

BLACK ORCHID
Neil Gaiman/Dave McKean

HEAVY LIQUID
Paul Pope

HOUSE OF SECRETS: FOUNDATIONS

HOUSE OF SECRETS: FACADE
Steven T. Seagle/Teddy Kristiansen

HUMAN TARGET
Peter Milligan/Edvin Biukovic

HUMAN TARGET: FINAL CUT
Peter Milligan/Javier Pulido

I DIE AT MIDNIGHT
Kyle Baker

IN THE SHADOW OF EDGAR ALLAN POE
Jonathon Scott Fuqua/
Stephen John Phillips/Steven Parke

JONNY DOUBLE
Brian Azzarello/Eduardo Risso

KING DAVID
Kyle Baker

MR. PUNCH
Neil Gaiman/Dave McKean

THE MYSTERY PLAY
Grant Morrison/Jon J Muth

THE NAMES OF MAGIC
Dylan Horrocks/Richard Case

NEIL GAIMAN & CHARLES VESS' STARDUST
Neil Gaiman/Charles Vess

NEIL GAIMAN'S MIDNIGHT DAYS
Neil Gaiman/Matt Wagner/
various

ORBITER
Warren Ellis/Colleen Doran

PREACHER: DEAD OR ALIVE (THE COLLECTED COVERS)
Glenn Fabry

PROPOSITION PLAYER
Bill Willingham/Paul
Guinan/Ron Randall

THE SANDMAN: THE DREAM HUNTERS
Neil Gaiman/Yoshitaka Amano

THE SANDMAN: DUST COVERS — THE COLLECTED SANDMAN COVERS 1989-1997
Dave McKean/Neil Gaiman

THE SANDMAN PRESENTS: THE FURIES
Mike Carey/John Bolton

THE SANDMAN PRESENTS: TALLER TALES
Bill Willingham/various

SHADE, THE CHANGING MAN: THE AMERICAN SCREAM
Peter Milligan/Chris Bachalo

TRUE FAITH
Garth Ennis/Warren Pleece

UNCLE SAM
Steve Darnall/Alex Ross

UNDERCOVER GENIE
Kyle Baker

UNKNOWN SOLDIER
Garth Ennis/Kilian Plunkett

V FOR VENDETTA
Alan Moore/David Lloyd

VEILS
Pat McGreal/Stephen John
Phillips/José Villarrubia

WHY I HATE SATURN
Kyle Baker

THE WITCHING HOUR
Jeph Loeb/Chris Bachalo/Art
Thibert

YOU ARE HERE
Kyle Baker

Visit us at www.vertigocomics.com for more information on these and many other titles from VERTIGO and DC Comics or call 1-888-COMIC BOOK for the comics shop nearest you, or go to your local book store.

VER0014